Fostoria Tableware

1944 – 1986

Milbra Long and Emily Seate

THE CRYSTAL FOR AMERICA

IDENTIFICATION & VALUE GUIDE

Fostoria Logo used from 1957 – 1986

COLLECTOR BOOKS
A Division of Schroeder Publishing Co., Inc.

The current values in this book should be used only as a guide. They are not intended to set prices, which vary from one section of the country to another. Auction prices as well as dealer prices vary greatly and are affected by condition as well as demand. Neither the authors nor the publisher assumes responsibility for any losses that might be incurred as a result of consulting this guide.

Searching For A Publisher?

We are always looking for knowledgeable people considered to be experts within their fields. If you feel that there is a real need for a book on your collectible subject and have a large comprehensive collection, contact Collector Books.

Front cover: 20" Pink Heirloom Vase
Peach Jenny Lind Cologne Flask and Stopper
Peach Hen and Nest
Pink Clover Apple Puff and Cover
Pink Facets Candlestick
Back cover: 1970 advertisement *Better Homes and Gardens*

Cover design by Michelle Dowling
Book design by Karen Smith
Color photography by Charles R. Lynch

COLLECTOR BOOKS
P.O. Box 3009
Paducah, Kentucky 42002-3009

Milbra Long and Emily Seate
P.O. Box 784
Cleburne, TX 76033-0784

Copyright © 1999 by Milbra Long and Emily Seate

Printed in the U.S.A. by Image Graphics Inc., Paducah, KY.

CONTENTS

ACKNOWLEDGMENTS

We are grateful to the Lancaster Colony Corporation, Inc. of Columbus, Ohio, for permission to use the materials and logo of the Fostoria Glass Company, Inc.

Our appreciation and respect for Collector Books grow with each book we author. We especially thank Billy Schroeder and Lisa Stroup for doing their best to bring to the reader this history of the patterns made by the Fostoria Glass Company as authentically and beautifully as is possible with today's technology.

DEDICATION

This book and all the other books of the "Crystal for America" series are dedicated to the employees of the Fostoria Glass Company, Inc. whose skilled hands created fine Fostoria crystal.

Every man's work . . .

Handmade Fostoria crystal is a source of pride for those who make it, as well as for those who own it. The work is challenging, not everyone can do it. It represents achievement and personal satisfaction for many skilled workers.

And for those who do own Fostoria ware, it is a link with the past—a time when virtually every household article was lovingly fashioned by hand. It brings with it a personal history lacking in the machine-made and mass-produced.

Fostoria has been around a long time—since 1887. And things aren't done a whole lot differently now than they were back then. Some of the products have changed, but the skills and processes are much the same. And there's still a lot of family involvement in the business—a kind of craftsmanship applied to management.

If you're ever in Moundsville, we invite you to tour the Fostoria plant. It's quite a spectacle to see hands making so many beautiful things from glass. It's an old-fashioned way of doing things. And the result is old-fashioned quality.

From Fostoria
Bicentennial Brochure

"Every man's work is always a portrait of himself."
– Samuel Butler

INTRODUCTION

When one places a price list from 1943 beside the price list from 1944, the difference in the sizes of the booklets is dramatic. The 1943 price list is pared down considerably from the listings found in the 1930s, but it still contains 90 pages while 1944 has only 30 pages, none of which lists any pieces in color.

The period from 1944 – 1986 was diverse both in products and in presentation. In addition to the shift from color to crystal evident in 1944, the post-war years saw the introduction of more and more giftware until in the last years, catalogs offered only stemware and giftware.

A three-digit number to identify a piece was added to the original numbering system in 1957. For example, 300 was used to identify an oblong butter and cover in any pattern, and 2056/300 was used to identify an American pattern oblong butter and cover. In 1976, Fostoria abandoned the numbering system that had served them for so long and developed a new system which used the first two letters of the pattern name followed by two numbers, a slash, and the three digits which identified the piece. Thus, the same American oblong butter and cover was described as AM01/300. Sometimes the two digits before the slash indicated the color of the piece, and sometimes it was simply the last two digits of the original four-digit number.

The lifetime of some patterns spanned all three numbering systems, making numbering difficult to keep consistent. Following a piece from start to finish involved wishing for a trail of bread crumbs and finding twists and turns instead. In order to be thorough, sometimes we have listed a piece with the post-1976 letter/digit, the original number, and the three-digit

piece identification even though Fostoria did not list pieces this way. In the case of the American pattern and the Navarre pattern, a few pieces introduced in the 1980s were assigned only letters and numbers from the last system.

By the 1970s most patterns had been reduced to stemware and sometimes one or two plates with a few serving pieces in the major patterns presented as Giftware in another part of the catalog. The etching of the company name on the bottom of most stems began in 1951 and continued through 1982 when blown ware was no longer made.

We have tried to present this complex period as simply as possible. Unfortunately, we have been unable to retain consistency in listing patterns and pieces either alphabetically or numerically. Most often, with Pressed Patterns, Etchings, Cuttings, and Decorations, the listings are numerical for the patterns and alphabetical for the pieces, but when faced with the three numbering systems described above, we had to resort at times to alphabetical listings for patterns, especially in Groups and Collections, and in Giftware, and numerical listings for pieces. With minimum effort, the reader should be able to find the pattern for which he is looking, and, if all else fails, we recommend the Index as a guide.

This volume completes the initial offerings of the Fostoria Glass Company, Inc., from 1924 through the close of the factory in Moundsville in 1986. A final volume, *Fostoria, Useful and Ornamental*, will feature a multitude of miscellaneous candlesticks, bowls, vases, comports, and shakers, and the section on Carvings that just would not fit into either this volume or the previous one.

HISTORY

In an article which appeared in the *Ceramic Industry of Chicago, Illinois* in May, 1951, titled "The Fostoria Story," one statement stands out as a subtle explanation of the success of the then sixty-year-old company: "Perceptive thinking is the Fostoria story." An impressive plant covering more than six acres and employing between 950 and 1,000 employees, the Fostoria Glass Company was at that time the largest manufacturer of hand-made table glassware in the country.

World War II caused changes at the Fostoria factory as in most industries of that time. Many of the older Fostoria molds were sacrificed as scrap metal for the war effort. Fuel was one of the few non-problem areas as Fostoria had the capacity to convert coal to producer gas. Some employees joined the armed services causing a shortage in man-power, and coupled with the shortages of supplies and slowed transportation, the greatest problem was servicing accounts. The demand for Fostoria glass continued.

Color production had declined and by the end of the war was no longer offered. It has been estimated that in 1929 – 1930, only 10% of Fostoria production was Crystal, whereas during the war, only 10% was color. The swing back to Crystal was undeniable. During the post-war period until about 1948, very few new items were offered, but by mid-century new ideas and new products were evident.

David Dalzell as sales manager worked with 19 salesmen headquartered in important cities in the United States and also in Canada and South America. In 1951 national distribution included over 5,000 dealers. Each dealer was furnished free sales aids including leaflets and folders on patterns, price lists, catalogs, radio commercials, display setups, and Lucite and electric signs. A 16mm film for use in schools and color stereo slides were also available and served to lay the foundation for the Bridal Registry so

Top row left to right: 6102 Goblet, Sherbet, Large Tulip Wine, Tulip Wine, Claret Wine. Bottom row left to right: 2630 Candy Jar and Cover, 4132 Highball, 4132 Double-Old Fashioned, 2667 7" Square Ashtray, 2364 12" Flared Bowl

popular from the mid 1950s through the company's closing: more evidence of long-range perception on the part of management.

Colors which were introduced were chosen to coordinate with housewares and decorating schemes and included olive green, smoke, and brown tones. Milk glass, which had not been made since before 1920, saw a resurgence in popularity, and Ebony was back in production in the early 1950s. Interest in figurals and ornamental creations persisted. Several Fostoria designs reflected the influence of the Swedish Modern look.

As foreign products came more and more to dominate the market, Fostoria began to seek ways to incorporate mechanical efficiencies, without sacrificing quality. In 1965 Fostoria built its first tank furnace which had automatic machinery for making glass. Although for a while the fire polishing was done by hand, eventually that, too, was done as part of the machine production especially after 1980. Around 1970, Fostoria began advertising lead crystal which comprised a large percentage of output from that date until the factory was closed. Several lines of lead crystal were inspired by the national bicentennial celebration.

From 1965 to 1971 the Fostoria Company produced glass at the Morgantown Glassware Guild plant in Morgantown, West Virginia. Fostoria had bought this factory and continued making some of the Morgantown patterns and pieces. One notable pattern was the "President's House" stemware that was chosen by Jacqueline Kennedy while she was First Lady. Fostoria was commissioned by the White House to manufacture this line of stemware with the Presidential seal. Presidential giftware and Congressional smoker items were made also. Special orders were filled for numerous political figures.

The Coventry line shows the Morgantown influence both in design and color.

Fostoria had a brief alliance with the Pickard China Company in the early 1970s. Stemware to coordinate with Pickard China was designed and manufactured and a joint brochure and other advertising created to show off the new wares.

Another client during the 1960s and 1970s was the Avon Company. Candle holders, vases, containers for soaps and cosmetics as well as special pieces for sales awards were among the items special ordered from Fostoria. The Avon Company (1886) was founded one year earlier than the Fostoria Company (1887), a fact evident in pieces of Coin Glass ordered by the Avon Company with the 1886 date on the coins.

The Fostoria Glass Company managed to stay in business longer than any other of the great glass houses of our recent past. In the 1980s management was still trying to read the market, seeking to provide products that were cost effective to an ever more casual market place. Before the factory was closed, this great glass house was offering its own line of foreign imports, as well as ice buckets that were not made from glass.

Perceptive thinking, the ability to take calculated risks, and an almost uncanny knowledge of where available monies could be best used were hallmarks of the Fostoria Glass Company. Management valued its skilled workers, and there is no record of any difficulties between labor and management. These factors were paramount to a company devoted to the manufacture of quality glassware for the American table. The Fostoria Glass Company's place in history is secure (see also *Fostoria Tableware: 1924 – 1943*).

The Crystal for America

Old-world grandeur and contemporary thought are blended in time-honored Fostoria stemware. Because of enduring excellence, we have been commissioned by the White House to manufacture special stemware with the Presidential seal. And our Presidential giftware has been gratefully received by dignitaries around the world.

What's more, Fostoria's reputation for craft and quality has resulted in commissions to produce special crystal giftware for numerous members of Congress over the years.

The care and quality which go into such pieces are reflected in the crystal and glassware we make for every American. Your tastes can be fulfilled in this same spirit of artistry. Whether you're buying that first set of wedding crystal, or choosing something to cherish for another chapter in your life.

Fostoria has an old-fashioned way of doing things. And the result is old-fashioned quality.

©1981 Fostoria Glass Company

PRICING

Normally, one bases prices on supply and demand, and the going rate in the market place. Since this book is primarily concerned with tableware, the authors have developed a set of criteria which, in addition to the above considerations, is based on the relationship of pieces within a pattern.

Each dinnerware pattern had typical pieces: some had more, some fewer. Just as the tiny cordial is more difficult to find and thus, more expensive in stemware patterns, some pieces are considered more valuable in tableware than others. Often times, value is determined by the fact that some pieces were used more than others, and some had harsher use. Dinner plates became scratched and chipped, vases were stained when water sat in them, and ice tubs were scratched by the tongs used to pick up the ice pieces. Therefore, one criteria is that prices differ within a pattern. Typically, the jug will be expensive, especially the 5000 jug, as will the dinner plate, vases, candelabra (with bobeches), and those pieces that were made for just a few years.

This book covers the last 42 years of a great glass company. Sometimes we have used the Fostoria prices of the time, especially from the late 1980s, since not enough time has passed, nor enough interest generated for the pieces to have market place prices.

Quality is another factor. Fostoria was proud of the clarity achieved in its crystal. The American pattern, from beginning to end, is typical of the care with which Fostoria finished each piece offered in that famous pattern, and generally, with all Fostoria glass.

The authors did use supply and demand as a factor. Some of the more popular etched patterns such as Navarre and Chintz will always be in short supply because of demand.

The current market place was also used as a factor in determining values. It did not weigh more heavily than quality or supply and demand. When one considers that all the patterns in this book were hand made, hand finished, and hand inspected by deftly skilled laborers who blew it into molds, pressed it, turned and twisted it with exquisite timing, the glassware becomes priceless. It represents a time in the history of America that will never be repeated: a time when glassware was mass produced by hand.

The authors decided to give just one value in this book instead of a range. The value is to be considered a retail price for the 1998 marketplace. A good rule of thumb is to consider that any value could vary as much as 20 per cent in either direction.

PRESSED PATTERNS

1372 Coin
2056 American
2364 Sonata
2412 Colony
2449 Lexington
2560 Coronet
2570-2745 Sculpture
2574 Raleigh
2630 Century
2638/2666 Contour
2643 Holiday
2650 Horizon
2685 Seascape
2691 Decorator Pattern
2700 Radiance
2703 Artisan
2718 Fairmont
2719 Jamestown
2737 Hawaiian
2739 Roulette
2752 Facets
2785 Gourmet
2806 Pebble Beach
2807 Glacier
2808 Caribbean
2816 Sierra/ Cutting 921, Sierra Ice
2834 Coventry/Crystal Print 24, Monaco
2844 Sea Shells Line
4186 Mesa

1372 COIN

Rare originals are in museums
but this Coin Glass you can own

Coin Glass first circulated in the 19th century. It was instantly popular. It was almost as instantly declared illegal and the molds broken ... because real coins were reproduced. (Counterfeiting!) Which explains why originals are in museum and private collections — and why lovers of Americana are so intrigued by the Fostoria reproduction. Many pieces are in amber and blue, as well as crystal — and you won't find more entrancing gifts for love or money. Where? Write Fostoria Glass Company, Dept. AH, Moundsville, West Virginia.

Fine Crystal with Fashion Flair ... made by hand in America

Courting Lamp
Oil (shown) — $8.75
Electric — $10.75

Fostoria

| 8" Bud Vase (Blue) $3.25 | 4½" Candleholders (Amber) (Pair) $7.00 | Quart Pitcher $4.50 | Handled Nappy $2.25 | Old Fashioned $1.95 | Wedding Bowl & Cover $7.00 | 9" Oval Bowl (Amber) $4.25 (All prices slightly higher west) |

When the United States government realized that the faces of real U.S. coins were being reproduced in glass, all production of that glass was determined to be illegal and was immediately halted in 1892. In 1959, the Fostoria Glass Company created its own version of coin glass with the date of the company's founding, 1887, incorporated into the design of the coins.

Fourteen Fostoria glassmakers combined their skills to re-create Coin Glass in crystal and five colors. The stemware, tumblers, and plates seem to be the most difficult to find currently. In the early 1960s four pieces in crystal were decorated with gold leaf on the coins, making them highly collectible. The green color is a bright emerald green and was made for a very short time.

Fostoria made some Coin Glass for the Avon Company and dated the coins on those pieces 1886, the founding of the Avon Company. A special issue was made commemorating the Centennial Celebration of Canada. The coins on those pieces show four different animals, Canada, and the date 1867.

The blue color was dropped in 1967 and added again in 1975. The two different periods of production may account for the variations in the shades, from a vibrant, intense blue to a pale or lighter shade.

Worthy of note is that the small round ash tray in the Cigarette Set also serves as a cover for the Cigarette. The Punch Bowl foot has no coins, and the cover for the 8½" footed Bowl has the coin on the finial. Note that the candlestick pictured on page 13 has a scalloped candle cup. The later candlestick had a flat-edged candle cup.

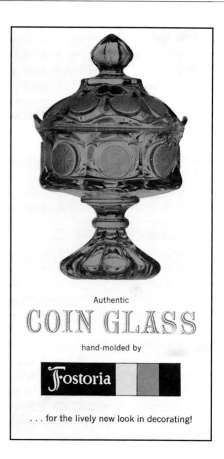

Authentic

COIN GLASS

hand-molded by

Fostoria

. . . for the lively new look in decorating!

Crystal, Amber, Olive Green, Blue, Ruby, Green.
Gold coins (Decoration 646) as noted. Stemware is featured in *Fostoria Stemware*, page 41.

Ash Tray, Small Round
    Crystal, 1961-1964; $32.00
    Amber, 1961-1964; $38.00
    Blue, 1961-1964; $45.00
    Green, 1963-1965; $75.00
Ash Tray, 4" Oblong
    Crystal, 1959-1973; $30.00
    Amber, 1961-1973; $35.00
    Olive Green, 1965-1973; $35.00
    Blue, 1961-1966; $45.00
    Green, 1963-1964; $75.00
Ash Tray, 5" One Coin
    Crystal, 1961-1981; $15.00
    Amber, 1961-1982; $18.00
    Olive Green, 1965-1981; $18.00
    Blue, 1961-1966; $28.00
    Ruby, 1968-1981; $24.00
    Green, 1963-1964; $75.00
Ash Tray, 7½" Four Coin
    Crystal, 1959-1981; $20.00
    Amber, 1959-1981; $22.00
    Olive Green, 1965-1981; $22.00
    Blue, 1961-1966; $35.00
    Ruby, 1967-1981; $25.00

    Green, 1963-1964; $78.00
Ash Tray, 7½" Center Coin
    Crystal, 1968-1980; $22.00
    Amber, 1968-1982; $22.00
    Olive Green, 1968-1981; $22.00
    Ruby, 1968-1982; $25.00
Ash Tray, 10" Large
    Crystal, 1960-1973; $26.00
    Amber, 1961-1973; $30.00
    Olive Green, 1965-1973; $30.00
    Blue, 1961-1966; $45.00
    Green, 1963-1964; $95.00
Bowl, 8" Round
    Crystal, 1959-1981; $38.00
    Amber, 1961-1982; $40.00
    Olive Green, 1965-1981; $40.00
    Blue, 1961-1966, 1975-1982; $68.00
    Ruby, 1967-1981; $55.00
    Green, 1963-1964; $125.00
Bowl, 8½" Footed
    Crystal, 1961-1981; $55.00
    Amber, 1961-1982; $55.00
    Olive Green, 1965-1981; $55.00
    Blue, 1961-1967; $85.00

Ruby, 1967-1982; $58.00
Green, 1963-1964; $135.00
Bowl, 8½", Footed and Cover
    Crystal, 1962-1964; $125.00
    Amber, 1962-1964; $125.00
    Blue, 1962-1964; $175.00
    Green, 1963-1964; $265.00
Bowl, 9" Oval
    Crystal, 1959-1981; $55.00
    Amber, 1961-1982; $55.00
    Olive Green, 1965-1981; $55.00
    Blue, 1961-1966, 1975-1982; $75.00
    Ruby, 1967-1982; $65.00
    Green, 1963-1964; $125.00
Bowl, Wedding and Cover
    Crystal, 1958-1980; $68.00
    Amber, 1962-1982; $65.00
    Olive Green, 1963-1980; $68.00
    Blue, 1962-1966, 1975-1982; $125.00
    Ruby, 1967-1982; $95.00
    Green, 1962; $200.00
    Gold Coin, 1960-1971; $195.00
Candlestick, 4½" (Pair)
    Crystal, 1960-1981; $45.00
    Amber, 1961-1982; $45.00
    Olive Green, 1965-1981; $48.00
    Blue, 1961-1966, 1975-1982; $65.00
    Ruby, 1967-1982; $58.00
    Green, 1963-1964; $125.00
Candlestick, 8", (pair)
    Crystal, 1968-1981; $100.00
    Amber, 1968-1982; $125.00
    Olive Green, 1968-1981; $110.00
    Ruby, 1968-1982; $125.00
Candy Box and Cover
    Crystal, 1960-1981; $58.00
    Amber, 1961-1982; $60.00

Bud Vase, Candy Jar and Cover, Shakers

Olive Green, 1965-1981; $60.00
Blue, 1961-1966; $125.00
Ruby, 1967-1982; $95.00
Green, 1963-1964; $175.00
Candy Jar and Cover
    Crystal, 1958-1981; $40.00
    Amber, 1961-1982; $42.00
    Olive Green, 1965-1981; $42.00
    Blue, 1961-1967, 1975-1982; $95.00
    Ruby, 1967-1982; $75.00
    Green, 1963-1964; $150.00
    Gold Coin, 1960-1971; $150.00
Cigarette Box and Cover
    Crystal, 1959-1964; $135.00
    Amber, 1964; $165.00
    Blue, 1964; $185.00
    Green, 1964; $275.00
    Gold Coin, 1960-1965; $275.00
Cigarette Holder and Cover
    Crystal, 1961-1964; $150.00
    Amber, 1961-1964; $150.00
    Blue, 1961-1964; $165.00
    Green, 1963-1964; $250.00
Cigarette Urn
    Crystal, 1964-1981; $42.00
    Amber, 1964-1981; $45.00
    Olive Green, 1965-1982; $45.00
    Blue, 1964-1966; $75.00
    Ruby, 1972-1981; $58.00
    Green, 1964; $125.00
Condiment Set (Cruet, shakers and tray)
    Crystal, 1964-1970; $195.00
    Amber, 1964-1970; $195.00
    Olive Green, 1965-1970; $195.00
    Blue, 1964-1966; $295.00
    Green, 1964; $500.00
Condiment Tray, 9⅝"
    Crystal, 1964-1970; $35.00
    Amber, 1965-1970; $40.00
    Olive Green, 1965-1970; $40.00
    Blue, 1965-1966; $65.00
Cream
    Crystal, 1959-1981; $28.00
    Amber, 1963-1982; $32.00
    Olive Green, 1965-1981; $32.00
    Blue, 1963-1966, 1975-1982; $50.00
    Ruby, 1973-1982; $35.00
    Green, 1963-1964; $60.00
Cruet and Stopper, 7 oz.
    Crystal, 1964-1970; $95.00
    Amber, 1964-1970; $95.00
    Olive Green, 1965-1970; $95.00
    Blue, 1964-1966; $135.00
    Green, 1964; $225.00
Decanter and Stopper
    Crystal, 1960-1965; $165.00
    Amber, 1964-1965; $225.00

Olive Green, 1965; $225.00
Blue, 1964-1965; $250.00
Green, 1964; $300.00
Gold Coin, 1960-1966; $300.00
Jelly
    Crystal, 1958-1981; $32.00
    Amber, 1961-1981; $38.00
    Olive Green, 1965-1981; $38.00
    Blue, 1961-1966; $50.00
    Green, 1963-1964; $75.00
Lamp, Coach, Electric
    Crystal, 1963-1967; $150.00
    Amber, 1963-1970; $150.00
    Blue, 1963-1966; $225.00
Lamp, Coach, Oil
    Crystal, 1963-1967; $150.00
    Amber, 1963-1970; $150.00
    Blue, 1963-1966; $225.00
Lamp, Handled Courting, Electric
    Amber, 1961-1963; $135.00
    Blue, 1963-1966; $150.00
Lamp, Handled Courting, Oil
    Amber, 1961-1973; $135.00
    Blue, 1963-1966; $150.00

Lamp, Tall Patio, Electric
    Crystal, 1961-1966; $195.00
    Amber, 1961-1970; $225.00
    Blue, 1963-1966; $285.00
Lamp, Tall Patio, Oil
    Crystal, 1961-1966; $200.00
    Amber, 1961-1970; $250.00
    Blue, 1963-1966; $295.00
Pitcher, Quart
    Crystal, 1959-1981; $95.00
    Amber, 1963-1981; $95.00
    Olive Green, 1965-1981; $95.00
    Blue, 1963-1966; $175.00
    Ruby, 1973-1981; $125.00
    Green, 1963-1964; $250.00
Nappy, 4½" Round
    Crystal, 1959-1964; $48.00
Nappy, 5⅜" Handled
    Crystal, 1959-1981; $22.00
    Amber, 1961-1981; $22.00
    Olive Green, 1965-1981; $22.00
    Blue, 1961-1966, 1975-1981; $38.00
    Ruby, 1967-1981; $34.00
    Green, 1963-1964; $40.00
Plate, 8"
    Crystal, 1969-1970; $75.00
    Olive Green, 1969-1970; $95.00
    Ruby, 1969-1970; $150.00
Punch Bowl, 14"
    Crystal, 1963-1973; $375.00
Punch Bowl Foot
    Crystal, 1963-1973; $150.00
Punch Cup
    Crystal, 1963-1973; $45.00
Salver, Cake
    Crystal, 1962-1973; $100.00
    Amber, 1962-1972; $125.00
    Olive Green, 1965-1972; $125.00

310   311   320   321   459   466

600　　602

Blue, 1962-1966; $250.00
Green, 1963-1964; $350.00
Shaker, Chrome Top "E", (pair)
　Crystal, 1964-1978; $65.00
　Amber, 1964-1978; $70.00
　Olive Green, 1964-1978; $70.00
　Blue, 1964-1966, 1975-1978; $95.00
　Ruby, 1973-1978; $95.00
　Green, 1964; $150.00
Smoker Set, 3-piece (Cigarette
　Holder, 2 ash tray covers)
　Crystal, 1961-1964; $200.00

Amber, 1961-1964; $225.00
Blue, 1961-1964; $250.00
Green, 1963-1964; $375.00
Sugar and Cover
　Crystal, 1959-1981; $38.00
　Amber, 1963-1982; $42.00
　Olive Green, 1965-1981; $42.00
　Blue, 1963-1966, 1975-1982; $65.00
　Ruby, 1973-1982; $50.00
　Green, 1963-1964; $120.00
Urn, 12¾" Ftd., and Cover
　Crystal, 1962-1981; $125.00
　Amber, 1962-1981; $125.00
　Olive Green, 1965-1981; $125.00
　Blue, 1962-1966; $175.00
　Ruby, 1967-1981; $150.00
　Green, 1963-1964; $300.00
Vase, 8" Bud
　Crystal, 1960-1981; $38.00
　Amber, 1961-1982; $38.00
　Olive Green, 1965-1981; $38.00
　Blue, 1961-1966, 1975-1982; $65.00
　Ruby, 1967-1982; $56.00
　Green, 1963-1965; $125.00
Vase, 10" Footed
　Crystal, 1961-1967; $67.00

1372/114—7½ in.
Round Ash Tray

1372/115
Oblong Ash Tray
Length 4 in.

1372/124—10 in.
Ash Tray

1372/179—8 in.
Bowl

1372/162
Wedding Bowl and Cover
Height 8-3/16 in.

1372/189—9 in.
Oval Bowl

1372/316—4½ in.
Candleholder

1372/347
Candy Jar and Cover
Height 6-5/16 in.

1372/354
Candy Box and Cover
Diameter 6⅜ in.
Height 4⅛ in.

1372/374
Cigarette Box and Cover
Height 1¾ in.
Length 5¾ in. Width 4½ in.

1372/400
Decanter and Stopper
Height 10-3/16 in.
Capacity 1 Pint

1372/448
Jelly

1372/453
Quart Pitcher
Height 6-9/16 in.

1372/495—4½ in.
Nappy
Height 3¾ in.

1372/499
Handled Nappy
Diameter 5⅜ in.

1372/673
Sugar & Cover
Height 5⅜ in.

1372/680
Cream
Height 3½ in.

1372/799—8 in.
Bud Vase

GOLD COIN DESIGN
Decoration No. 646
Gold Decorated Coins

1372/162
Wedding Bowl and Cover
Height 8-3/16 in.
Length 5¾ in. Width 4½ in.

1372/347
Candy Jar and Cover
Height 6-5/16 in.

1372/400
Decanter and Stopper
Height 10-3/16 in.
Capacity 1 Pint

1372/374
Cigarette Box and Cover
Height 1¾ in.

Crystal Cake Salver, Amber Condiment Set

Candy Jar, Blue Wedding Bowl

*Gold Coin Cigarette Box
and Cover, Decanter*

Photograph by Milbra Long

*Green Nappy
Cruet and
WeddingBowl*

2056 AMERICAN

In this second period, the American pattern continued to be the hallmark of the Fostoria Glass Company, selling better than any other pattern made. Some of the pieces added were unique to this period, some were reintroduced from the earlier period under new names. The Ice Cream set became the Appetizer Set and the Catsup Bottle became the Condiment Bottle. Notable among the introductions of this period were the Wedding Bowl and Cover, the Jam Pot and Cover and the Jam Pot Set, the footed Mayonnaise, the Chrome Top for the Shakers, the Shrimp Bowl, the Dripcut Syrup, the 3-toed Tid Bit, the Handled Muffin Tray, the Handled Utility Tray, and the 8½" Bud Vases. Most interesting is the addition of a Youth Set, and a Bell in the 1980s. A Toddler Set had been offered in 1957 and both sets used the Baby Bowl.

Better Homes and Gardens, December 1940

We have included all the pieces which were being made between 1944 and 1986, or which were introduced during that period. Though other publications list an 8' footed round bowl, we found no listing for this item. It may have been a special order or made for sampling and sold through the Fostoria Outlet Stores. A few pieces were offered in Milk Glass, the Bud Vase in colored Milk Glass. In 1983 – 1986 five pieces appeared in the price list in Ruby. Other Ruby pieces continued to be offered through the outlet stores into the 1990s: 9" Handled Serving Dish, 11" Centerpiece, 10" Handled Cake, 9" Handled Utility Tray, 8" Handled Muffin, and possibly others. Several pieces of American in crystal were also made by other factories and sold in the outlet stores.

Appetizer, Individual Square
    (Also listed as Square Ice Cream),
    1934-1943; 1957-1958; $34.00
Appetizer Set, 7 piece, 1934-1943; 1957-1958
    Included 10½" Oblong Tray and
    6 Individual Square Appetizers; $365.00
Ash Tray, 2⅞" Square, 1936-1973; $12.00
Ash Tray, 5" Square, 1957-1974; $97.00
Basket, Reed Handle, 1940-1958; $95.00
Bell, July 1981-May 1982; $500.00/market
Boat, Sauce, and Plate, 1938-1958; $68.00
Bon Bon, 3-toed, 1925-1982; $32.00
Bottle, Condiment and Stopper
    (Same as Catsup), 1957-1958; $125.00
Bowl, Baby, No. 142, 1957-1958; $65.00
Bowl, Baby, No. 150, 1980-1982; $65.00
Bowl, 7" Cupped, 1939-1971; $58.00
Bowl, 8" Footed Round, 1979-1983; $135.00
Bowl, 12" Footed Fruit
    (Same as Tom and Jerry), 1915-1970; $220.00
Bowl, 16" Footed Fruit, 1915-1965; $200.00
Bowl, 8" Footed, Handled, 1924-1945; $95.00
Bowl, 8½" Handled, 1934-1972; $62.00
Bowl, Handled Serving, 1948-1982; $54.00

Addition to American Pattern

**Bell
AM01/047**

Bowl, 11¾" Oval, 1938-1982; $65.00
Bowl, Oval Vegetable, 1939-1982; $35.00
Bowl, 2-part Vegetable, 1940-1974; $37.00
Bowl, 14" Punch, with 2056½
    High Foot, 1942-1958; $375.00
Bowl, 14" Punch, with Low
    Foot, 1915-1982; $325.00
Bowl, 18" Punch, Low
    Foot, 1915-1980; $475.00
Punch Bowl Ladle (Plastic), 1953-1982; $20.00
Bowl, 11½" Rolled Edge, 1940-1974; $50.00
Bowl, 3½" Rose, 1918-1958; $24.00
Bowl, 5" Rose, 1935-1958; $37.00
Bowl, 13" Shallow Fruit, 1939-1974; $95.00
Bowl, 7" Square Footed, 1952-1958; $200.00
Bowl, 10½" 3-toed, 1937-1985; $39.00
Bowl, 6½" Wedding, 1948-1973; $85.00
Bowl, 6½" Wedding
    and Cover, 1948-1973; $115.00
    Milk Glass, 1954-1960; $125.00
Box, 4¾"x3½" Cigarette and Cover,
    1936-1958; $48.00
Box, Flower (same as Oblong Butter Cover),
    1940-1948; $22.00
Butter, Oblong and Cover, 1940-1985; $35.00
Butter, Round and Cover, 1915-1974; $95.00
Cake Stand, Footed, 1979-1985; $110.00
Candlestick, Chamber, (pair) 1980-1982; $65.00
Candlestick, Duo, (pair) 1936-1958; $175.00
Candlestick, 3", (pair) 1937-1982; $32.00
Candlestick, 6", (pair) 1933-1982; $87.00

2056½ Candlestick, 7",
    (pair) 1924-1944; $245.00
Candlestick, Twin, (pair) 1937-1982; $140.00
Candy, 7" Footed and Cover, 1948-1982; $52.00
Candy Jar and Cover, 1937-1974; $40.00
Celery, 10" Tray, 1916-1985; $27.00
Centerpiece, 11" 3-cornered, 1940-1982; $48.00
Centerpiece, 9½", 1935-1982; $65.00
Centerpiece, 11", 1935-1980; $75.00
Centerpiece, 15", 1935-1944; $195.00
Cheese and Cracker, 1939-1970; $64.00
Coaster, All-over design, 1937-1980; $11.00
Coaster, Rayed Bottom, 1980-1982; $9.00
Comport, 5" High Foot, 1924-1982; $38.00
Comport and Cover, 5" High Foot,
    1924-1982; $54.00
Condiment Set, 6-piece, 1938-1943,
    1952-1958; $465.00
    Included 9" Cloverleaf Tray, two 5 oz.
    Oil Bottles (D.S.), two No. 2 Shakers
    (FGT), Mustard, Cover, and Spoon
Cream, 4¾ oz. Individual, 1916-1982; $12.00
Cream, 9½ oz. Large, 1915-1982; $16.00
Cream, 3 oz. Tea, 1939-1974; $14.00
Cup, Footed No. 614 (Punch),
    1972-1982; $12.00
Cup, Footed No 396 (Coffee),
    1932-1985; $12.00
Decanter and Stopper, 24 oz., 1934-1965; $95.00
Decanter Set, 8-piece, 1934-1943; 1957-1960,
    Included 10½" Oblong Tray, 24 oz.

Decanter and Stopper, and six 2 oz.
Whiskeys; $240.00
Floating Garden, 10" (Same as Oval, 10"),
1934-1973; $78.00
Floating Garden, 11½" (Same as Oval, 11½"), 1934-
1958; $85.00
Ice Bucket with Metal Handle, 1940-1970; $65.00
Ice Dish, 1940-1958; $48.00
Liners: Tomato Juice, Crab Meat,
Fruit Cocktail; $20.00
Ice Tub, Small, and 8" Plate, 1925-1958; $88.00
Ice Tub, Large, and 9" Plate, 1916-1958; $115.00
Jam Pot and Cover, 1948-1971; $68.00
Jam Pot Set, 3-piece, 1948-1971; $150.00
Included Sugar and Cream Tray, 2
Jam Pots and Covers.
Jar, Cookie, and Cover (Same as Cracker and
Pretzel), 1957-1970; $265.00
Jar, Pretzel, and Cover (Same as Cookie and
Cracker), 1933-1944; $265.00
Jelly, Footed Regular, 1916-1982; $35.00
Jelly, Footed Regular and Cover,
1916-1982; $48.00
Jug, 7¼" Quart, 1918-1974; $90.00
Jug, 6½" 3-pint Ice, 1938-1982; $85.00
Jug, 8", 3-pint, 1918-1974; $125.00
Jug, 8", ½-Gallon, 1918-1973; $125.00
2056½ Jug, 8¼", ½-Gallon Ice Lip,
1918-1982; $125.00
Lamp, Candle (3" Candle, Peg Candle Insert,
Wax Pot, Shade), 1939-1943;
(pair) 1954-1970; $250.00
Lamp, 12" Hurricane (Base and Chimney),
1939-1943; (pair) 1953-1958; $500.00
Lemon Dish, 1915-1944; $30.00
Lemon Dish and Cover, 1915-1944;
1947-1970; $54.00
Lily Pond, 12", 1940-1974; $95.00
Mayonnaise, 2-part, 2 Ladles, 1939-1974; $64.00
Mayonnaise, Plate, Ladle, 1935-1973; $64.00
Mayonnaise, Footed, and Ladle,
1948-1973; $53.00
Mug, 12 oz. Tankard (Same as Beer),
1974-1982; $85.00
Mug, Tom and Jerry, 1935-1944; $45.00
Mug, Youth (Same as Tom and Jerry),
1980-1982; $45.00

*Party Server with
two metal spoons*

Mustard, Cover, and Spoon, 1935-1965; $64.00
Napkin Ring, 2", 1973-1982; $35.00
Nappy, 4½" Regular, 1915-1982; $18.00
Nappy, 4¾" Fruit, 1915-1982; $18.00
Nappy, 5" Regular, 1915-1985; $15.00
Nappy, 5" Regular and Cover, 1924-1982; $25.00
Nappy, 6" Regular, 1915-1982; $18.00
Nappy, 7" Regular, 1915-1982; $20.00
Nappy, 8" Regular, 1915-1985; $20.00
Nappy, 8" Deep, 1915-1959; $55.00
Nappy, 10" Deep, 1916-1985; $55.00
Nappy, 4½" Handled Regular,
1915-1982; $15.00
Nappy, 4½" Handled Square,
1915-1982; $15.00
Nappy, 5" Handled, 3-cornered,
1915-1982; $15.00
Nappy, 5½" Handled Flared, 1915-1944; $24.00
Oil, 5 oz., D.S., G. S., 1915-1982; $54.00
Oil, 7 oz., D.S., G.S., 1915-1972; $60.00
Olive, 6", 1916-1982; $18.00
Oval, 4½" (commonly called
an Almond), 1918-1958; $24.00
Party Server, 5½" Divided, 2 metal
spoons, 1980-1983; $30.00
Pickle, 8", 1916-1982; $22.00
Picture Frame, 1980-1985; $32.00
Pitcher, Pint Cereal, 1937-1973; $37.00
Plate, 6" Bread and Butter, 1932-1982; $10.00
Plate, Cream Soup, 1939-1958; $15.00
Plate, Crescent Salad, 1937-1944; $75.00
Plate, 6½" Youth, 1980-1982; $60.00
Plate, 7" Salad, 1934-1982; $15.00
Plate, 8" Crushed Ice Tub, 1915-1958; $25.00
Plate, 8½" Salad, 1935-1982; $23.00
Plate, 9" Sandwich, 1915-1974; $33.00
Plate, 9½" Dinner, 1932-1982; $24.00

Plate, 10" Handled Cake, 1948-1982; $46.00
Plate, 10½" Sandwich, 1915-1982; $30.00
Plate, 11½" Sandwich, 1915-1974; $36.00
Plate, 12" Footed Cake, 1938-1983; $48.00
Plate, 13½" Oval Torte, 1939-1973; $98.00
Plate, 14" Torte, 1934-1985; $45.00
Plate, 18" Torte, 1935-1980; $175.00
Platter, 10½" Oval, 1933-1970; $55.00
Platter, 12" Oval, 1933-1973; $65.00
Preserve, Handled and Cover, 1915-1944; $80.00
Relish, 2-Part, 1935-1985; $30.00
Relish, 3-Part, 1935-1944; $65.00
2056½ Relish, Combination 3-part, 1939-1982; $68.00
2056½ Relish, 4-division, 1939-1971; $47.00
Salad Set, 3-piece, 1935-1982; $110.00
    Included 14" Torte Plate, 10" Deep
    Nappy (Salad Bowl), Salad
    Fork and Spoon (Wood)
Salt, Individual, 1924-1982; $8.00
Salver, 10" Round, 1916-1982; $165.00
Salver, 10" Square, 1924-1982; $185.00
Saucer, 6", Plain Center, 1932-1982; $6.00
Shaker, No. 1, 3", (pair) 1916-1945
    HNT(Heavy Nickle Top), $50.00
    HST (Heavy Silver Top), $55.00
    FGT (Fostoria Glass Top), $75.00
    SPT (Silver Plated Top), $65.00
    W (Glass disc with heavy nickle
    band), $75.00
    above available at different times
2056½ Shaker, No. 2, 3¼" (pair)
    "S" (Silver) Top, 1941-1943;
    1947-1948; $65.00
    Chrome "A" , 1949-1985; $32.00
Shaker, 2" Individual
    FGT (Fostoria Glass Top), 1938-1949; $48.00
    Chrome Top "C", 1939-1983; $38.00
Shaker Set, 3-piece, 1938-1949
    Included Individual Shaker Tray and
    2 Individual Shakers
    FGT, 1938-1949; $68.00
    Silver/Chrome Tops, 1941-1974; $48.00
Shaker, Sugar, Chrome Top, 1979-1982; $125.00

Shaker, Cheese, Chrome Top (Same as
    Sugar with larger holes; also bottom
    same as Dripcut Syrup), 1979-1982; $125.00
Shrimp Bowl, 1959-1973; $425.00
Smoker Set, 5-piece, 1935-1958; $100.00
    Included Cigarette Box and Cover
    and four 4½" Square Ash Trays
Soup, Handled Cream, 1938-1958; $54.00
Sugar and Cover, 6¼", 1915-1982; $40.00
Sugar, 5¼" Handled and Cover, 1924-1982; $45.00
Sugar, 2½" Individual, 1916-1982; $12.00
Sugar and Cream Set, Individual,
    3-piece, 1939-1974; $38.00
    Included Sugar and Cream Tray,
    Individual Sugar and Cream
Sugar and Cream Set, Tea, 3-piece,
    1939-1974; $45.00
    Included Sugar and Cream Tray,
    Tea Sugar and Cream
Sugar, 2¼" Tea, 1939-1974; $14.00
Syrup, 6½ oz. Dripcut, 1957-1982; $75.00
Syrup, 10 oz., Cover and Plate, 1939-1944; $300.00
Tid Bit, 3-toed, 1949-1982; $28.00
Toddler Set, 2-piece, 1957-1958
    Included No. 141 Baby Tumbler and
    No. 142 Baby Bowl; $565.00/market
Tom and Jerry Set, 9-piece, 1935-1944; $550.00
    Included 12" Footed Fruit Bowl and
    8 Tom and Jerry Mugs
Toothpick, 2⅜", 1916-1981; $20.00
Topper, Ash Tray, 1939-1958; $28.00
    Milk Glass, 1954-1960; $38.00
Topper, 2½" for matches, 1939-1958; $30.00
    Milk Glass, 1954-1961; $34.00
Topper, 3" Cigarette Holder, 1939-1958; $35.00
    Milk Glass, 1954-1965; $36.00
Topper, 4", 1940-1958; $45.00
    Milk Glass, 1954-1959; $95.00
Tray, Individual Shaker, 1939-1974; $20.00
Tray, 9" Cloverleaf Condiment,
    1938-1943; 1952-1958; $165.00
Tray, 10½" Oblong, 1932-1958; $110.00
Tray, Handled Lunch, 1939-1973; $85.00
Tray, Handled Muffin, 1948-1973; $50.00
Tray, Handled Utility, 1942-1982; $50.00
Tray, Sugar and Cream, 1939-1974; $15.00
Tumbler, No. 141, Baby, 1957-1958; market
Urn, 6" Square, 1940-1970; $75.00
Urn, 7½" Square, 1939-1970; $85.00
Vase, 6" Footed Cupped Bud, 1940-1982; $30.00
Vase, 6" Footed Flared Bud, 1940-1982; $30.00
    Milk Glass, 1954-1965; $42.00
    Aqua, 1957-1959; $125.00
    Peach, 1957-1959; $125.00
Vase, 8½" Footed Cupped Bud, 1948-1983; $42.00
Vase, 8½" Footed Flared Bud, 1948-1983; $42.00
    Milk Glass, 1954-1965; $75.00

New additions by popular request

Cheese Shaker, Footed Cake Stand

Vase, 6" Flared, 1935-1970; $35.00
Vase, 7" Flared (High Foot for Punch Bowl),
    1918-1959; $125.00
Vase, 8" Flared, 1935-1970; $50.00
Vase 10" Flared, 1939-1970; $90.00
Vase, 9" Square Footed, 1933-1974; $85.00
    Milk Glass, 1954-1960; $125.00
Vase, 6" Straight, 1933-1970; $56.00
Vase, 8" Straight, 1915-1970; $55.00
Vase, 10" Straight, 1915-1958; $95.00
Vase, 12" Straight, 1915-1944; $145.00

Vase, Sweetpea, 1935-1958; $65.00
Vase, Swung, 9" to 12", 1937-1944; $165.00
Youth Set, 3-piece, 1980-1982; $165.00
    Included No. 544 6" Plate (actually
    6½"), No. 150 Baby Bowl, and No. 708 Mug.
Ruby (1983-1986):
AM02/347 Candy and Cover, Footed; $100.00
AM02/763 Vase, Footed Flared Bud; $58.00
AM02/137 Bon Bon, 3-toed; $65.00
AM02/211 Bowl, 10" Salad; $95.00
AM02/567 Plate, 14" Torte; $95.00

Ruby American
Handled Utility Tray
Handled Cake
Candy Jar and Cover
Handled Bowl
Handled Muffin Tray
Bon Bon

Milk Glass
Square Footed Vase
Wedding Bowl and Cover
8½" and 6" Bud Vases
Topper Vase
Topper Cigarette
Topper Matchholder

2056—7 in.
Bowl, Cupped
Height 4½ in.

2056—12 in.
Footed Fruit Bowl
Small Punch Bowl or
Tom and Jerry Bowl
Capacity 1¾ gal.
Height 7¼ in.

2056—16 in.
Footed Fruit Bowl
Height 4¼ in.

2056—8½ in.
Handled Bowl
Height 3¾ in.

2056—11¾ in.
Oval Bowl
Height 2⅞ in.
Width 7½ in.

2056—11½ in.
Rolled Edge Bowl
Height 2¾ in.

2056—13 in.
Shallow Fruit Bowl
Height 3 in.

2056—10½ in.
3 Toed Bowl
Height 3½ in.

2056—6 ½ in.
Wedding Bowl and Cover
Height 8 in.

2056—6 ½ in.
Wedding Bowl
Height 5 ¼ in.

2056—9 ½ in.
Centerpiece
Height 3 ⅝ in.

2056—11 in.
Centerpiece
Height 4 ⅜ in.

2056—11 in.
3-Cornered Centerpiece
Height 3 ¾ in.

2056—10 in.
Floating Garden

2056—11 ½ in.
Floating Garden

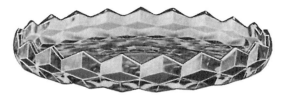

2056—12 in.
Lily Pond
Height 2 ¼ in.

2056—3 in.
Candlestick

2056—6 in.
Candlestick

2056
Duo Candlestick
Height 6 ½ in, Spread 8 ¼ in.

2056 ½
Twin Candlestick
Height 4 ⅜ in., Spread 8 ½ in.

2056—8½ in.
Small Boat
2056—12 in.
Large Boat

2056
Butter and Cover

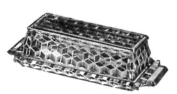

2056½
Oblong Butter and Cover
Length 7½ in., Height 2⅛ in.
Width 3¼ in.

2056—5 in.
Comport and Cover
Height 9 in.

2056
Footed Cup
Cup Capacity 7 oz.
2056
Saucer

2056—9 in.
Handled Serving Dish
Height 2⅜ in.

2056—9 in.
Oval Vegetable Dish
Width 6¾ in.

2056½
2 part Vegetable Dish
Length 10 in., Height 2⅛ in.
Width 7 in.

2056½
3 Pc. Jam Pot Set

2056½
Jam Pot and Cover
Height 4½ in.

2056
Jelly and Cover
Height 6¾ in.
Diameter 4½ in.

2056—4½ in.
Oval

2056—6 in.
Olive

2056—8 in.
Pickle

2056—10 in.
Celery

2056—6 in.
B. & B. Plate

2056—7 in.
Salad Plate

2056—8½ in.
Salad Plate

2056—9½ in.
Dinner Plate

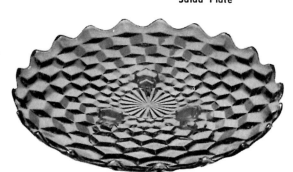

2056—12 in.
Footed Cake Plate

2056—10 in.
Handled Cake Plate

2056—9 in.
Sandwich Plate

2056—10½ in.
Sandwich Plate

2056—11½ in.
Sandwich Plate

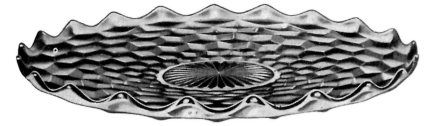

2056—14 in.
Torte Plate

2056—18 in.
Torte Plate

2056—13½ in.
Oval Torte Plate

2056—10½ in.
Oval Platter

2056—12 in.
Oval Platter

2056
2 Part Relish
Length 9 in., Width 5½ in.
12 in. Overall

2056½
3 Part Combination Relish
Length 11 in., Width 7½ in.

2056½
4 Division Relish
Length 9 in., Width 6½ in.

2056
Individual Salt
Height 1 in.

2056
Sauce Boat
Length 6¾ in., Width 5 in.
2056
Sauce Boat Plate
Length 8 in., Width 6½ in.

2056
Cream Soup
2056
Cream Soup Plate

2056—3 Piece Ind. Shaker Set
Length 4 in., Height 2¼ in.
Consisting of:
1/12 doz. 2056
Ind. Shaker Tray
1/6 doz. 2056
Ind. Shaker, Silver Top "C"

2056½
Shaker
Silver Top "A"
Height 3½ in.

2056
Ind. Shaker
Silver Top "C"
Height 2⅞ in.

2056
Sugar and Cover
Height 6¼ in.
also
Candy Jar and Cover

2056
Cream
Height 4¼ in.
Capacity 9½ oz.

2056½
Handled Sugar and Cover
Height 5¼ in.

2056—3 Piece Ind.
Sugar and Cream and Tray
Consisting of:
1/12 doz. 2056—6¾ in.
S. & C. Tray
1/12 doz. 2056—Ind. Sugar
1/12 doz. 2056—Ind. Cream
2056½—3 Piece Tea Sugar
and Cream and Tray
Consisting of:
1/12 doz. 2056—6¾ in.
S. & C. Tray
1/12 doz. 2056½—Tea Sugar
1/12 doz. 2056½—Tea Cream

2056—14 in. Punch Bowl
and High Foot (Illustrated)
Low Foot can also be furnished
for 14 in. Punch Bowl
Capacity 2 Gallons
2056—18 in. Punch Bowl
Capacity 3 ¾ Gallons
Low Foot is used with
18 in. Punch Bowl

2056—Ice Bucket
Height 4 ½ in. Top Dia. 6 in.
Metal Handle and Tongs
Tongs Priced Separately

2056
Punch Cup, Reg.

2056
Punch Cup, Fld.

2056
Decanter and Stopper
Cap. 24 oz. Height 9 ¼ in.

2056
3 Pint Ice Jug
Height 6 ½ in.

2056 ½
Ice Jug, Lipped
Cap. ½ Gallon, Height 8 ¼ in.

2056
Pint Cereal Pitcher
Height 5 ⅜ in.
2056
Quart Jug
Height 7 ¼ in.

2056
3 Pint Jug
Height 8 in.
2056
½ Gallon Jug
Height 8 in.

2056
Small Ice Tub and Plate
Top Dia. 5 ⅝ in., Height 3 ¾ in.
2056
Large Ice Tub and Plate
Top Dia. 6 ½ in., Height 4 ½ in.

2056
Footed Mayonnaise and Ladle
Height 4⅝ in.

2056
2 Part Mayonnaise and 2 Ladles
Dia. 6¼ in., Height 3¾ in.

2056
Mayonnaise and Plate
and Ladle
Height 3 in.

2056—10 in., 3 Piece Salad Set
Height 5 in.
Consisting of
1/12 Doz. 2056— 10 in. Salad
Bowl
1/12 Doz. 2056—14 in. Torte
Plate
1/12 Doz. 2056—Salad Fork
and Spoon, Wood

2056
Basket, Reed Handle
Height 4 in. Length 9 in.
Width 7 in.

2056
3 Toed Bon Bon
Diameter 7 in.

2056
Footed Candy and Cover

2056
3 Part Candy Box and Cover
Height 4 in. Width 6⅛ in.

2056
3 Toed Tid Bit
Diameter 8 in. Height 1½ in.

**2056
Cheese and Cracker
Height 4 in.
Diameter Plate 11½ in.
Diameter Cheese 5¾ in.**

**2056
Coaster
Diameter 3¾ in.**

**2056
Ice Dish
Tomato Juice Liner Illustrated**

**2451—4 oz.
Crab Meat Liner
Blown**

**2451—5 oz.
Fruit Cocktail Liner
Blown**

**2451—5 oz.
Tomato Juice Liner
Blown**

**2056
Lemon and Cover
Height 3½ in., Dia. 5½ in.**

**2056
Mustard and Cover and Spoon
Height 3¾ in.**

**2056—5 oz. Oil, D/S
Height 6¼ in.
2056—7 oz. Oil, D/S
Height 6¾ in.**

**2056—10 in.
Round Salver
Height 7¼ in.**

**2056—10 in.
Square Salver
Height 7¼ in.**

2056—12 in.
Handled Lunch Tray

2056
Handled Muffin Tray
Length 8 in. Width 10 in.

2056—9 in.
Handled Utility Tray
Diameter 9½ in.

2056—4¾ in.
Nappy (Fruit)

2056—4½ in.
Nappy
2056—5 in.
Nappy
2056—6 in.
Nappy
2056—7 in.
Nappy

2056—5 in.
Nappy and Cover
Height 5 in.

2056—8 in.
Nappy, Reg.
2056—8 in.
Nappy, Deep
2056—10 in.
Nappy, Deep

2056—4½ in.
Hld. Nappy, Square

2056—4½ in.
Hld. Nappy, Reg.

2056—5 in.
Hld. Nappy, 3 Cor.

2056
Cigarette Box and Cover
Length 4¾ in. Width 3½ in.

2056
Oval Ash Tray
Length 5½ in.

2056
Square Ash Tray
2⅞ in. Square

2056
5 Piece Smoker Set
Consisting of:
1/12 Doz. 2056—Cigarette
Box and Cover
1/3 Doz. 2056—Square
Ash Trays

2056—2½ in.
Topper
Top Diameter 3¾ in.

2056—3 in.
Topper
Top Diameter 4½ in.

2056
Topper Ash Tray
Top Diameter 2⅛ in.

2056—3½ in.
Rose Bowl
2056—5 in.
Rose Bowl

2056—6 in.
Vase
2056—8 in.
Vase
2056—10 in.
Vase

2056½—6 in.
Vase, Flared

2056½—7 in.
Vase, Flared

2056½—8 in.
Vase, Flared
2056½—10 in.
Vase, Flared

2056½—9½ in.
Vase, Flared

2056—9 in.
Square Footed Vase

2056
Sweetpea Vase
Height 4½ in.

2056—6 in.
Square Urn
2056—7½ in
Square Urn

2056—4 in.
Topper
Top Diameter 6 in.

2056/259
Shrimp Bowl
Diameter 12¼"

2056—6 in.
Footed Bud Vase, Cupped

2056—6 in.
Footed Bud Vase, Flared

2056—8½ in.
Footed Bud Vase, Cupped

2056—8½ in.
Footed Bud Vase, Flared

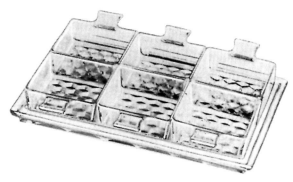

2056
7 Pc. Appetizer Set
consisting of:
1/12 Doz. 2056
10½ in. Oblong Tray
½ Doz. 2056
Individual Appetizers
Height 1¾ in., Length
10½ in., Width 8¾ in.

2056
8 Pc. Decanter Set
consisting of:
1/12 Doz. 2056
Decanter & Stopper
½ Doz. 2056 2 oz. Whiskey
1/12 Doz. 2056
10½ in. Oblong Tray

2056
3¼ in. Individual Appetizer

2056
Toddler Set
consisting of:
1/12 Doz. 2056 Baby Tumbler
1/12 Doz. 2056 Baby Bowl

2056
Cookie Jar & Cover
Height 8⅞ in.
Diameter 5¾ in.

2056
Condiment Bottle & Stopper
Height 6¾ in.
Capacity 8½ oz.

2056
Dripcut Syrup
Height 5¼ in.
Capacity 6½ oz.

2056
10½ in. Oblong Tray

2056
5 in. Ash Tray

American

Youth Gift Set

Additions to AMERICAN PATTERN

		Retail Price Each	
☐	AM01/737	Boxed Youth Gift Set Consisting of:	$35.00
☐	AM01/150	Bowl	12.50
☐	AM01/708	Handled Mug	12.50
☐	AM01/544	6" Plate	10.00
☐	AM01/866	Picture Frame	7.50
☐	AM01/311	Chamber Candleholder	11.50

150

708

544

866

311

2364 SONATA

Sonata made its debut in 1940 and was offered in Crystal only. Since pieces from this line were used throughout the 1944 – 1986 period, it seemed only natural to include Sonata in this book rather than in the 1924 – 1943 volume. The utter simplicity of this pattern defines it.

One of only a few lines to have its very own Cigarette Holder, this plain pattern with its graceful elegance holds other charms as well. The Cigarette Holder and the Individual Almond are very difficult to find, as is the Candy Box and Cover. A few pieces, especially those with flat rims, seem to have been borrowed from the earlier 2350 Pioneer line. Suspiciously familiar are the 5" Fruit, the 6" Baked Apple, the 8" Rim Soup, the 8" Pickle, and the 11" Celery. We first noticed the similarities when finding a Baked Apple with the Romance etching prompted further research on these flat-rimmed pieces.

Many other patterns used pieces from the Sonata line. The Duo Candlestick has a different number but obviously was meant to be part of Sonata. The 6" Comport retained its original number, but when the same comport was made two inches taller, it was given the 2364 designation. Basically, these two comports are identical except for size.

Interestingly, a 2364 Torte Plate was offered in 1931 in color. It was not called Sonata and was listed with other numbered plates.

Almond, Individual, 1949-1959; $7.00
Ash Tray, Individual, 1941-1943; $7.00
Bowl, 5" Fruit, 1942-1944; $12.00
Bowl, 6" Baked Apple (2350), 1942-1944;
    1957-1965; $15.00
Bowl, 8" Rim Soup (2350), 1941-1943;
    1957-1968; $18.00
Bowl, Oval Sauce, 1949-1959; $30.00
Bowl, 9" Salad, 1940-1973; $30.00
Bowl, 9" Lily Pond, 1961-1973; $32.00
Bowl, 10½" Salad, 1940-1973; $35.00
Bowl, 12" Flared, 1940-1976; $40.00
Bowl, 12" Lily Pond, 1940-1965; $40.00
Bowl, 13" Fruit, 1940-1965; $45.00
Candlestick, Duo (6023),
    (pair) 1943-1964; $48.00
Candy Box and Cover, 1941-1943; $67.00
Celery, 11", 1942-1957; $22.00
Cheese and Cracker, 1941-1959; $34.00

Cigarette Holder, 1941-1943; $22.00
Comport, 6" (2400), 1947-1959; $22.00
Comport, 8", 1942-1957; $30.00
Mayonnaise, Plate and Ladle, 1941-1973; $46.00
Mayonnaise, 2 part, Plate and Ladle,
    1949-1962; $48.00
Pickle, 8", 1942-1958; $18.00
Plate, Crescent, 1941-1973; $18.00
Plate, 11" Sandwich, 1941-1973; $20.00
Plate, 14" Torte, 1940-1976; $40.00
Plate, 16" Torte, 1946-1970; $45.00
Relish, 2-part, 1942-1973; $22.00
Relish, 3-part, 1942-1973; $45.00
Salad Set, 9", 1946-1970; $65.00
Salad Set, 10½", 1946-1973; $75.00
Shaker, Individual, Top "E",
    (pair) 1942-1976; $18.00
Shaker, Large, Top "B", (pair) 1953-1976; $25.00
Tray, Handled Lunch, 1942-1965; $35.00

2364—10½ in. Salad Bowl
Height 4 in.

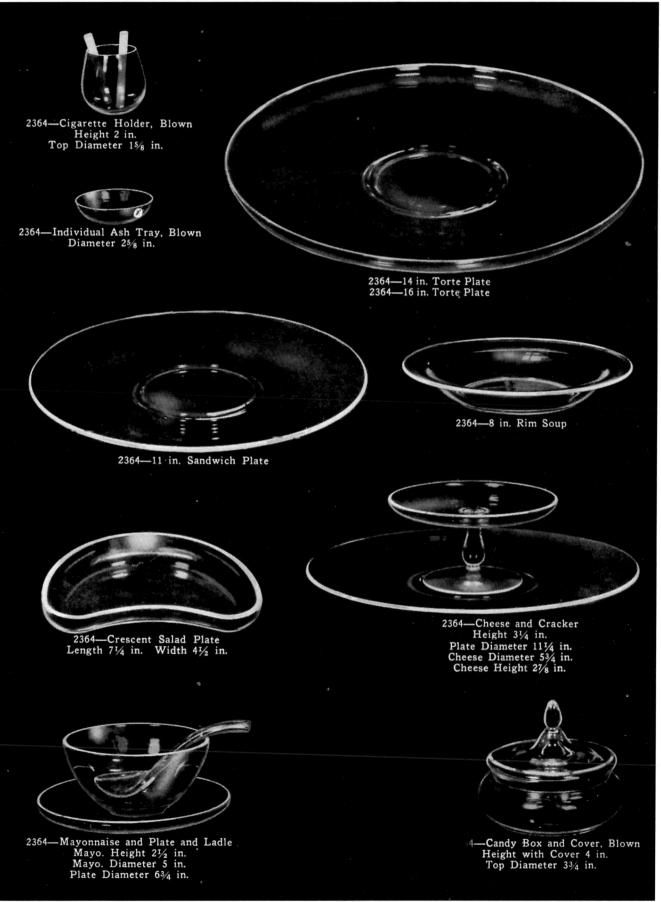

2364—Cigarette Holder, Blown
Height 2 in.
Top Diameter 1⅝ in.

2364—Individual Ash Tray, Blown
Diameter 2⅝ in.

2364—14 in. Torte Plate
2364—16 in. Torte Plate

2364—11 in. Sandwich Plate

2364—8 in. Rim Soup

2364—Crescent Salad Plate
Length 7¼ in.   Width 4½ in.

2364—Cheese and Cracker
Height 3¼ in.
Plate Diameter 11¼ in.
Cheese Diameter 5¾ in.
Cheese Height 2⅞ in.

2364—Mayonnaise and Plate and Ladle
Mayo. Height 2½ in.
Mayo. Diameter 5 in.
Plate Diameter 6¾ in.

4—Candy Box and Cover, Blown
Height with Cover 4 in.
Top Diameter 3¾ in.

2364—12 in.
Bowl, Flared
Height 2⁷⁄₈ in.

2364—13 in.
Fruit Bowl
Height 2³⁄₄ in.

2364—12 in.
Lily Pond
Height 2¹⁄₄ in.

6023
Duo Candlestick
Height 5¹⁄₂ in. Spread 6 in.

2400—6 in.
Comport
2364—8 in.
Comport

2364—8 in.
Pickle
Height 1 in.
2364—11 in.
Celery

2364
Crescent Salad Plate
Length 7¹⁄₄ in. Width 4¹⁄₂ in.

2364 — 11 in.
Sandwich Plate

2364 — 14 in.   2364 — 16 in.
Torte Plate   Torte Plate

2364
3 part Relish
Height 1-1/2 in. Length 10 in.
Width 7-1/4 in.

2364
Shaker
Chrome Top "C"
Height 2-5/8 in.

2364
Oval Sauce Dish
Height 2-3/4 in.

2364
2-part Mayonnaise
and 2 Ladles
Height 2-3/4 in.

2364
Mayonnaise and Plate
and Ladle
Mayo. Height 2-1/2 in.
Mayo. Diameter 5 in.
Plate Diameter 6-3/4 in.

2364
Individual Almond

2364
Cheese and Cracker
Height 3-1/4 in.
Plate Diameter 11-1/4 in.
Cheese Diameter 5-3/4 in.
Cheese Height 2-7/8 in.

2364 — 9 in.   Also 2364 — 10-1/2 in.
3 Piece Salad Set (Illustrated   3 Piece Salad Set
Consisting of: Consisting of:
1/12 Doz. 2364 — 9 in. Salad   1/12 Doz. 2364 — 10-1/2 in.
Bowl Ht. 2-5/8 in.   Salad Bowl — Ht. 4 in.
1/12 Doz. 2364 — 11 in.   1/12 Doz. 2364 — 14 in.
Sandwich Plate   Torte Plate
1/12 Doz. 2364 — Fork and   1/12 Doz. 2364 — Fork and
Spoon — Wood   Spoon — Wood

2364
Handled Lunch Tray
Diameter 11-1/4 in.

2412 COLONY

Of all Fostoria's pressed dinnerware, the Colony pattern is second only to the American pattern in popularity. The short-lived Queen Anne pattern shown in *Fostoria Tableware: 1924 – 1943* had exclusive rights to the 2412 number at first. When Colony was offered, most pieces from the Queen Anne pattern were included in the Colony line. Earlier, Fostoria had introduced 112 Cascade as its first swirl pattern. Curiously, the 14½" Lustre has the 2412 number when shown with Queen Anne, and the 1103 number when shown with Colony.

Colony was made in crystal except for some few pieces made in Milk Glass in the 1950s (see Milk Glass), and the Maypole and Ruby Giftware. It was a complete dinner service and was introduced in 1938. However since many pieces were added in the late 1940s and early 1950s, Colony is shown here instead of in the earlier volume. As late as 1981, the 3" and 9" Candlesticks still were being made in crystal, and the Sugar and Cream and 6" Bud Vase were offered in Ruby for a very short run through May of 1982. (See Maypole and Holly and Ruby Giftware for additional pieces and colors.)

Of particular interest to collectors are the early pieces made with plain surface and swirl trim. This style of Colony was offered in 1939 and 1940. The square ash trays, cigarette and cover, the rectangular shaped relishes, celery, divided sweetmeat, pickle, olive, low comport, mayonnaise and plate, and urn and cover were all made plain. The ash trays continued to be made through 1959.

The Colony pattern has its unique features, with a blown jug, swirled handles, swirled cruet tops, and distinctive, almost beaded handles on the sweetmeat, lemon, bon bon and whip cream. The center handled tray has an extraordinarily swirled handle, and one of three cornucopia-like pieces Fostoria ever made was in the Colony pattern.

Good Housekeeping, November 1939

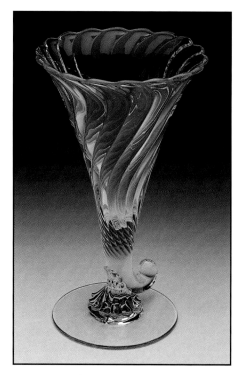

Cornucopia Vase

Stemware is featured in *Fostoria Stemware*, page 46.

Almond, Footed, 1940-1957; $24.00

Ash Tray, 3" Square, 1939-1959; $10.00

Ash Tray, 3½" Square, 1939-1959; $12.00

Ash Tray, 4½" Square, 1938-1959; $20.00

Ash Tray, 3" Round, 1949-1959; $15.00

Ash Tray, 4½" Round, 1949-1959; $15.00

Ash Tray, 6" Round, 1949-1959; $20.00

Ash Tray Set, 3-piece Square, 1941-1959; $42.00

Ash Tray Set, 3-pc. Round, 1949-1959; $50.00

Bon Bon, 5", 1939-1963; $18.00

Bon Bon, 3-toed, 1940-1965; $26.00

Bon Bon, Footed, 1949-1959; $34.00

Bowl, 4½" Ice, 1948-1962; $25.00

Bowl, 4½" Round Nappy, 1939-1970; $12.00

Bowl, 4¾" Finger; 1941-1944, $18.00

Bowl, 5" Round Nappy, 1939-1970; $14.00

Bowl, 7¼" Ice, 1940-1943; $36.00

Bowl, 8" Cupped, 1938-1959; $40.00

Bowl, 8¼" Flared, 1949-1959; $40.00

Bowl, 8½" Serving, 1941-1970; $42.00

Bowl, 9" Rolled Edge, 1948-1959; $45.00

Bowl, 9¾" Salad, 1939-1972; $45.00

Bowl, 10" Fruit, 1948-1959; $48.00

Bowl, 10½" Fruit, 1938-1959; $48.00

Bowl, 10½" Oval Vegetable, 1948-1970; $34.00

Bowl, 10½" 2-part Oval Vegetable, 1948-1971; $38.00

Bowl, 11" Footed Oval; 1941-1958, $68.00

Bowl, 11" Flared; $50.00

Bowl, 14" Fruit, 1941-1959; $75.00

Bowl, High Footed, 1938-1944; $125.00

Bowl, Low Footed, 1938-1959; $95.00

Bowl, 3-toed Nut, 1940-1944; $54.00

Bowl, Ice Cream, Square, 1938-1965; $48.00

Bowl, Punch, 1952-1973; $500.00/market

Bowl, Rose, 1949-1960; $37.00

Bowl, Tricorne, 3-toed, 1940-1944; $54.00

Butter and Cover, 1948-1970; $45.00

Candelabra, 2-light, (pair) 1938-1965; $150.00

Candle, Duo, (pair) 1938-1965; $95.00

Candle, 6" Lustre, (pair) 1938-1942; $95.00

Candle, 7½" Lustre, (pair) 1938-1959; $125.00

Candle, 14½" Lustre (1103), (pair) 1934-1942; $250.00

Candle, Lustre No. 4, (pair) 1934-1942; $175.00

Candlestick, 3", (pair) 1940-1966; $30.00

Candlestick, 7", (pair) 1939-1973; $48.00

Candle Lamp, 1941-1945; $95.00

Candy Box and Cover, 1948-1959; $62.00

Celery, 9⅝", 1949-1965; $22.00

Celery, 11½", 1941-1948; $32.00

Celery, 10½" Rectangle, 1938-1940; $45.00

Centerpiece, 13", 1941-1965; $70.00

Cheese and Cracker, 1940-1959; $70.00

Cigarette Box and Cover, 1939-1944; $95.00

Comport, Low and Cover, 1945-1959; $65.00

Comport, Low, Plain, and Cover, 1939-1944; $85.00

Cream Soup, 1940-1965; $57.00

Cup and Saucer, 1940-1973; $14.00

Cup, Punch, 1952-1973; $16.00

Jelly and Cover, Footed, 1948-1959; $54.00

Jug, 3-pint, 1952-1970; $135.00

Jug, 2-quart, 1940-1959; $150.00

Lemon, 6½", 1939-1959; $18.00

Lily Pond, 9", 1953-1959; $40.00

Lily Pond, 10", 1941-1959; $40.00

Lily Pond, 13", 1941-1959; $57.00

Mayonnaise, Plate, Ladle, Plain, 1939-1944; $75.00

Mayonnaise, Plate, Ladle, 1945-1970; $47.00

Oil and Stopper, 1940-1958; $58.00

Olive, 6¼", 1948-1959; $18.00

Olive, 6½" Rectangle, 1939-1940; $24.00

Olive, 7", 1941-1948; $20.00

Pickle, 8" Rectangle, 1938-1940; $30.00

Pickle, 8", 1949-1959; $22.00

Pickle, 9½", 1941-1948; $25.00

Pitcher, Cereal, 1948-1959; $85.00

Plate, 6", 1940-1973; $10.00

Plate, 7", 1940-1975; $12.00

Plate, 8", 1940-1973; $14.00

Plate, 9", 1940-1973; $37.00

Plate, 13" Torte, 1938-1972; $57.00

Plate, 15" Torte, 1941-1959; $65.00

Plate, 18" Torte, 1952-1959; $95.00

2412—Finger Bowl
Height 2 in.
Diameter 4¾ in.

2412—2-Quart Ice Jug
Height 7¾ in.

Plate, Handled Cake, 1941-1970; $38.00
Platter, 12½", 1948-1959; $57.00
Relish, 7¼" Rectangle, 1939-1940; $28.00
Relish, 10" Rectangle, 1939-1940; $38.00
Relish, 2-part, 1941-1972; $25.00
Relish, 3-part, 1941-1972; $35.00
Salad Set, 3-piece; $100.00
    Salad Bowl, 13" Torte, Wooden Fork and Spoon
Salver, 12" Cake, 1938-1942; $125.00

Shaker (pair)
    Chrome Top B, 1942-1978; $18.00
    Silver Top B, 1940-1973; $20.00
    Glass Top F, 1940-1948; $35.00
Shaker Set, 3-pc., Individual
    Chrome Top C, 1949-1973; $28.00
    Silver Top C, 1940-1973; $30.00
    Glass Top F, 1942-1968; $38.00
Sugar and Cream, 1940-1970; $25.00

2412—Footed Cup
2412—Saucer
Cup Capacity 6 oz.

2412—Cream Soup

2412—Mayonnaise and Plate and Ladle
Mayo. Height 3⅜ in.   Mayo. Diameter 4⅝ in.
Plate Diameter 6¾ in.

2412—Individual Sugar
Height 2⅞ in.

2412—Individual Cream
Height 3¼ in.
Capacity 4¼ oz.

2412—7 in. Olive
2412—9½ in. Pickle
2412—11½ in. Celery

2412—Individual Shaker and E Top
Height 1⅞ in.

2412—3 Piece Ind. Shaker Set
Length 4½ in.   Height 2¼ in.
Consisting of:
1/12 Doz. 2412—Ind. Shaker Tray
1/6 Doz. 2412—Ind. Shaker and E Top

2412—Ind. Sugar and Cream and Tray
Height 3½ in.
Consisting of:
1/12 Doz. 2412—6¾ in. S. & C. Tray
1/12 Doz. 2412—Ind. Sugar
1/12 Doz. 2412—Ind. Cream

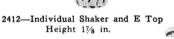

2412—Shaker and F Top
Height 2¾ in.

2412—Footed Sugar
Height 3⅜ in.

2412—Footed Cream
Height 3⅞ in.
Capacity 7 oz.

2412—Footed Almond
Height 1⅜ in.
Length 2¾ in.

2412—4 oz. Oil and Stopper
Ground Stopper
Height 5⅞ in.
Capacity 4½ oz.

Sugar and Cream, Individual, 1940-1972; $25.00
Sweetmeat, 5", 1939-1959; $18.00
Sweetmeat, Divided Rectangle, 1939-1941; $26.00
Tid Bit, 3-toed, 1940-1944; $54.00
Tid Bit, 7" Footed, 1939-1944; $75.00
Tray, Sugar and Cream, 1940-1970; $18.00
Tray, Handled Lunch, 1939-1969; $65.00
Tray, Muffin, 1941-1970; $57.00
Tray, 10½" Snack, 1941-1959; $40.00

Urn and Cover, Footed; 1940-1944, $125.00
Urn and Cover, Ftd., Plain, 1940-1944; $165.00
Vase, Flared Bud, 1941-1971; $18.00
Vase, 7" Cupped, Footed, 1940-1959; $62.00
Vase, 7½" Flared, Footed, 1940-1959; $68.00
Vase, 9¼" Cornucopia, 1952-1959; $74.00
Vase, 12", 1938-1944; $175.00
Vase, 14", 1938-1944; $195.00
Whip Cream, 4¾", 1939-1965; $20.00

2412—4½ in. Round Nappy
2412—5 in. Round Nappy

2412—Ice Cream
5½ in. Square

2412—13 in. Torte Plate

2412—12 in. Salver
Height 4½ in.

2412—Handled Lunch Tray
Diameter 11½ in.

2412—Low Comport—No. Cover
Height 4 in.
2412—Low Comport and Cover
Height 6⅜ in.

2412—Cheese and Cracker
Height 3½ in.
Plate Diameter 12½ in.
Cheese Diameter 5¼ in.

2412—Handled Muffin Tray
Length 8⅜ in.   Width 9¾ in.

2412—7 in. Footed Tid Bit
Height 2⅞ in.

2412—3-Toed Tricorne
Length 7 in.
Height 2⅞ in.

2412—8½ in. Serving Dish, 2 Handles
Height 2⅜ in.

2412—3-Toed Tid Bit
Diameter 7½ in.
Height 1⅜ in.

2412—3-Toed Bon Bon
Diameter 7 in.
Height 2 in.

2412—3-Toed Nut Bowl
Diameter 5⅝ in.
Height 2⅝ in.

2412—10 in. Cake Plate, 2 Handles

2412—Ice Bowl
Height 4 in.
Diameter 7¼ in.

2412—Sweetmeat
Diameter 5 in.
Height 1½ in.

2412—Bon Bon
Length 5 in.
Width 6 in.

2412 Whip Cream
Diameter 4¾ in.
Height 1¾ in.

2412—Lemon
Diameter 6½ in.

2412—3 Piece Ash Tray Set
Consisting of:
1/12 Doz. 2412—3 in. Ind. Ash Tray
1/12 Doz. 2412—3½ in. Small Ash Tray
1/12 Doz. 2412—4½ in. Large Ash Tray

2412—Oblong Cigarette Box and Cover
Length 6 in.   Width 4¾ in.
Height 1⅜ in.   Holds 38 Cigarettes

2412—3 in. Individual Ash Tray

2412—3½ in. Small Ash Tray

2412—4½ in. Large Ash Tray

43

2412—3 in. Candlestick

2412—10 in. Lily Pond
Height 2¼ in.

2412—7½ in Vase, Flared

2412—7 in. Ftd. Vase, Cupped

2412—6 in.
Footed Bud Vase, Flared

2412—11 in. Footed Oval Bowl
Height 4 in.

2412—Footed Urn No Cover
Height 6⅝ in.
2412—Footed Urn and Cover
Height 9 in.

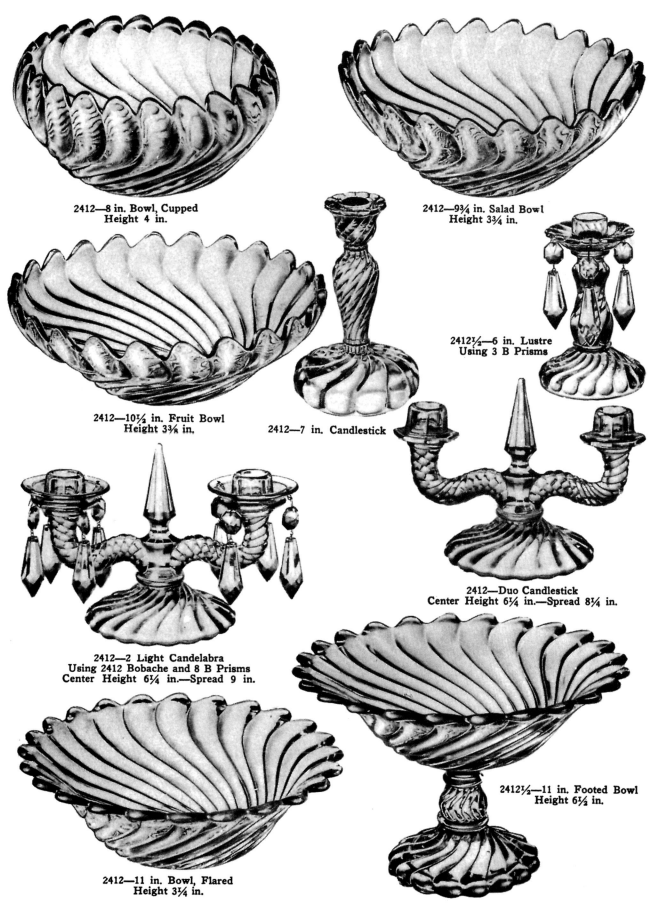

2412—8 in. Bowl, Cupped
Height 4 in.

2412—9¾ in. Salad Bowl
Height 3¾ in.

2412—10½ in. Fruit Bowl
Height 3⅜ in.

2412—7 in. Candlestick

2412½—6 in. Lustre
Using 3 B Prisms

2412—2 Light Candelabra
Using 2412 Bobache and 8 B Prisms
Center Height 6¼ in.—Spread 9 in.

2412—Duo Candlestick
Center Height 6¼ in.—Spread 8¼ in.

2412½—11 in. Footed Bowl
Height 6½ in.

2412—11 in. Bowl, Flared
Height 3¼ in.

2412 COLONY

No. 4 Lustre (10 UDP)
Height 9¾ in.

2412—Low Foot Bowl
Diameter 10½ in. Height 5⅝ in.

2412—7½ in. Lustre
8 U Drop Prisms

2412—12 in. Vase
2412—14 in. Vase

2412—High Foot Bowl
Diameter 10½ in. Height 8¼ in.

1103—14½ in. Lustre
10 U Drop Prisms

2412
Vegetable Dish
Length 10½ in. Height 2⅛ in.
Width 6⅞ in.

2412
Pint Cereal Pitcher
Height 5⅞ in.

2412
Candy Box and Cover
Height 4 in. Diameter 6½ in.

2412—2 Pt.
Vegetable Dish
Length 10½ in. Height 2⅛ in.
Width 6⅞ in.

2412—10½ in.
Snack Tray

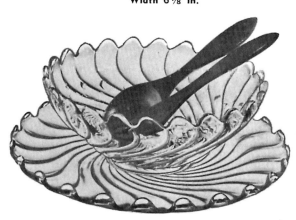

2412—9¾ in.
3 Piece Salad Set
Consisting of:
1/12 Doz. 2412—9¾ in. Salad
Bowl—Height 3¾ in.
1/12 Doz. 2412—13 in.
Torte Plate
1/12 Doz. 2412—Salad Fork
and Spoon—Wood

2412
Footed Bon Bon
Diameter 5 in. Height 4⅛ in.

2412
Oblong Butter and Cover
Length 7½ in. Height 2 in.
Width 3½ in.

2412
Ice Bowl
Top Diameter 4½ in.
Height 6¼ in.

2412
Jelly and Cover

2412—6 in.
Plate
2412—7 in.
Plate
2412—8 in.
Plate
2412—9 in.
Plate

2412—6¼ in.
Olive

2412—8 in.
Pickle

2412—9⅝ in.
Celery

2412—12½ in.
Platter

2412
2 Part Relish
Length 7 in. Height 1¾ in.
Width 4⅞ in.

2412
Shaker
Silver Top "B"
Height 3⅝ in.

2412
Ind. Shaker
Silver Top "C"
Height 2⅜ in.

2412—10 in.
Lily Pond
Height 2¼ in.
2412—13 in.
Lily Pond
Height 2¾ in.

2412—3 Piece Ind. Shaker Set
Length 4½ in. Height 2¼ in.
Consisting of:
1/12 Doz. 2412
Ind. Shaker Tray
1/6 Doz. 2412
Ind. Shaker, Silver Top "C"

2412—14 in.
Fruit Bowl
Height 2¾ in.

2412—10 in.
Fruit Bowl
Height 2⅝ in.

2412
3 Part Relish
Length 10½ in. Height 1¾ in.
Width 7¼ in.

2412—13 in.
Centerpiece
Height 2⅝ in.

2412—9 in.
Lily Pond
Height 2¼ in

2412—9 in.
Bowl, Rolled Edge
Height 2⅞ in.

2412—8¼ in.
Bowl, Flared
Height 3⅝ in.

2412—3 Piece Ash Tray Set
Consisting of:
1/12 Doz. 2412—3 in. Ind. Ash Tray
1/12 Doz. 2412—3 ½ in. Small Ash Tray
1/12 Doz. 2412—4 ½ in. Large Ash Tray

2412—3 ½ in.
Small Ash Tray

2412—3 in.
Individual Ash Tray

2412—4 ½ in.
Large Ash Tray

2412 ½—4 ½ in.
Round Ash Tray

2412 ½—3 in.
Round Ash Tray

2412½—3 Piece Round Ash Tray Set
Consisting of:
1/12 doz. 2412½—3 in. Round Ash Tray
1/12 doz. 2412½—4 ½ in. Round Ash Tray
1/12 doz. 2412½—6 in. Round Ash Tray

2412½—6 in.
Round Ash Tray

2412—6 in.
Rose Bowl

2412—7 ½ in.
Vase, Flared

2412—7 in.
Ftd. Vase, Cupped

2412—6 in.
Footed Bud Vase, Flared

49

2412
3 Pint Ice Jug
Height 8-½ in.

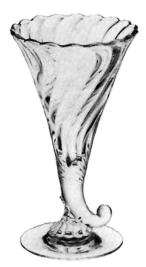

2412 — 9-¼ in.
Cornucopia Vase

2412
Punch Bowl
Capacity 2 gal.
Height 8-⅛ in.
Top Diameter 13-¼ in.

2412
Punch Cup
Capacity 5-¼ oz.
Height 2-⅞ in.

2412 — 18 in.
Torte Plate

2449 LEXINGTON

Reintroduction of Hermitage, 1974
Olive Green, Brown, Yellow

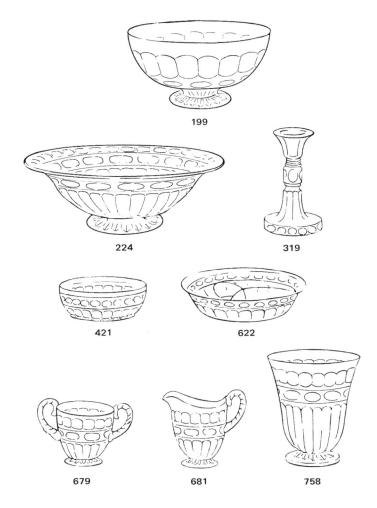

199 Bowl, 8" Footed; $32.00
224 Bowl, 10" Footed
    Flared; $32.00
319 Candleholder, 6"; $64.00
421 Bowl, 5" Fruit; $15.00
622 Relish, 3-part; $26.00
679 Sugar, Footed; $13.50
681 Cream, Footed; $13.50
758 Vase, 6" Footed; $38.00

Lexington Olive Green 10" Bowl and 6" Candleholders

2560 CORONET

One of Fostoria's most distinctive patterns, Coronet is easily identified through the three graceful, wavy lines which decorate the edge of each piece, with the notable exception of the Cup, and the handles which resemble ram's horns. The ram's horns are most noticeable in the 4½" single Candlestick and the duo Candlestick. The 4" Candlestick and 6" Comport have an unusual stem that is reminiscent of a Greek column. The Comport has an additional decoration at the top of the stem that is quite striking.

The Coronet line was first introduced in 1938, with several pieces not offered until 1939, for example, the Sugar and Cream Tray. Much of the line was discontinued after the watershed year of 1943, and the entire line was no longer being made by 1960. Pieces are elusive in this short-lived pattern. The salad bowl, for example, was made the full time; however, the two-part salad survived for only five years.

Some slight similarities exist between Coronet and Colony. The handle of the Center Handled Tray is the same for both patterns. Cup handles and Sugar and Cream handles are similar, but the Coronet handles are a continuous swirl, whereas the Colony handles are smooth at first and end with swirls.

Often confused with Heisey's Rose pattern, Willowmere (Etching 333) was offered on the Coronet blank. Unfortunately, not many of Fostoria's patterns used Coronet dinnerware; Etching 332, Mayflower, Cutting 785, Cynthia, and Decoration 515, Richlieu were among the few. Truly, the flowing design and brilliance of the crystal cause Coronet to be desireable with or without any ornamentation.

The Muffin Tray pictured has been made into a basket using metal filigree. It was not offered by Fostoria with the metal container.

Handled Muffin Tray with Metal Filigree Frame, Handled Vase

Sugar and Cream with Tray, Pansy Vase

Bon Bon, 2 Handles, 1938-1959; $26.00
Bon Bon, 3-toed, 1938-1959; $34.00
Bowl, 5" Fruit, 1938-1943; $18.00
Bowl, 6" Cereal, 1938-1943; $20.00
Bowl, 3-toed Nut, Cupped, 1938-1959; $34.00
Bowl, 8½" Handled Serving, 1938-1959; $38.00
Bowl, 8½" Cupped, 1938-1944; $47.00
Bowl, 10" Salad, 1938-1959; $45.00
Bowl, 2-part Salad, 1938-1943; $65.00
Bowl, 11" Handled, 1938-1959; $65.00
Bowl, 11½" Crimped, 1938-1959; $65.00
Bowl, 12" Flared, 1938-1959; $65.00
Bowl, 13" Fruit, 1938-1959; $68.00
Cake, 10½" Handled, 1938-1959; $42.00
Candlestick, 4", (pair) 1938-1957; $36.00
Candlestick, 4½", (pair) 1938-1959; $36.00
Candlestick, Duo, (pair) 1938-1959; $48.00
Celery, 11", 1938-1957; $28.00
Cheese and Cracker, 1938-1944; $48.00

Comport, 6", 1938-1943; $34.00
Cup and Saucer, 1938-1959; $14.00
Ice Bucket, Chrome Handle, 1938-1943; $57.00
Lemon Dish, 2 Handles, 1938-1959; $18.00
Mayonnaise, Plate, Ladle, 1938-1959; $37.00
Mayonnaise, 2-part, 2 Ladles, 1938-1943; $37.00
Oil and Stopper, 3 oz., 1938-1943; $47.00
Olive, 6¾", 1938-1959; $14.00
Pickle, 8¾", 1938-1959; $16.00

Plate, 6", 1938-1959; $5.00
Plate, 7", 1938-1959; $8.00
Plate, 8", 1938-1959; $8.00
Plate, 9", 1939-1959; $12.00
Plate, 14" Torte, 1938-1959; $50.00
Relish, 2-part, 1938-1959; $28.00
Relish, 3-part, 1938-1959; $37.00
Relish, 4-part, 1938-1943; $46.00
Relish, 5-part, 1938-1943; $48.00

2560—Plate
See Price List for Sizes

2560—Individual Sugar
Height 3 in.

2560—Individual Cream
Height 3¼ in.
Capacity 4 oz.

2560—Footed Sugar
Height 3½ in.

2560—Footed Cream
Height 4⅛ in.
Capacity 7 oz.

2560—Mayonnaise and Plate and Ladle
Height 3½ in.

2560—2-Part Relish
Length 6½ in. Width 5¼ in.

2560—3-Part Relish
Length 10 in. Width 7¾ in.

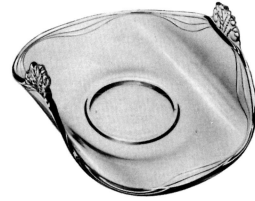

2560—Handled Muffin Tray
Length 8¼ in. Width 10 in.

2560—Cheese and Cracker
Height 3¼ in.
Diameter Plate 11 in.
Diameter Cheese 5¾ in.

Salad Set, 1942-1959; $95.00
    10" Salad Bowl, 14" Torte,
    Salad Fork and Spoon, Wood
Shaker, FGT, (pair) 1938-1944; $35.00
Sugar and Cream, 1938-1959; $34.00
Sugar and Cream, Individual, 1938-1959; $34.00
Sugar and Cream Set, 1939-1959; $49.00
    Individual Sugar and Cream,
    Sugar and Cream Tray

Sweetmeat, 2 Handled, 1938-1959; $26.00
Tid Bit, 3-toed, 1938-1959; $28.00
Tray, Handled Muffin, 1938-1959; $42.00
Tray, 11½" Lunch, 1938-1959; $46.00
Tray, Sugar and Cream, 1939-1959; $14.00
Vase, 3¾" Pansy, 1938-1943; $37.00
Vase, 6" Handled, 1939-1943; $75.00
Whip Cream, 2 Handles, 1938-1959; $26.00

2560—Sweetmeat, 2 Hdles.
Diameter 5½ in.
Height 1½ in.

2560—Whip Cream, 2 Hdles.
Diameter 5 in.
Height 1¾ in.

2560—Lemon Dish, 2 Hdles.
Diameter 6¼ in.

2560—3-Toed Bon Bon
Diameter 7¼ in.
Height 2⅜ in.

2560—6 in. Comport
Height 4⅝ in.

2560—Bon Bon, 2 Hdles.
Length 5¾ in.
Width 6¼ in.

2560—3-Toed Tid Bit, Flat
Diameter 8¼ in.
Height 1¼ in.

2560—3-Toed Nut Bowl, Cupped
Diameter 5⅞ in.
Height 3 in.

2560—10 in. Salad Set
Consisting of:
1/12 doz. 2560—10 in. Salad Bowl—Ht. 4⅛ in.
1/12 doz. 2560—14 in. Torte Plate
1/12 doz. 2560—Salad Fork and Spoon—Wood

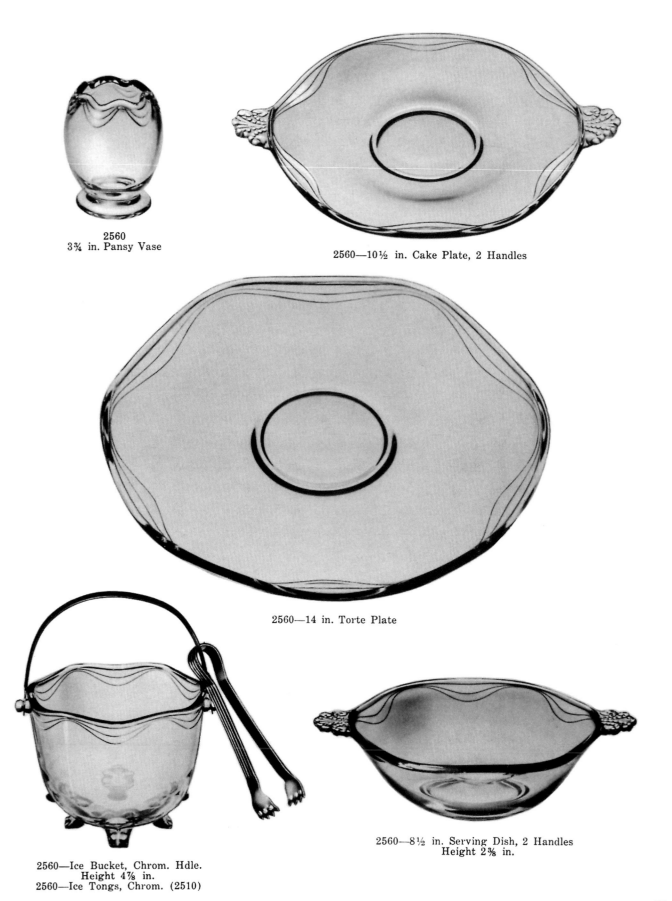

2560
3¾ in. Pansy Vase

2560—10½ in. Cake Plate, 2 Handles

2560—14 in. Torte Plate

2560—Ice Bucket, Chrom. Hdle.
Height 4⅞ in.
2560—Ice Tongs, Chrom. (2510)

2560—8½ in. Serving Dish, 2 Handles
Height 2⅜ in.

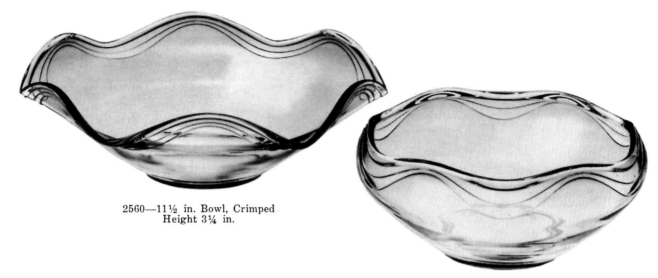

2560—11½ in. Bowl, Crimped
Height 3¼ in.

2560—8½ in. Bowl, Cupped
Height 4 in.

2560—4½ in. Candlestick

2560—11 in. Handled Bowl
Height 3¼ in.

2560—4½ in. Candlestick

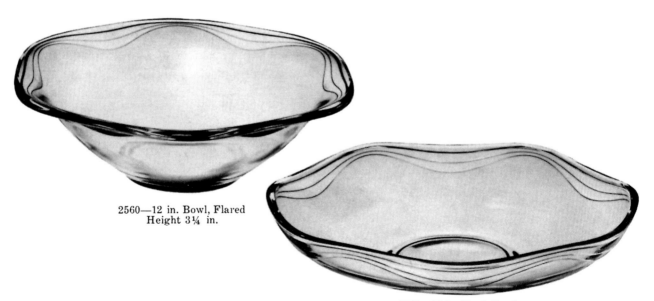

2560—12 in. Bowl, Flared
Height 3¼ in.

2560—13 in. Fruit Bowl
Height 2½ in.

2560—6¾ in. Olive

2560—6 in. Cereal

2560—8¾ in. Pickle

2560—5 in. Fruit

2560—Footed Shaker, F.G.T.
Height 2⅞ in.

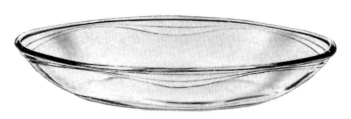

2560—11 in. Celery

2560—4 Part Relish
Length 10 in.
Width 6¾ in.

2560—Footed Cup
2560—Saucer
Cup Capacity 5½ oz.

2560—3 oz. Footed Oil and Stopper
Height 4½ in.

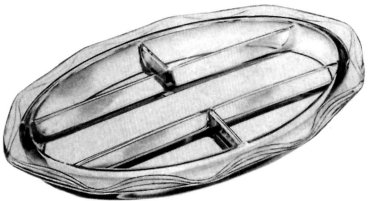

2560—5 Part Relish
Length 13¼ in.
Width 9⅝ in.

2560—2 Part Salad Bowl
with Fork and Spoon, Wood
Height 3⅞ in.
Top Diameter 10½ in.

2560½—4 in. Candlestick

2560—Duo Candlestick
Height 5⅛ in.—Spread 9 in.

2560—11½ in. Handled Lunch Tray

2560—2 Part Mayonnaise
with 2 Ladles
Height 3½ in.
Top Diameter 6¾ in.

2570 – 2745 SCULPTURE

1961 – 1971

The Sculpture Pattern borrowed pieces from other lines at its advent in July 1961. The two 2570 pieces were originally part of the Artisan Pattern. Only a few molds were needed as several different shapes could be made by pulling, cupping in, and swinging the molten piece of glass. Each mold was assigned a number and beginning in 1957, each piece made from that basic mold shape was given a second number which appears with the mold number separated by a slash. For example, the mold shape number was 2570, with 189 and 795 differentiating two pieces created from the original shape by skilled hands. Three different pieces were created from 2740: the Spire Bowl, the Oblong Bowl, and the Float.

Originally offered in Crystal only, Gray Mist was added in 1963 and both colors continued to be offered through 1971. The color Gray Mist may be misleading as usually "Mist" meant an acid etch or satin finish. In this case, Gray Mist is indicative of a smokey color. All sizes are length except the candleholder and vases, which are height.

2570/795 Basket, 17"; $38.00
2745/208 Bowl, 5¾" Ruffled; $21.00
2756/208 Bowl, 5¾" Triton; $22.00
2740/168 Bowl, 8" Spire; $22.00
2745/183 Bowl, 8½" Trindle; $21.00
2743/179 Bowl, 10¾" Petal; $32.00
2740//126 Bowl, 13½" Oblong; $35.00
2744/174 Bowl, 13½" Tricorne; $35.00
2741/266 Bowl, 14" Oval; $35.00
2570/189 Bowl, 14" Shell; $35.00

2740/415 Bowl, 14" Float; $35.00
2741/279 Bowl, 18" Lineal; $38.00
2742/311 Candleholder, 3½" (pair); $22.00
2757/313 Candle Twist, 2" (pair); $18.00
2756/168 Cosmic, 8½"; $28.00
2743/767 Vase, 7¼" Star; $24.00
2745/758 Vase, 8¼" Florette; $24.00
2741/755 Vase, 11½" Pinch; $32.00
2744/830 Vase, 12½" Swung; $32.00

2744/830 Crystal Vase, 2740/168 Spire Bowl in Gray Mist

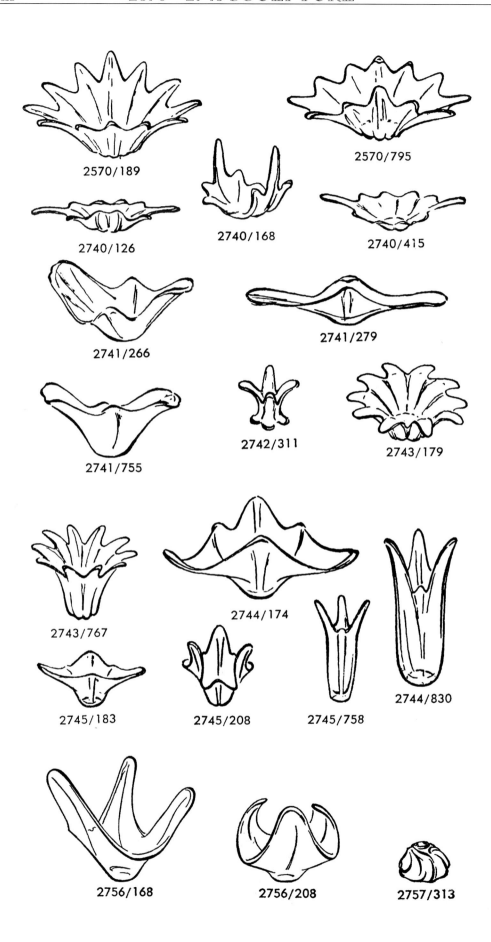

2570/189

2570/795

2740/126

2740/168

2740/415

2741/266

2741/279

2741/755

2742/311

2743/179

2743/767

2744/174

2744/830

2745/183

2745/208

2745/758

2756/168

2756/208

2757/313

2574 RALEIGH

With twig handles and paneled base, each piece in this line is made of the clearest hand-finished crystal. The stem on the comport is reminiscent of the columnar effect found in Coronet, and the entire line has that solid, masculine, no-nonsense feel of post-war America, even though it was introduced in 1939. Sold as a pressed pattern or used for numerous etched and cut patterns, it continued to be an important line in Fostoria's offerings until 1965. No stemware was offered with the line, but it coordinates well with stemware from the Dolly Madison and Georgian patterns.

Bon Bon, 1939-1944; $15.00
Bowl, 8½" Serving Dish, 1939-1965; $28.00
Bowl, 9½" Handled, 1939-1944; $35.00
Bowl, 12" Flared, 1939-1965; $34.00
Bowl, 13" Fruit, 1939-1958; $37.00
Candlestick, 4", (pair) 1939-1944; $38.00
Candlestick, Duo, (pair) 1940-1965; $44.00
Celery, 10½", 1939-1958; $18.00
Comport, 5", 1939-1943; $22.00
Cup and Saucer, 1939-1965; $14.00
Ice Tub and Tongs, 1939-1944; $28.00
Lemon, 1939-1944; $15.00
Mayonnaise, Plate, Ladle, 1939-1958; $36.00
Oil, 4¼ oz., Ground Stopper, 1939-1943;
    1955-1965; $35.00
Olive, 6", 1939-1958; $12.00

Pickle, 8", 1939-1958; $14.00
Plate, 6", 1939-1965; $5.00
Plate, 7", 1939-1965; $6.00
Plate, 8", 1939-1965; $8.00
Plate, 9", 1939-1944; $18.00
Plate, 10" Cake, 1939-1965; $24.00
Plate, 14" Torte, 1939-1965; $30.00
Relish, 3-part, 1939-1965; $30.00
Shaker, (pair) 1939-1965; $22.00
Sugar and Cream, 1939-1965; $22.00
Sugar and Cream, Individual, 1939-1965; $22.00
Sugar and Cream Set, 1940-1965; $34.00
Sugar and Cream Tray, 1940-1965; $12.00
Sweetmeat, 1939-1944; $15.00
Tray, Handled Muffin, 1939-1958; $25.00
Whip Cream, 1939-1944; $15.00

Individual Sugar and Cream, Oil Bottle, Cup and Saucer

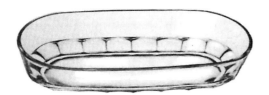

2574—10½ in. Celery

2574—8 in. Pickle

2574—6 in. Olive

2574—Mayonnaise and Plate and Ladle
Mayo Height 3 in.
Mayo Diameter 4¾ in.
Plate Diameter 7¼ in.

2574—3 Part Relish
Length 10 in. Width 7 in.
Height 1¾ in.

2574—Plate
see Price List for sizes

2574—Individual Sugar
Height 2⅞ in.

2574—Individual Cream
Height 3½ in.
Capacity 4½ oz.

2574—Footed Sugar
Height 3¾ in.

2574—Footed Cream
Height 4 in.   Capacity 7 oz.

2574—5 in. Comport
Height 4⅞ in.

2574—10 in. Cake Plate

2574—Handled Muffin Tray
Length 8 in.   Width 10 in.

2574—Lemon
Diameter 6½ in.

2574—8½ in. Serving Dish
Height 2½ in.

2574—Sweetmeat
Diameter 5¼ in.
Height 1⅛ in.

2574—Whip Cream
Diameter 5 in.
Height 1¾ in.

2574—Bon Bon
Length 5 in.
Width 6⅜ in.

2574—Ice Tub
Top Diameter 6½ in.
Height 4⅛ in.
Chromium Tongs
Tongs priced separately

2574—9½ in. Handled Bowl
Height 3⅜ in.

2574—4 in. Candlestick

2574—12 in. Bowl, Flared
Height 3 in.

2574—Footed Cup
2574—Saucer
Cup Capacity 6 oz.

2574—3 Piece Sugar and Cream Set
Consisting of:
1/12 Doz. 2574—S. & C. Tray
1/12 Doz 2574—Ind. Sugar
1/12 Doz. 2574—Ind. Cream

2574—Shaker, F.G.T.
Height 2⅝ in.

2574—14 in. Torte Plate

2574—4¼ oz. Oil, Ground Stopper
Height 5⅝ in.

2574—13 in. Fruit Bowl
Height 2¾ in.

2574—Duo Candlestick
Height 5¼ in.   Spread 8½ in.

2630 CENTURY

Century was the first pressed dinnerware pattern introduced after the war and became the workhorse for Fostoria dinnerware in 1950. A few pieces had been introduced in 1949, but Century became a full-fledged dinner service in 1950 and continued to be made until 1982. Century has fine handles shaped like a backwards "c", a center handled tray whose handle is made up of a forward "c" and a backwards "c", and edges that resemble an elaborately fluted pie crust. Finials on lids are quite remarkable and closely resemble a treble clef symbol. The stoppers to the cruets incorporate the finial, as does the tiny mustard. The Oval Vase is an unusual piece, as is the Handled Vase with its backwards "c" handles looking like arms akimbo. The Trindle Candlestick incorporates three "c's" in an elaborate design complete with pie-crust edges on the "c's".

Two Jug shapes were made. The first (page 71) was made from 1950 – 1952. During 1952 the shape was modified as shown on page 72. The earlier one may be found with Bouquet, Heather, Starflower, and possibly Camelia etchings.

Most pieces still may be found by collectors, although it is difficult to find pieces without scratches, since the pattern features large, plain surfaces which are vulnerable. The tiny individual ash tray, though made for a relatively long time, is seldom seen, and the 9½" Ice Jug has to be the rarest piece. Century was a favorite of the American housewife from its inception, rivaled only by American and Colony.

Stemware is featured in *Fostoria Stemware*, page 48.

Century Condiment Set, Two-tiered Tid Bit, Individual Shaker Set, Jelly and Cover

Ash Tray, Individual, 1950-1972; $20.00
Basket, Reed Handle, 1950-1958; $82.00
Bon Bon, 3-toed, 1949-1974; $24.00
Bowl, 4½" Handled Nappy,
    1949-1982; $18.00
Bowl, 5" Fruit, 1950-1974; $20.00
Bowl, 6" Cereal, 1950-1974; $28.00
Bowl, 8" Flared, 1952-1973; $30.00
Bowl, 10¾" Footed, Flared, 1949-1970; $45.00
Bowl, 12" Flared, 1949-1965; $50.00
Bowl, 11" Rolled Edge,
    Footed, Flared, 1949-1965; $52.00
Bowl, Handled Serving, 1949-1974; $40.00
Bowl, 10" Large, 1980-1982; $40.00
Bowl, Oval Utility, 1949-1982; $38.00
Bowl, Oval Vegetable, 1950-1982; $22.00
Bowl, 8½" Salad, 1950-1973; $30.00
Bowl, 10½" Salad, 1949-1974; $40.00
Bowl, 6" Small, 1980-1982; $28.00
Bowl, Snack, 1952-1970; $20.00
Butter, Oblong, 1949-1974, 1980-1982; $46.00
Cake, Handled, 1949-1982; $48.00
Candlestick, 4½", (pair) 1949-1982; $36.00
Candlestick, Duo, (pair) 1949-1978; $75.00
Candlestick, Trindle, (pair) 1950-1978; $125.00
Candy Jar and Cover, 1950-1982; $48.00
Cheese and Cracker, 1950-1970; $45.00
Comport, 4⅜", 1949-1972; $34.00
Condiment Set, 3-piece, 1950-1973; $125.00
Cup and Saucer, 1949-1982; $18.00
Ice Bucket, Metal Handle, Tongs,
    1950-1969; $95.00
Jug, 9½", 3-pint, 1950-1952; $175.00
Jug, 3-pint Ice, 1952-1974; $125.00
Lily Pond, 9", 1952-1974; $46.00
Lily Pond, 11¼", 1949-1973; $52.00
Mayonnaise, Plate, Ladle, 1949-1971; $48.00

Mayonnaise, 2-part set, 1952-1965; $57.00
Mustard, Cover, Spoon, 1950-1966; $48.00
Oil, 5 oz., 1950-1973; $58.00
Pickle, 8¾", 1949-1982; $18.00
Pitcher, Pint, Cereal, 1950-1974; $67.00
Plate, 6", 1949-1974; $10.00
Plate, 7", 1949-1982; $10.00
Plate, 8", 1949-1982; $15.00
Plate, 9", 1949-1974; $27.00
Plate, 10½", 1950-1976; $40.00
Plate, Crescent Salad, 1950-1976; $47.00
Plate, Party, and Cup, 1950-1958; $44.00
Plate, 14" Torte, 1949-1982; $40.00
Plate, 16" Torte, 1950-1972; $50.00
Platter, 12" Oval, 1950-1970; $75.00
Preserve and Cover, 1950-1973; $47.00
Relish, 2-part, 1949-1982; $20.00
Relish, 3-part, 1949-1982; $32.00
Salad set, 3-piece, 1949-1974; $90.00
Salver, Cake, 1949-1973; $95.00
Shaker, Regular Chrome Top "B", (pair) 1949-1982; $26.00
Shaker, Individual, Chrome Top "C", (pair)
    1949-1982; $22.00
Shaker, Individual set with tray, 1949-1970; $37.00
Sugar and Cream, Regular, 1949-1974; $24.00
Sugar and Cream, Individual, 1949-1974; $24.00
Sugar and Cream, Individual set, 1949-1974; $40.00
Tid Bit, 3-toed, 1949-1982; $23.00
Tid Bit, 2-tier, Metal Handle, 1950-1970; $65.00
Tray, Handled Lunch, 1952-1974; $45.00
Tray, Handled Muffin, 1949-1974; $48.00
Tray, Handled Utility, 1949-1974; $48.00
Tray, 10½" Snack, 1952-1974; $45.00
Tricorne, 3-toed, 1949-1974; $28.00
Vase, 6" Bud, 1950-1973; $35.00
Vase, 7½" Handled, 1950-1958; $95.00
Vase, 8½" Oval, 1950-1958; $85.00

2630
Footed Preserve & Cover
Height 6 in.

2630
Oval Vegetable Dish
Length 9½ in. Height 1¾ in.
Width. 6½ in.

2630
6 in. Cereal
5 in. Fruit

2630
Party Plate Set
Consisting of:
2630—8'' Party Plate
2630—Ftd. Cup

2630
Crescent Salad Plate
Length 7½ in. Width 4⅜ in.

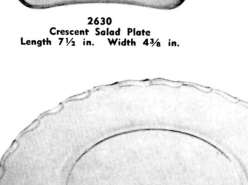

2630—12 in.
Oval Platter

2630
Trindle Candlestick
Height 7¾ in. Spread 7½ in.

2630
Individual Ash Tray
Length 2¾ in.

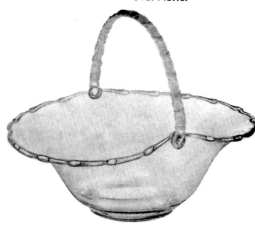

2630
Basket, Reed Handle
Height. 4 in. Length 10¼ in.
Width 6½ in.

2630
3 Piece Condiment Set
Consisting of:
1/6 doz. 2630 — 5 oz. Oil, D/S
1/12 doz. 2630—Sugar and Cream Tray

2630 — 12 in.
Bowl, Flared
Height 2-7/8 in.

2630 — 10-3/4 in.
Footed Bowl, Flared
Height 4-1/4 in.

2630 — 11 in.
Footed Bowl, Rolled Edge
Height 3-1/4 in.

2630
Duo. Candlestick
Height 7 in. Spread 6-5/8 in.

2630 — 4 1/2 in.
Candlestick

2630 — 11-1/4 in.
Lily Pond
Height 2-1/4 in.

2630
Oblong Butter & Cover
Length 7-1/2 in. Height 2 in.
Width 3-3/8 in.

2630
Comport
Height 4-3/8 in.

2630
Footed Cup
Cup Capacity 6 oz.
2630
Saucer

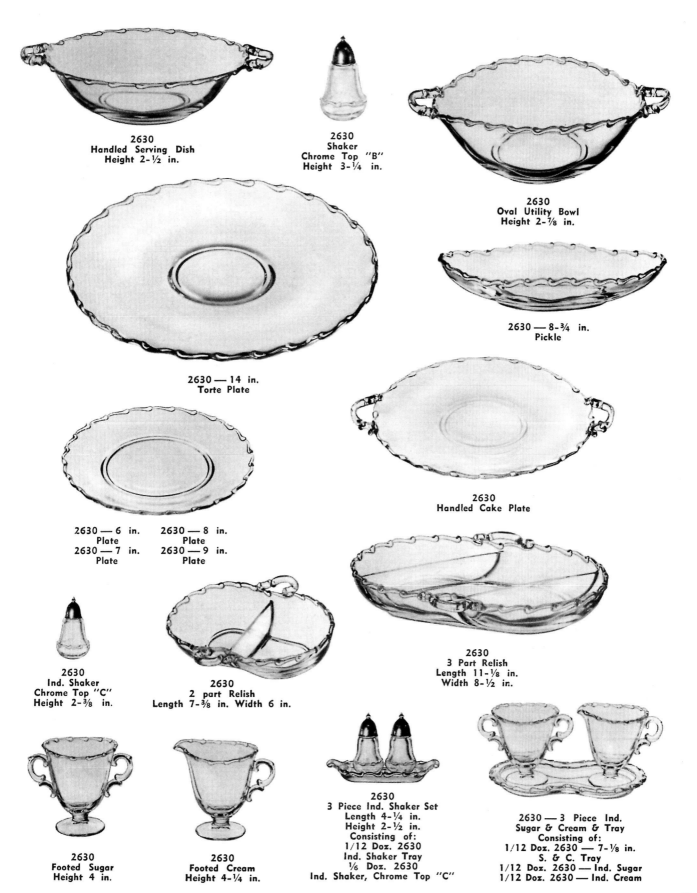

2630
Handled Serving Dish
Height 2-1/2 in.

2630
Shaker
Chrome Top "B"
Height 3-1/4 in.

2630
Oval Utility Bowl
Height 2-7/8 in.

2630 — 8-3/4 in.
Pickle

2630 — 14 in.
Torte Plate

2630
Handled Cake Plate

2630 — 6 in.
Plate
2630 — 7 in.
Plate

2630 — 8 in.
Plate
2630 — 9 in.
Plate

2630
Ind. Shaker
Chrome Top "C"
Height 2-3/8 in.

2630
2 part Relish
Length 7-3/8 in. Width 6 in.

2630
3 Part Relish
Length 11-1/8 in.
Width 8-1/2 in.

2630
Footed Sugar
Height 4 in.

2630
Footed Cream
Height 4-1/4 in.

2630
3 Piece Ind. Shaker Set
Length 4-1/4 in.
Height 2-1/2 in.
Consisting of:
1/12 Doz. 2630
Ind. Shaker Tray
1/6 Doz. 2630
Ind. Shaker, Chrome Top "C"

2630 — 3 Piece Ind.
Sugar & Cream & Tray
Consisting of:
1/12 Doz. 2630 — 7-1/8 in.
S. & C. Tray
1/12 Doz. 2630 — Ind. Sugar
1/12 Doz. 2630 — Ind. Cream

2630
Mayonnaise and Plate
and Ladle
Height 3-¼ in.

2630
3-Toed Tricorne
Height 2-½ in.
Length 7-⅛ in.

2630 — 10½ in.
3 Piece Salad Set (illustrated)
Height 4¼ in.
Consisting of:
1/12 doz. 2630—10½ in.
Salad Bowl
1/12 doz. 2630 — 14 in.
Torte Plate
1/12 doz. 2630 — Salad Fork &
Spoon (wood)

Also 2630—8½ in.
3 Piece Salad Set.
Height 3¼ in.
Consisting of:
1/12 doz. 2630 — 8½ in.
Salad Bowl
1/12 doz. 2630 — 11 in.
Cracker Plate
1/12 doz. 2630 — Salad Fork &
Spoon (wood)

2630
3-Toed Bon Bon
Diameter 7-¼ in.
Height 2-¼ in.

2630
3-Toed Tid Bit
Diameter 8⅛ in.
Height 1¼ in.

2630
Salver
Diameter 12-¼ in.
Height 2-⅛ in.

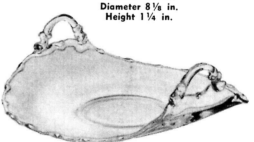

2630
Handled Muffin Tray
Length 9-½ in.
Width 8-½ in.

2630
Handled Utility Tray
Diameter 9-⅛ in.
Height 1-¼ in.

2630 — 4-½ in.
Handled Nappy

2630
3 Pint Ice Jug
Height 9½ in.

2630
Pint Cereal Pitcher
Height 6⅛ in.

2630
Ice Bucket
Height 4⅞ in. Top Dia. 7⅜ in.
Chromium Handle and Tongs
Tongs priced separately

2630
Candy Jar and Cover
Height 7 in.

2630
Mustard, Cover and Spoon
Height 4 in.

2630
3 Piece Tid Bit Set
Metal Handle
Height 10¼ in.

2630
Cheese and Cracker
Height 2¾ in.
Plate Diameter—10¾ in.
Cheese Diameter—5⅜ in.
Cheese Height—2½ in.

2630 — 7½ in.
Handled Vase

2630 — 6 in.
Bud Vase

2630 — 8½ in.
Oval Vase

2630
3 Pint Ice Jug
Height 7-1/8 in.

2630
Handled Lunch Tray
Diameter 11-1/4 in.

2630 — 9 in.
Lily Pond
Height 1-5/8 in.

2630 — 8 in.
Bowl Flared
Height 3-5/8 in.

2630 — 10-1/2 in.
Snack Tray

2630
Snack Bowl
Height 3-1/2 in.

2630
2-part Mayonnaise
and 2 Ladles
Height 3-3/8 in.

2638/2666 CONTOUR

In the twentieth century every decade seemed to have one predominant theme. The fifties saw the birth of convenience in the home, and a shift from formal to informal. Formal dining and dressing were generally reserved for special occasions. Swedish Modern was imported both in furniture design and glassware, and new products available in plastic were found everywhere. A favorite new invention (innovation) of the fifties, and one for which we will always be grateful, was the fitted bedsheet, trademarked the "Contour" sheet.

Since Fostoria paid close attention to style and design trends, it seems only natural that the company had already introduced a "Contour" line by January 1, 1949. The line number was 2638 and included mostly serving and accessory pieces. None of these pieces were ever listed with cut, etched, or decorated patterns. The 10½" Oblong Bowl was included with the Garden Center items but was offered only in crystal. The Candlestick was made in Ebony beginning in 1954.

On January 1, 1952, Fostoria introduced 2666, and by September also named it "Contour." Thus, the September price list contains two Contour lines with two different numbers in two different parts of the booklet. The shapes of the 2666 Contour pieces follow the same basic style as the 2638 Contour, but are not as heavy. The crystal in both lines is excellent quality.

Besides the 2638 Candlestick, several of the 2666 pieces were made in Ebony as shown in the list. The 8¼" Oval Bowl was made in Silver Mist when part of the Garden Center offering. The Mardi Gras design used four shapes in its unique design of decorated Milk Glass. A 6" Pitcher Vase was part of the Decorator Collection and was not listed with Contour even though it had the same number (2666).

The Oil and Stopper and the Shaker were listed in the "New Goods" notice sent to retail dealers July 1, 1954. The two pieces appeared in the 1955 catalog, but were not listed in the July, 1955 supplement. They will undoubtedly be difficult to find.

The Contour pattern was used to fill in or complete several dinnerware and luncheon sets. Some patterns used only a few pieces, most often the Sugar and Cream and the Oval Bowl. The Quart Pitcher was the only piece used with Navarre, Meadow Rose, Chintz, Romance, and Willowmere etchings, and Bridal Wreath, Sprite, Rose, and Cynthia cuttings.

Similarities to pieces of the Seascape pattern are inescapable. Some of the pieces seem to be identical, i.e., the Sugar and Cream, and Tray. However, they were given different numbers for identification.

Ebony pieces are shown in the Ebony section.

2638 CONTOUR

Ash Tray, 6", 3 lips, 1949-1965; $12.00
Ash Tray, 7", 1 lip, 1950-1965; $15.00
Ash Tray, 7", 2 lips, 1949-1965; $15.00
Bowl, 5½", 1949-1965; $20.00
Bowl, 5½" Square, 1949-1965; $20.00
Bowl, 7" Deep, 1949-1965; $20.00
Bowl, 7½" 3-Cornered, 1949-1963; $22.00
Bowl, 8½" Oval, 1949-1963; $22.00

Bowl, 8½" Square, 1949-1965; $24.00
Bowl, 10½" Oblong, 1949-1972; $25.00
   Garden Club Line, 1960-1964
Candlestick, 4½" (pair)
   Crystal, 1949-1965; $65.00
   Ebony, 1953-1958; $125.00
Tray, 7", 1950-1965; $18.00

2638
Ash Tray — 1 Lip

2638 — 7 in.
Tray

2638 — 10-¾ in.
Bowl
Height 3-⅛ in.

2638 — 6 in.
Ash Tray — 3 Lips
Height 2-⅞ in.

2638 — 8-½ in.
Square Bowl
Height 4-⅜ in.

2638 — 10-½ in.
Oblong Bowl
Height 4-½ in.

2638 — 7 in.
Ash Tray — 2 Lips
Height 3 in.

2638 — 7 in.
Deep Bowl
Height 5 in.

2638 — 8-½ in.
Oval Bowl
Height 5-⅜ in.

2638 — 5-½ in.
Square Bowl
Height 2-⅞ in.

2638 — 7-½ in.
3-Cornered Bowl
Height 5-¼ in.

2638 — 5-½ in.
Bowl
Height 3 in.

2638 — 4-½ in.
Candlestick

2666 CONTOUR

Ash Tray, 6½", 1953-1958; $12.00
Bon Bon, 1953-1965; $18.00
Bowl, 8¼" Oval
    Crystal, 1953-1965; $35.00
    Silver Mist, 1960-1964; $38.00
    Ebony, 1954-1957; $38.00
Bowl, 9" Salad
    Crystal, 1953-1972; $35.00
    Ebony, 1954-1958; $40.00
Bowl, 11" Salad
    Crystal, 1952-1972; $40.00
    Ebony, 1954-1958; $45.00

Bowl, Individual Salad, 1952-1970; $15.00
Butter, Oblong, 1955-1970; $22.00
Butter Pat, 1952-1959; $10.00
Candle, Flora (pair)
    Crystal, 1953-1965; $34.00
    Ebony, 1954-1958; $38.00
Celery, 1952-1968; $14.00
Coaster, Utility, 1952-1966; $10.00
Cup and Saucer, 1952-1970; $18.00
Mayonnaise, Plate, Ladle
    Crystal, 1952-1970; $55.00
    Ebony, 1954-1958; $55.00
Oil and Stopper, 1955; $55.00

2666
Shaker
Chrome Top "E"
Height 2¾ in.

2666
Oblong Butter and Cover
Length 7 in.   Height 2 in.

2666
Oval Plate
Length 8⅜ in.   Width 5 in.

2666
Oil and Stopper
Height 5⅜ in.
Capacity 6 oz.

2666
Sauce Pitcher and Plate
Overall Length 8½ in.

2666
Sauce Pitcher
Length 8½ in.

Pickle, 1952-1965; $10.00
Pitcher, Pint, 1952-1976; $20.00
Pitcher, 3-Pint, 1952-1976; $35.00
Pitcher, Quart, 1952-1976; $30.00
Plate, 7", 1952-1970; $10.00
Plate, 10", 1952-1959; $20.00
Plate, Party, and Cup,
    1952-1959; $26.00
Plate, Canape, 1952-1965; $30.00
Plate, 10" Snack, 1953-1972; $30.00
Plate, 14" Serving, 1952-1972; $47.00
Preserve, Handled, 1955-1966; $28.00
Relish, 2-part, 1952-1972; $24.00

Relish, 3-part, 1952-1972; $32.00
Salver, Cake, 1955-1961; $50.00
Sauce Pitcher, 1955-1962; $30.00
Sauce Plate, Oval, 1955-1962; $10.00
Shaker, Chrome Top, (pair) 1955; $48.00
Sugar and Cream,
    Regular, 1952-1972; $35.00
Sugar and Cream,
    Individual, 1952-1972; $34.00
Tray, Individual Sugar and
    Cream, 1952-1972; $10.00
Vase, Pitcher (see Groups: Decorator
    Collection)

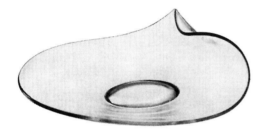

2666—10 in.
Snack Plate

2666—9 in.
Salad Bowl
Height 2¾ in.

2666
Oval Bowl
Diameter 8¼ in.
Height 3¼ in.

2666
Bon Bon
Diameter 6⅞ in.
Height 3 in.

2666
Ash Tray
Diameter 6½ in.

2666
Canape Plate
Diameter 7⅜ in.
Height 2 in.

2666
Flora-Candle
Diameter 6 in.

2666
Cup
Cup Capacity 8 oz.
2666
Saucer

2666
Butter Pat
Diameter 3-½ in.

2666 — 7 in.
Plate
2666 — 10 in.
Plate

2666
Party Plate & Cup
Consisting of:
2666 — 8-½ in. Party Plate
2666 — Cup

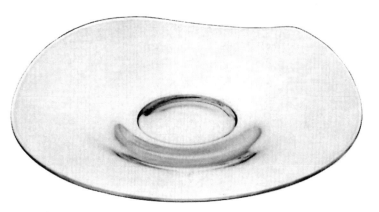

2666 — 14 in.
Serving Plate

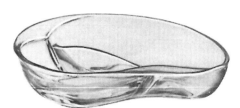

2666
2 Part Relish
Length 7-⅜ in.   Width 6 in.

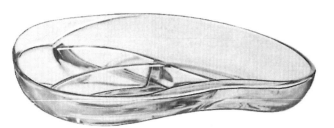

2666
3 Part Relish
Length 10-¾ in.   Width 7-⅞ in.

2666
Sugar
Height 2-⅝ in.

2666
Cream
Height 3-½ in.

2666 — 3 Piece
Ind. Sugar & Cream & Tray
Consisting of:
1/12 doz. 2666 S. & C. Tray
1/12 doz. 2666 Ind. Sugar
1/12 doz. 2666 Ind. Cream

**2666
Pint Pitcher
Height 5-¼ in.**

**2666
Quart Pitcher
Height 6-⅞ in.**

**2666
3 Pint Pitcher
Height 8-¾ in.**

**2666
Mayonnaise and Plate
and Ladle
Height 3-¼ in.**

**2666
4 Pc. Salad Set
Height 4-⅞ in.
Consisting of:
1/12 doz. 2666 Salad Bowl
1/12 doz. 2666 14 in. Serving Plate
1/12 doz. Salad Fork & Spoon (Wood)**

**2666
Ind. Salad/Dessert
Height 2-¼ in.**

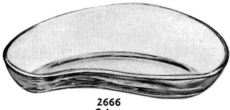

**2666
Celery
Length 9 in.**

**2666
Pickle
Length 7-¼ in.**

**2666
Utility Coaster
Length 4-¾ in.
Coaster Diameter 3-⅜ in.**

2643 HOLIDAY

1950 – 1958

Holiday tumblers are shown in *Fostoria Stemware*, page 151. Tumblers came first in this pattern, having been made since 1949. All pieces listed here were made with Horizontal Optic except the coaster.

Coaster; $10.00
Cocktail Mixer, 20 oz. Handled; $45.00
Cocktail Mixer, 30 oz. Handled; $55.00
Decanter and Stopper; $70.00
Ice Bowl; $30.00

2643
20 oz. Cocktail Mixer
30 oz. Cocktail Mixer

2643
Decanter & Stopper
Capacity 24 oz. Height 10¼ in.

2643
Coaster
Diameter 4 in.

2643
Ice Bowl
Height 5 in.
Diameter 6⅝ in.

2650 HORIZON

1951-1954, Cinnamon and Spruce
Stemware was made through 1958, and is featured in *Fostoria Stemware*, page 156.

Bowl, Dessert/Finger; $12.00
Bowl, Fruit; $12.00
Bowl, Cereal; $14.00
Bowl, Handled Serving; $20.00
Bowl, 8½" Salad; $22.00
Bowl, 10½" Salad; $25.00
Coaster; $10.00
Cup and Saucer; $18.00
Mayonnaise/Plate/Ladle; $34.00
Nappy and Cover, 5"; $18.00

Plate, 7"; $8.00
Plate, 10" Dinner; $18.00
Plate, 11" Sandwich; $20.00
Plate, 14" Torte; $25.00
Platter, 12" Oval; $35.00
Relish, 3-part; $30.00
Salad Set, 4-piece, 8½" Bowl; $48.00
Salad Set, 4-piece, 10½" Bowl; $57.00
Server, 4-part; $40.00
Sugar and Cream; $30.00

Spruce Torte Plate; Cinnamon Sugar, Cream, and Coaster

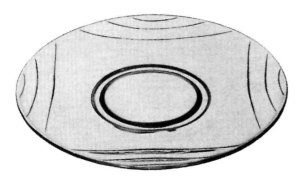

2650-11 in.
Sandwich Plate

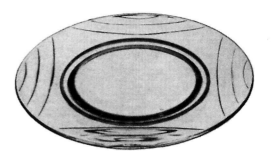

2650-10 in
Dinner Plate
2650-7 in.
Plate

2650
Sugar
Height 3-1/8 in.

2650
Cream
Height 3-1/2 in.

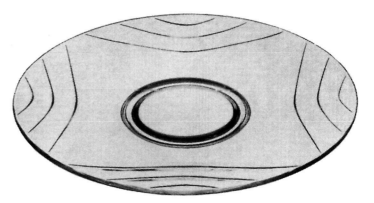

2650-14 in.
Torte Plate

2650-12 in.
Oval Platter

2650
Cup
Cup Capacity 8-1/2 oz.
2650
Saucer

2650
Mayonnaise and Plate
and Ladle
Height 2⅞ in.

2650
3 Part Relish
Length 12-½ in.
Width 7-⅝ in.

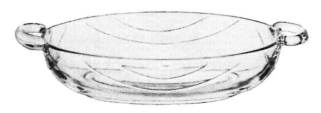

2650
Handled Serving Dish
Height 2-½ in.

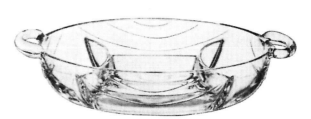

2650
4 Part Server
Length 11-½ in.
Height 2-½ in.

2650
5 in. Nappy and Cover
Height 3-½ in.

2650
Coaster

2650
Cereal

2650
Fruit

2650-8½ in.
4 Piece Salad Set (illustrated)
Height 3-¼ in.
Consisting of:
1/12 doz. 2650-8½ in.
Salad Bowl
1/12doz. 2650-11 in.
Sandwich Plate
1/12 doz. 2650-Salad Fork &
Spoon (Wood)

Also 2650-10-½ in.
4 Piece Salad Set
Height 4 in.
Consisting of:
1/12 doz. 2650-10-½ in.
Salad Bowl
1/12 doz. 2650-14 in.
Torte Plate
1/12 doz. 2650-Salad Fork &
Spoon (Wood)

2685 SEASCAPE

July 1954 – 1957, Caribee Blue and Coral Sand
Seascape was taken directly from the 2666 Contour line.

VINTAGE

Plate Etching 347

1955 – 1956, Caribee Blue and Coral Sand
The Vintage Etching was used on several pieces from the Seascape Line as indicated by the asterisk.

Bowl, Square; $55.00
*Bowl, Footed; $85.00
Bowl, Pansy; $24.00
*Bowl, 10" Salad; $55.00
*Bowl, 8" Shallow; $55.00
*Bowl, 11½" Shallow; $65.00
*Candleholder (pair); $75.00
Mayonnaise, Plate, Ladle; $58.00
*Plate, 14" Buffet; $72.00
*Preserve, Handled; $46.00
Relish, 2-part; $38.00
Relish, 3-part; $45.00
*Salver; $135.00
Sugar and Cream; $65.00
Sugar and Cream, Individual; $65.00
Sugar and Cream Tray; $25.00

Sugar and Cream and Tray, Individual Set; $90.00
*Tray, Mint; $37.00
*Tray, Oval; $44.00

Vintage, Plate Etching No. 347

Caribee Blue Footed Bowl with Vintage etching

Coral Sand Preserve, Mayonnaise, Plate and Ladle, Tea Sugar, Cream, and Tray

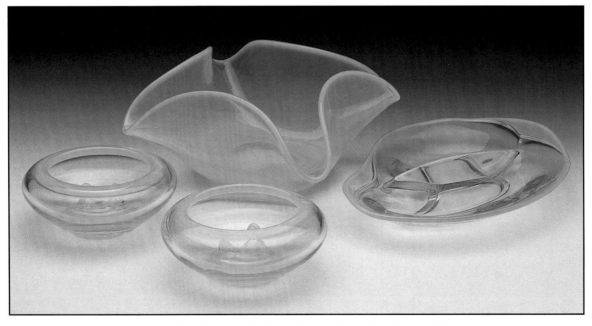

Caribee Blue Candlesticks, Square Bowl, Two-Part Relish

2685—14 in.
Buffet Plate

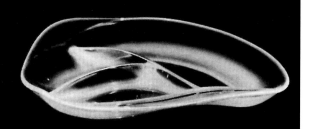

2685
3 Part Relish
Length 11³₄ in. Width 8½ in.

2685
2 Part Relish
Length 9 in. Width 6 in.

2685—3 Piece
Individual Sugar and Cream and Tray
Consisting of:
1/12 Dz. 2685—S. & C. Tray
1/12 Dz. 2685—Ind. Sugar
1/12 Dz. 2685—Ind. Cream

2685
Sugar
Height 2⁷₈ in.

2685
Cream
Height 3³₈ in.

2685—10 in.
Salad Bowl

2685
Mayonnaise and Plate
and Ladle
Height 2³₈ in.

2685
Handled Preserve
Length 6½ in.

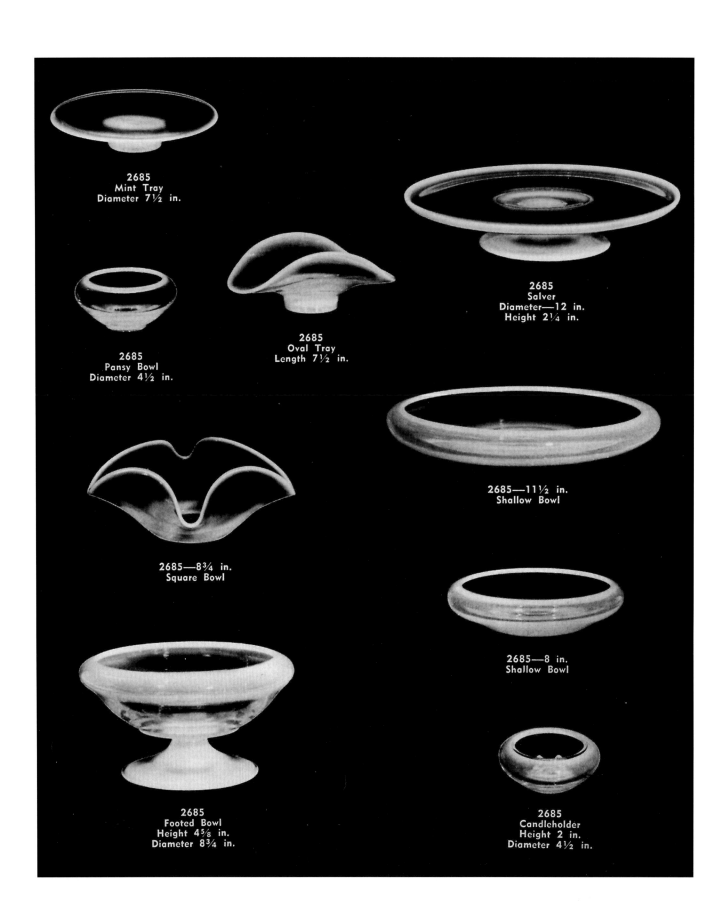

2685
Mint Tray
Diameter 7½ in.

2685
Pansy Bowl
Diameter 4½ in.

2685
Oval Tray
Length 7½ in.

2685
Salver
Diameter—12 in.
Height 2¼ in.

2685—11½ in.
Shallow Bowl

2685—8¾ in.
Square Bowl

2685—8 in.
Shallow Bowl

2685
Footed Bowl
Height 4⅝ in.
Diameter 8¾ in.

2685
Candleholder
Height 2 in.
Diameter 4½ in.

2691 DECORATOR PATTERN

1955 – 1957, Crystal

Ash Tray; $14.00
Cigarette Holder, Individual; $20.00
Cup and Saucer; $16.00
Cup and Saucer, Demitasse; $15.00
Dessert, 4⅞"; $12.00
Plate, 7"; $10.00
Preserve, Handled; $16.00
Sauce Bowl, Plate, Ladle; $34.00

Server, 2-part; $20.00
Server, 3-part; $22.00
Shaker, Chrome Top "A" (pair); $20.00
Soup; $14.00
Sugar and Cream; $25.00
Sugar and Cover; $15.00
Tray, Sugar and Cream; $12.00

2691—7 in.
Plate

2691
2 Part Server
Height 1½ in. Width 6⅜ in.

2691
3 Part Server
Length 9¾ in. Width 7½ in.
Height 1½ in.

2691
Demitasse Cup
Capacity 2¼ oz.
2691
Demitasse Saucer

2691
Sugar and Cream and Tray
Consisting of:
1/12 doz. 2691 Sugar and Cream and Tray
1/12 doz. 2691 Sugar and Cover
1/12 doz. 2691 Cream

2691
Sugar and Cover
Height 3¼ in.

2691
Cream
Height 3¼ in.

2691
Dessert
Diameter 4⅞ in.

2691
Cup
Capacity 7½ oz.
2691
Saucer

2691
Soup
Diameter 4¾ in.

2691
Shaker and Chrome Top "A"
Height 3 in.

2691
Sauce Bowl and Plate and Ladle
Height 2¾ in.

2691
Handled Preserve
Width 4 in.

2691
Individual Cigarette Holder
Height 2½ in.

2691
Individual Ash Tray
Diameter 2⅝ in.

Decorator Pattern Cream and Sugar

2700 RADIANCE

1956 – 1957, Crystal

1957 – White, Aqua, and Peach Milk Glass (see Milk Glass, pages 214 and 215)

Stemware in this pattern is featured in *Fostoria Stemware*, page 49.

A lead crystal pattern called Radiance (3113) was offered in the 1980s in stemware only.

Basket, Pansy
   White, 1957-1960; $18.00
   Aqua, 1957-1959; $22.00
   Peach, 1957-1959; $22.00
Bowl, Serving; $12.00
Bowl, Cereal/Dessert; $10.00
Bowl, 12" Salad; $20.00
Bowl, Violet
   White, 1957-1962; $18.00
   Aqua, 1957-1959; $22.00
   Peach, 1957-1959; $22.00

Cup and Saucer; $12.00
Plate, 7"; $4.00
Plate, 10"; $10.00
Plate, 14" Buffet; $18.00
Platter, 15"; $20.00
Salad Set; $38.00
Sauce Bowl, Plate, Ladle; $26.00
Server, 3-part; $18.00
Shaker, Gold top (pair); $18.00
Sugar and Cream; $18.00

Radiance Sauce Bowl, Plate and Ladle, Cup and Saucer

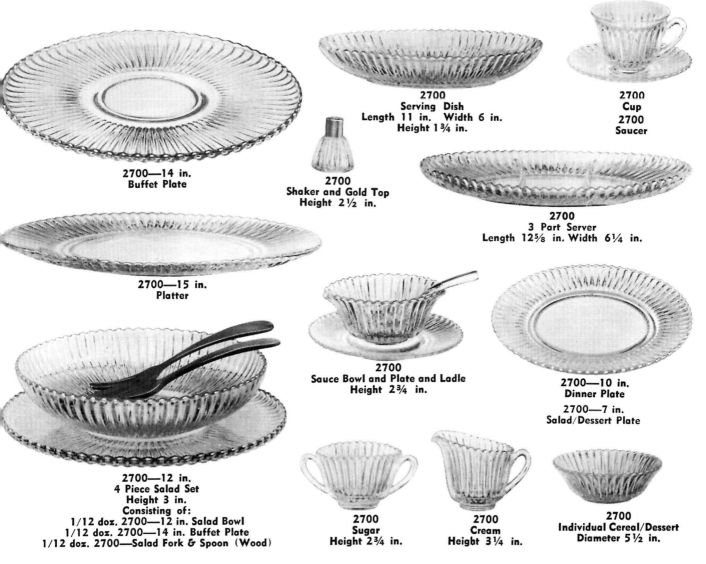

2700—14 in.
Buffet Plate

2700
Serving Dish
Length 11 in.   Width 6 in.
Height 1¾ in.

2700
Shaker and Gold Top
Height 2½ in.

2700
Cup
2700
Saucer

2700
3 Part Server
Length 12⅝ in. Width 6¼ in.

2700—15 in.
Platter

2700
Sauce Bowl and Plate and Ladle
Height 2¾ in.

2700—10 in.
Dinner Plate

2700—7 in.
Salad/Dessert Plate

2700—12 in.
4 Piece Salad Set
Height 3 in.
Consisting of:
1/12 doz. 2700—12 in. Salad Bowl
1/12 doz. 2700—14 in. Buffet Plate
1/12 doz. 2700—Salad Fork & Spoon (Wood)

2700
Sugar
Height 2¾ in.

2700
Cream
Height 3¼ in.

2700
Individual Cereal/Dessert
Diameter 5½ in.

2703 ARTISAN

1958 – 1963, Crystal, Amethyst, and Marine

In 1958 there were five pieces listed in the Artisan pattern. By 1960, the 2570 Shell Bowl and the 2570 Basket Vase ha been transferred to the Sculpture pattern and made in Lead Crystal and Gray Mist. The Oblong Bowl and the Square Bu fet Plate were listed with Miscellaneous as being made in Silver Mist, Silver Mist Spruce, and Silver Mist Amethyst in 19 – 1964. The Artisan pattern was listed through 1963 with the three 2703 pieces. Prices for colors would be about 15% mo than those listed.

Bowl, 12", 3-cornered; $30.00
Bowl, 14¾" oblong; $40.00
Plate, 13" square; $40.00
2570 Bowl, Shell, September 1957-1959; $38.00
2570 Vase, Basket, September 1957-1959; $38.00

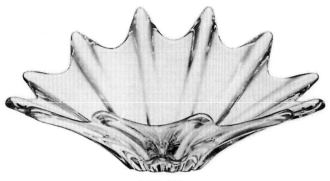

2570/189
Shell Bowl
Length 13½ in. Width 10 in.

2703/174
Bowl, 3 Cornered
Diameter 12 in.

2703/189
Oblong Bowl
Length 14¾ in. Width 10¼ in.

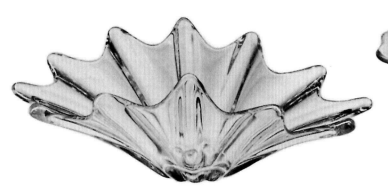

2570/795
Basket Vase
Length 14½ in. Width 9 in.

2703/191—13 in.
Square Buffet Plate

2718 FAIRMONT

1960 – 1965, Crystal, Amber, Blue, and Green
Stemware was made 1958 – 1965 and is featured in *Fostoria Stemware*, page 49.

360 Celery, 9¼"; $18.00
421 Dessert, 5"; $14.00
447 Jelly and Cover, 6"; $26.00
540 Pickle, 7¾"; $14.00

550 Plate, 8"; $8.00
630 Relish, 2-part; $18.00
635 Sauce Dish and Cover; $20.00
679 Sugar and Cream; $22.00

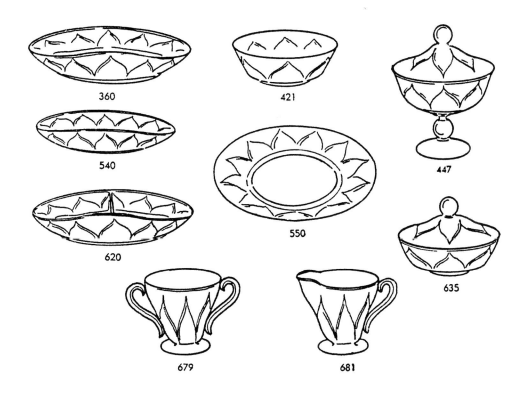

360   421   447
540   550   620   635
679   681

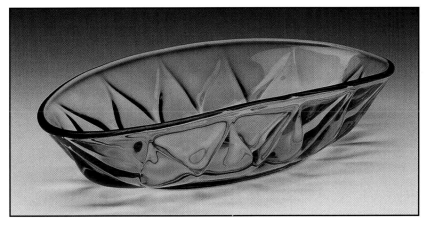

Green Pickle

2719 JAMESTOWN

In 1607 a hearty group of brave souls founded the first successful English settlement in America. One of the major reasons for establishing the settlement was glassmaking. In fact, the American glass industry dates from the second year of the Jamestown settlement, 1608.

When the United States began making plans to celebrate the 350th anniversary of the founding of the Jamestown colony, key personnel in the glass industry at that time joined together to create a Glasshouse for the newly envisioned Jamestown Island Colonial National Historical Park. Carl H. Gustkey, president of Imperial Glass Corporation, Mr. W. Dalzell, president of the Fostoria Glass Company, Inc., and T. Clarence Heisey, president of A. H. Heisey and Company were the original committee for this project. They were later joined by Richard B. Tucker, retired vice-president of Pittsburgh Plate Glass Company, Harry H. Cook, international president of the American Flint Glass Workers' Union, and William H. Blenko, president of Blenko Glass Company. These men chartered the Jamestown Glasshouse Foundation, Inc., in 1956, and succeeded in funding and building a glasshouse to specifications not seen or used in America for several centuries.

Every effort was made to construct an authentic glasshouse, true to the original insofar as was possible from historical and archeological records. The Glasshouse was the first exhibit of the Jamestown Festival begun and the first completed. Local materials were used in the construction including hand-hewed oak logs weighing as much as two tons. Workmen

skilled in the use of an ax were employed and taught to weave small branches for the wattle of the walls, to daub the wattle with clay laced with straw, and to thatch the roof with swamp reeds and rushes. The only concession to modern times was the natural gas-fired furnace. Once the Glasshouse was a reality, members of the Flint Glass Workers' Union were on hand in seventeenth century costume to staff the factory (from the "Report of the 350th Anniversary Celebration Corporation"). It has been reported that a glass "shop" from the Fostoria factory was sent to man the Glasshouse during the celebration of the opening of the Jamestown Festival Park.

The reconstructed Glasshouse of 1608, built as a permanent exhibit by the American glass industry and the National Park Service. *National Park Service Photo.*

The Fostoria Glass Company offered the beautiful Jamestown pattern for the first time in 1958, the 350th anniversary of glassmaking at Jamestown. The Jamestown pattern came into being during a resurgence of interest in Early American designs, and its graceful sturdiness reflects that trend. Even the green color is similar to the green bottles, flasks, and candleholders produced at the Glasshouse in Jamestown Festival Park. From its introduction, Jamestown was a favorite of brides and remains one of Fostoria's most popular casual patterns. (See also *Fostoria Stemware*, p. 50.)

Bowl, Dessert, 4½"
    Crystal, 1958-1970; $30.00
    Blue, 1958-1970; $32.00
    Green, 1958-1970; $32.00
    Amber, 1958-1970; $25.00
    Pink, 1961-1970; $34.00
    Amethyst, 1959-1970; $32.00
    Brown, 1961-1970; $20.00
    Ruby, 1965-1970; $34.00
Bowl, 10" Salad
    Crystal, 1959-1972; $65.00
    Green, 1959-1965; $75.00
    Amber, 1959-1965; $65.00
Butter, Oblong and Cover
    Crystal, 1959-1970; $65.00
    Blue, 1959-1970; $95.00
    Green, 1959-1970; $85.00
    Amber, 1959-1970; $65.00
Celery, 9¼"
    Crystal, 1958-1965; $38.00
Cream
    Crystal, 1958-1973; $32.50
    Blue, 1958-1973; $37.50
    Green, 1958-1973; $35.00
    Amber, 1958-1973; $25.00
    Pink, 1961-1973; $37.50
    Amethyst, 1959-1965; $35.00
    Brown, 1961-1973; $20.00
Dish, Handled Serving
    Crystal, 1959-1970; $65.00
    Blue, 1959-1966; $85.00
    Green, 1959-1966; $75.00
    Amber, 1959-1966; $65.00
Jelly and Cover, 6⅛"
    Crystal, 1958-1970; $70.00
    Amber, 1958-1965; $70.00

Jug, 3-Pint
    Crystal, 1959-1970; $135.00
    Blue, 1959-1970; $175.00
    Green, 1959-1970; $160.00
    Amber, 1959-1970; $135.00
    Pink, 1961-1970; $200.00
    Amethyst, 1959-1965; $150.00
    Brown, 1961-1970; $95.00
Pickle, 8⅜"
    Crystal, 1958-1967; $34.00
Relish, 2-part
    Crystal, 1958-1970; $36.00
    Blue, 1958-1970; $43.00
    Green, 1958-1966; $40.00
    Amber, 1958-1970; $36.00
Plate, 8"
    Crystal, 1958-1970; $18.00
    Blue, 1958-1972; $30.00
    Green, 1958-1974; $28.00
    Amber, 1958-1982; $18.00
    Pink, 1961-1982; $32.00
    Amethyst, 1959-1970; $28.00
    Brown, 1961-1982; $15.00
    Ruby, 1964-1982; $35.00
Plate, 9½" Handled Cake
    Crystal, 1959-1970; $65.00
    Blue, 1959-1965; $85.00
    Green, 1959-1965; $75.00
    Amber, 1959-1965; $65.00
Plate, 14" Torte
    Crystal, 1959-1972; $65.00
    Blue, 1959-1965; $85.00
    Green, 1959-1965; $75.00
    Amber, 1959-1965; $65.00
Salad Set, including 10" Salad Bowl, 14" Torte,
    Wooden Salad Fork and Spoon

Crystal, 1959-1972; $130.00
Green, 1959-1965; $150.00
Amber, 1959-1965; $130.00
Salver, 10" Round
    Crystal, 1959-1965; $150.00
Sauce Dish, 4½" and Cover
    Crystal 1958-1970; $54.00
    Blue, 1958-1966; $64.00
    Green, 1958-1966; $60.00
    Amber, 1958-1966; $54.00
Shaker and Chrome Top "A" (pair)
    Crystal, 1959-1973; $65.00
    Blue, 1959-1973; $85.00
    Green, 1959-1973; $75.00
    Amber, 1959-1973; $65.00
    Pink, 1961-1973; $85.00

Amethyst, 1959-1965; $75.00
Brown, 1961-1973; $55.00
Sugar
    Crystal, 1958-1973; $32.50
    Blue, 1958-1973; $37.50
    Green, 1958-1973; $35.00
    Amber, 1958-1973; $25.00
    Pink, 1961-1973; $37.50
    Amethyst, 1960-1965; $35.00
    Brown, 1961-1973; $20.00
Tray, 9⅜" Handled Muffin
    Crystal, 1959-1970; $65.00
    Blue, 1959-1966; $85.00
    Green, 1959-1966; $75.00
    Amber, 1959-1966; $65.00

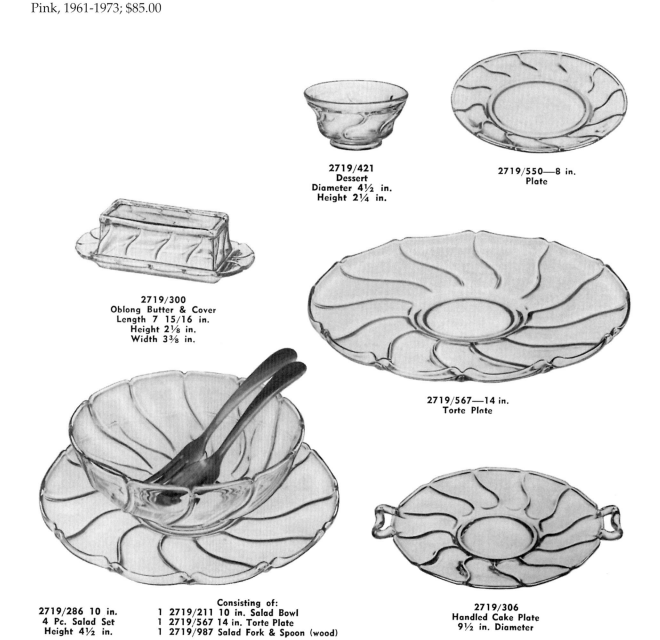

2719/421
Dessert
Diameter 4½ in.
Height 2¼ in.

2719/550—8 in.
Plate

2719/300
Oblong Butter & Cover
Length 7 15/16 in.
Height 2⅛ in.
Width 3⅜ in.

2719/567—14 in.
Torte Plate

2719/286 10 in.
4 Pc. Salad Set
Height 4½ in.

Consisting of:
1 2719/211 10 in. Salad Bowl
1 2719/567 14 in. Torte Plate
1 2719/987 Salad Fork & Spoon (wood)

2719/306
Handled Cake Plate
9½ in. Diameter

2719/635
Sauce Dish & Cover
Height 4½ in.
Diameter 4½ in.

2719/360
Celery
Length 9¼ in.

2719/540
Pickle
Length 8⅜ in.

2719/620
Two-part Relish
Length 9⅛ in.   Width 4¾ in.

2719/648
Handled Serving Dish
Height 2½ in.

2719/726
Handled Muffin Tray
Length 9⅜ in.   Width 7⅞ in.

2719/653
Shaker & Chrome Top "A"
Height 3½ in.

2719/679
Footed Sugar
Height 3½ in.

2719/681
Footed Cream
Height 4 in.

2719/456—3 pt.
Ice Jug
Height 7 5/16 in.

2719/447
Jelly & Cover
Height 6⅛ in.

2719/630
Round Salver
Diameter 10 in.   Height 7 in.

2737 HAWAIIAN

1961 – 1963
Amber with Brown accent color
Amber with Peacock Blue accent color

This unusual pattern is a two-color design and was difficult to make. A precise amount of the accent color was gathered from the furnace and dropped into the mold. Then a glob of the amber base glass was dropped over this. As it was pressed, the accent color fused into the amber to create the Hawaiian design. When the piece was removed from the mold, it was hand shaped to form one of the pieces in the pattern. Several pieces were most likely shaped from the same mold. For example, the Ruffled Vase might have been flattened to make the 14" Torte or reshaped to become the 8" Deep Bowl, the 11½" Shallow Bowl, or the Shrimp Bowl.

106 Appetizer Set (Cracker Plate and
    solid Amber Sauce Dish; $95.00
126 Basket, 9"; $48.00
179 Bowl, 8" Ruffled; $54.00
208 Bowl, 8" Deep; $57.00
415 Bowl, 8" Flower Float; $48.00
188 Bowl, 9" Handled; $54.00
239 Bowl, 11½" Shallow; $60.00
266 Bowl, 15" Oval; $75.00

500 Candy, 8" Handled; $40.00
369 Cheese and Cracker (Cracker Plate and
    wooden Cheese Block); $85.00
567 Plate, 14" Torte (same as Cracker); $75.00
394 Shrimp and Dip, 2-piece (Shrimp Bowl
    and solid Amber Footed Dip); $125.00
767 Vase, 6¾" Ruffled; $45.00
807 Vase, 8⅞" Pitcher; $65.00

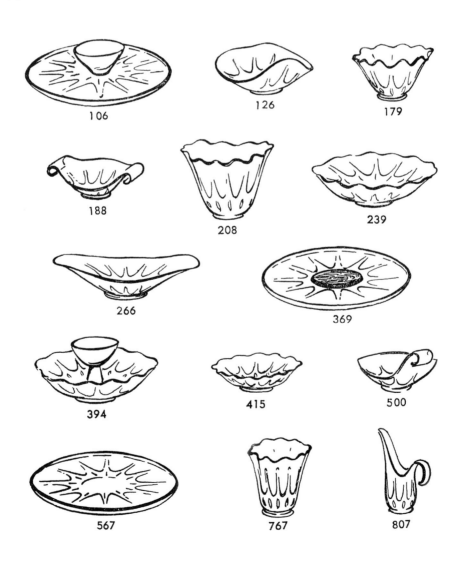

106   126   179

188   208   239

266   369

394   415   500

567   767   807

Amber/Brown Oval Bowl and Handled Candy; Amber/Peacock Shallow Bowl and Handled Bowl

Facets Pink Candlesticks, Crystal Ash Tray, Gold Candlestick

2739 ROULETTE

January 1968 New Goods.
Made in Ebony with Crystal and Ruby with Crystal except where noted.

This line never appeared in a price list. However, the candlestick was borrowed from 2638 Contour and several pieces seem to have been slightly reshaped and put into the Sculpture line. Some of these pieces may have been made on a trial basis.

208 Bowl, Star, 5" tall; $65.00
231 Bowl, 11" tall Quadrangle; $85.00
316 Candlestick, Crystal only (pair); $65.00
248 Tricorne Bowl, 3½" tall; $60.00
266 Centerpiece, 17" Oval; $95.00
267 Vase, 7" Petal; $65.00
785 Vase, 8" Basket; $70.00
792 Vase, 8½" Trident; $70.00
832 Vase, 15" Flame; $125.00

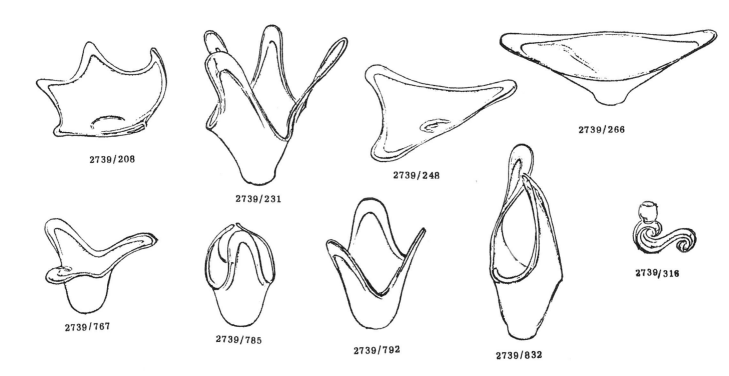

2739/208
2739/231
2739/248
2739/266
2739/767
2739/785
2739/792
2739/832
2739/316

2752 FACETS

Several pieces of the Facets line are pictured page 97. The Facets Candlestick is shown on the cover of this book.

2752/120 Ash Tray, 8"
  Crystal, 1961-1967; $15.00
  Pink, 1962-1965; $15.00
2752/124 Ash Tray, 11" Oblong
  Crystal, 1962-1967; $15.00
  Pink, 1962-1965; $20.00
2752/189 Bowl, 9" Oval
  Crystal, 1962-1965; $20.00
  Pink, 1962-1965; $24.00
  Gold, 1962-1965; $24.00
2752/211 Bowl, 10"
  Crystal, 1962-1965; $22.00
  Pink, 1962-1965; $28.00
2752/347 Bowl, Footed and Cover
  Crystal, 1962-1965; $35.00
  Pink, 1962-1965; $45.00
2752/350 Bon Bon and Cover

Crystal, 1962-1965; $30.00
Pink, 1962-1965; $40.00
Gold, 1962-1965; $35.00
2752/314 Candlestick, 3½" (pair)
  Crystal, 1962-1965; $30.00
  Pink, 1962-1965; $37.00
  Gold, 1962-1965; $35.00
2752/354 Candy Box and Cover
  Crystal, 1962-1965; $30.00
  Pink, 1962-1965; $40.00
2752/374 Cigarette Box, Oblong and Cover
  Crystal, 1961-1965; $25.00
  Pink, 1962-1965; $35.00
2752/653 Shaker, Chrome Top A (pair)
  Crystal, 1962-1965; $30.00
  Pink, 1962-1965; $35.00

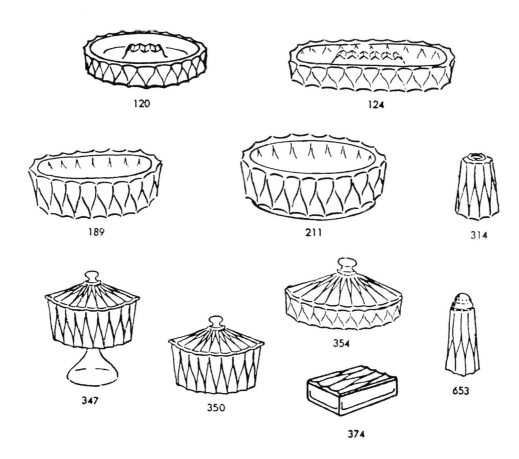

120

124

189

211

314

347

350

354

653

374

2785 GOURMET

1964 – 1970

The Gourmet line was introduced as the Hostess pattern in 1964. From 1966 through 1970, it was also offered with two decorations: Platinum, Decoration 669; and Gold, Decoration 668.

Bowl, 10" Footed; $35.00
Plate, 14" Torte (not decorated); $40.00
Relish, 2-part; $30.00
Relish, 4-part; $35.00
Relish, 5-part; $42.00
Shaker, Chrome Top "A" (not decorated)
 (pair); $35.00
Sugar and Cream, Footed; $38.00

Gourmet Sugar with Gold Decoration, Cream with Platinum Decoration

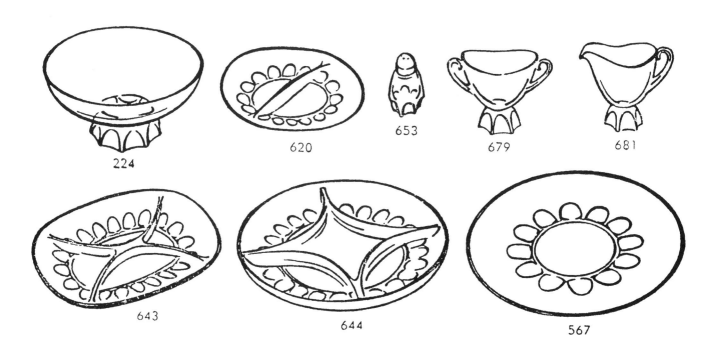

224

620

653

679

681

643

644

567

2806 PEBBLE BEACH

1969 – 1970 except as noted.
Crystal, Black Pearl, Lemon Twist, Pink Lady, and Mocha
Stemware is featured in *Fostoria Stemware*, page 51.

211 Bowl, 10" Salad; $40.00
600 Bowl, 11½" Salad/Punch
  Crystal only, 1969-1972; $65.00
615 Cup, 6½ oz. Punch
  Crystal only, 1969-1972; $15.00
421 Dessert; $14.00
  Also made in Flaming Orange,
  1969-1970
550 Plate, 8"; $14.00
  Also made in Flaming Orange,
  1969-1970
558 Plate, 11" Cake; $50.00
567 Plate, 14" Torte; $65.00
454 Pitcher, Quart; $75.00
622 Relish, 10" 3-part; $65.00
652 Shaker, Chrome Top E (pair); $26.00
676 Sugar and Cover; $16.00
680 Cream; $14.00

Lemon Twist Plate, Flaming Orange Dessert

2807 GLACIER

1969 – 1972, Crystal
The Cigarette Lighter is pictured on the back cover.

Ash Tray, Small 3¾"; $9.00
Ash Tray, Medium, 5½"; $12.00
Ash Tray, Large 8¾"; $15.00
Cigarette Lighter, Gold or Silver Fitting; $18.00
Cigarette Lighter Set
    Included Cigarette Lighter and 5½"
    Medium Ash Tray; $30.00

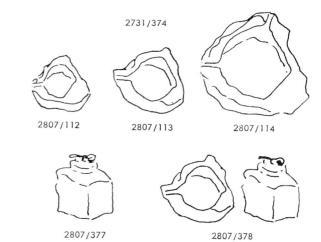

2731/374

2807/112   2807/113   2807/114

2807/377   2807/378

2808 CARIBBEAN

1969 – 1970, Crystal and Steel Gray
Blown lead glass with metal tripod base. The 830 Vase is pictured on the back cover..
The 6112 line of stemware is similar in design and is featured in *Fostoria Stemware*, page 136.

194 Bowl, 9" Footed; $35.00
347 Candy and Cover, 10" Footed; $45.00
318 Candleholder, 5½" Footed (pair); $45.00

829 Urn and Cover, 15" Footed; $54.00
830 Vase, 13" Footed; $45.00

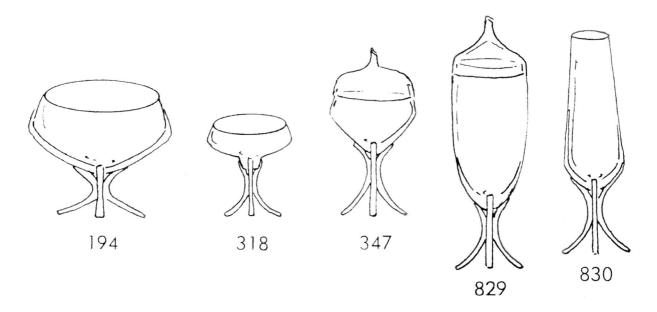

194   318   347   829   830

2816 SIERRA

July 1969 – 1970, Blank
Gift Items in Crystal

SIERRA ICE

Cutting 921
July 1969 – 1970, Blank
Gift Items in Crystal

110 Ash Tray, 4½"; $12.00
111 Ash Tray, 5½"; $15.00
178 Bowl, 8" Accent; $18.00
219 Centerpiece, 10" Footed; $35.00
325 Candle Pedestal, 8" (Single); $35.00

630 Server, 11½" Footed; $35.00
645 Tri-Server, 6½"; $20.00
757 Vase, 6" Flora; $20.00
768 Urn, 7" Footed; $28.00

Sea Shells Green Candlestick, Bowl, Copper Blue Vase

2834 COVENTRY LINE

1970 – 1971

MONACO

Crystal Print 24 on 2834 Line
Crystal and Honey Gold

135 Bon Bon; $12.00
191 Bowl, 8"; $18.00
195 Bowl, 9"; $20.00
300 Butter and Cover, Oblong; $35.00
540 Pickle, 8"; $16.00
560 Plate, 12" Square; $22.00
567 Plate, 14" Service; $26.00
620 Relish, 8" 2-part; $18.00
651 Shaker, Chrome Top E (pair); $18.00
677 Sugar and Cream; $20.00

Monaco Honey Gold Butter and Cover

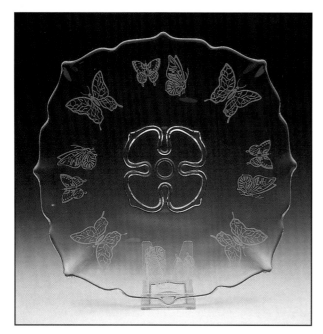

Square Plate with unlisted Butterfly etching

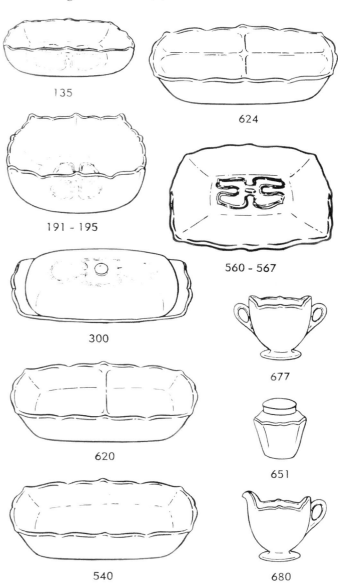

135

624

191 - 195

560 - 567

300

677

620

651

540

680

2844 SEA SHELLS

1971 – 1973, Crystal, Copper Blue and Green
One piece in Crystal, Black Pearl, and Lemon Twist
One piece in Crystal Luster, Black Pearl Luster, and Lemon Twist Luster.

2844/172 Bowl, 7" Rolled Edge
  Crystal; $30.00
  Copper Blue; $45.00
  Green; $45.00
2844/758 Bowl, 7½" Shallow
  Crystal; $30.00
  Copper Blue; $45.00
  Green; $45.00
2844/193 Bowl, 8½" Rolled Edge
  Crystal; $38.00
  Copper Blue; $50.00
  Green; $50.00
2844/208 Bowl, 10" Flared Edge
  Crystal; $47.00
  Copper Blue; $62.00
  Green; $62.00
2844/231 Bowl, 11" Flared
  Crystal; $50.00
  Copper Blue; $65.00
  Green; $65.00
2844/257 Bowl, 12½" Rolled Edge
  Crystal; $47.00
  Copper Blue; $65.00
  Green; $65.00
2844/275 Bowl, 15" Rolled Edge
  Crystal; $55.00
  Copper Blue; $68.00
  Green; $68.00
2844/311 Candlestick, 2⅝" Flora (pair)
  Crystal; $45.00
  Copper Blue; $65.00
  Green; $65.00
2844/317 Candlestick, 3½" Flared (pair)
  Crystal; $50.00

  Copper Blue; $70.00
  Green; $70.00
2803/380 Coaster, Shell
  Crystal; $8.00
  Black Pearl; $9.00
  Lemon Twist; $9.00
2823/421 Dessert, Shell
  Crystal Luster; $10.00
  Black Pearl Luster; $12.00
  Lemon Twist Luster; $12.00
2825/201 Small Shell, 9½"
  Crystal; $40.00
  Copper Blue; $55.00
  Green; $55.00
2825/259 Medium Shell, 13"
  Crystal; $50.00
  Copper Blue; $70.00
  Green; $70.00
2825/280 Large Shell, 18"
  Crystal; $55.00
  Copper Blue; $75.00
  Green; $75.00
2844/575 Torte Plate, 17"
  Crystal; $55.00
  Copper Blue; $75.00
  Green; $75.00
2844/751 Vase, 4"
  Crystal; $20.00
  Copper Blue; $30.00
  Green; $30.00
2844/785 Vase, 8"
  Crystal; $38.00
  Copper Blue; $50.00
  Green; $50.00

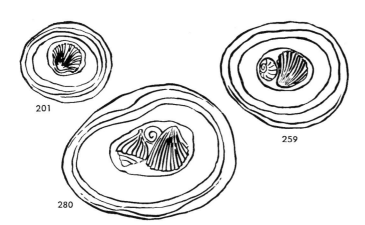

201

259

280

380

421

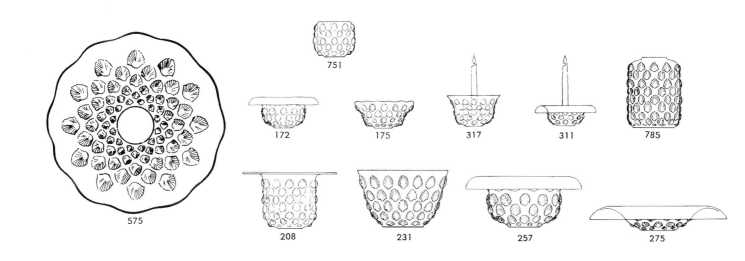

751

172   175   317   311   785

575   208   231   257   275

4186 MESA

Stemware is featured in *Fostoria Stemware*, page 61.

380 Coaster
  Crystal, 1968-1970; $5.00
  Olive Green, 1968-1970; $6.00
  Brown, 1968-1970; $4.00
  Amber, 1968-1970; $5.00
  Blue, 1968-1970; $6.00
495 Dessert, 4¾"
  Crystal, 1967-1974; $10.00
  Olive Green, 1967-1974; $12.00
  Brown, 1967-1970; $10.00
  Amber, 1967-1974; $10.00
  Blue, 1967-1974; $14.00
  Ruby, 1967-1970; $18.00
454 Pitcher, Quart
  Crystal, 1967-1970; $45.00
  Olive Green, 1967-1970; $45.00
  Brown, 1967-1970; $35.00
  Amber, 1967-1970; $40.00
  Blue, 1967-1970; $65.00
458 Pitcher, 2-Quart
  Crystal, 1967-1970; $55.00
  Olive Green, 1967-1970; $55.00
  Brown, 1967-1970; $45.00
  Amber, 1967-1970; $50.00
  Blue, 1967-1970; $75.00

550 Plate, 8"
  Crystal, 1967-1974; $10.00
  Olive Green, 1967-1974; $10.00
  Brown, 1967-1970; $6.00
  Amber, 1967-1974; $8.00
  Blue, 1967-1974; $12.00
  Ruby, 1967-1970; $18.00
653 Shaker, Chrome Top A (pair)
  Crystal, 1968-1972; $24.00
  Olive Green, 1968-1972; $24.00
  Brown, 1968-1970; $16.00
  Amber, 1968-1972; $20.00
  Blue, 1968-1972; $35.00
673 Sugar and Cover
  Crystal, 1968-1970; $18.00
  Olive Green, 1968-1970; $18.00
  Brown, 1968-1970; $14.00
  Amber, 1968-1970; $16.00
  Blue, 1968-1970; $22.00
680 Cream
  Crystal, 1968-1970; $15.00
  Olive Green, 1968-1970; $15.00
  Brown, 1968-1970; $10.00
  Amber, 1968-1970; $12.00
  Blue, 1968-1970; $18.00

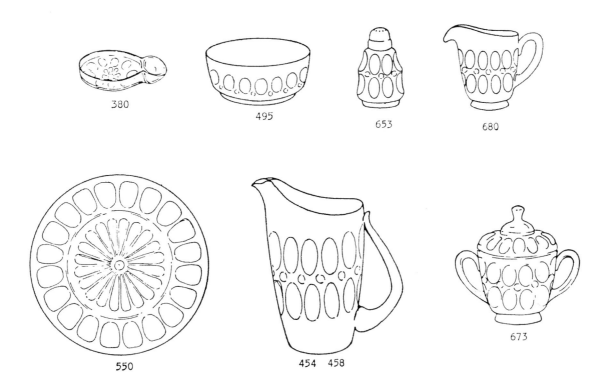

380

495

653

680

550

454 458

673

Ruby Plate; Blue Shaker, Coaster, and Pitcher

ETCHINGS AND CRYSTAL PRINTS

Plate Etchings

327 Navarre

332 Mayflower

333 Willowmere

334 Colonial Mirror

335 Willow

336 Plymouth

337 Sampler

340 Buttercup

341 Romance

342 Bouquet

343 Heather

344 Camelia

345 Starflower

346 Thistle

Crystal Prints

1 Sylvan

2 Skyflower

6 Lacy Leaf

7 Milkweed

ETCHINGS

Etchings continued to be a prominent part of Fostoria production during this period with the Navarre etching vying with the American pattern for longevity. Some of the etchings shown here were introduced before World War II but continued to be made long into the 1944 – 1986 period. A few patterns introduced just before the war were offered mostly during the war years, such as Colonial Mirror, Plymouth, Willow, and Sampler. Crystal Prints were a new offering for Fostoria and were essentially a more delicate version of the plate etching. One of the most diverse and beautiful of the etchings shown here is Mayflower. In addition to the Coronet dinnerware blank, Mayflower used pieces from Diadem and Flame (see *Fostoria Tableware: 1924 – 1943*).

Since many of these patterns used the same pieces, in most cases sample pages are shown instead of the entire pattern. By looking through all the etchings or referring back to the Pressed Patterns in this book and in *Fostoria Tableware: 1924 – 1943*, one may locate pictures of each piece in each pattern.

NAVARRE

Plate Etching 327

For pieces discontinued before 1944, see *Fostoria Tableware: 1924 – 1943*, pages 232 – 239.
Stemware is featured in *Fostoria Stemware*, pages 87 and 88.

Navarre tableware pieces were discontinued from time to time until in 1971, only stemware and 7- and 8-inch plates were being made. In 1974 a number of pieces were reintroduced as Navarre Giftware. These continued being made until May 1982. Note that the top picture on page 111 shows the Flared Handled Nappy with a collar-type base rather than the earlier 3-toed base. The Navarre pattern was one of the few major dinnerware patterns not to have a Jelly until 1974 when the regular Baroque (2496) Comport became the Jelly. It was never offered with a cover. Some of these later items are heavier, slightly thicker glass.

We have listed two Carates, a Puff Box and Cover, and a Perfume Bottle and Stopper which were listed in New Goods in January 1982 only. These never made it beyond the sample stage and are rare indeed.

The 2482 Candlestick when plain (unetched) was pictured and listed with both one central bobache and with two bobaches in the late 1960s. Although the Navarre pattern never offered the 2482 Candlestick with bobache, one might assume that the etched candlestick could have sported bobaches since it was being offered during the same period.

2482 Candlestick with one bobache and two bobaches

2375 Mayonnaise, Plate and Ladle

2496 Bon Bon, 1938-1982; $48.00
2496 Bowl, Regular Nappy, 1938-1944; $32.00
2496 Bowl, Flared Nappy, 1938-1982; $25.00
2496 Bowl, Square Nappy, 1938-1944; $32.00
2496 Bowl, 3-cornered Nappy, 1938-1970; $27.00
2496 Bowl, 3-toed Nut, 1938-1944; $58.00
2496 Bowl, 8½" Handled Serving, 1954-1961; $75.00
2496 Bowl, 10" Floating Garden, 1936-1959; $150.00
2470½ Bowl, 10½", 1936-1963; $95.00
2496 Bowl, 12" Flared, 1936-1970; $95.00
2545 Bowl, 12½" Flame, 1936-1959; $110.00
2496 Candlestick, 4", (pair) 1936-1979; $70.00
2496 Candlestick, 5½", (pair) 1936-1959; $85.00
2496 Candlestick, Duo, (pair) 1936-1970; $95.00
2496 Candlestick, Trindle, (pair) 1936-1959; $135.00
2472 Candlestick, Duo, (pair) 1936-1959; $150.00
2482 Candlestick, Trindle, (pair) 1936-1970; $175.00
2545 Candlestick, Duo, (pair) 1936-1959; $200.00
2496 Candy and Cover, 1938-1962; $125.00
2440 Celery, 11½", 1936-1944; $58.00
2496 Cheese and Cracker, 1938-1959; $115.00
2496 Comport, 5½", 1937-1959; $50.00
2400 Comport, 6", 1936-1959; $55.00
2440 Cup and Saucer, 1936-1970; $34.00
2496 Ice Bucket and Tongs, 1936-1959; $130.00
2496 Jelly, 1974-1982; $57.00
5000 Jug, 1936-1959; $495.00
2375 Mayonnaise, Plate, Ladle, 1936-1945; $85.00
2496 Mayonnaise, 2-part, 1936-1944; $50.00
2496½ Mayonnaise, Plate, Ladle, 1949-1959; $85.00

2440 Pickle, 8½", 1936-1944; $42.00
2496 Pickle, 8", 1949-1959; $39.00
2666 Pitcher, Quart, 1958-1970; $450.00
2440 Plate, 6", 1936-1967; $14.00
2440 Plate, 7", 1936-1982; $18.00
2440 Plate, 8" 1936-1982; $23.00
2440 Plate, 9", 1936-1959; $68.00
2496 Plate, 10" Cake, 1937-1982; $75.00
2440 Plate, Oval Cake, 1936-1946; $95.00
2496 Plate, 14" Torte, 1936-1982; $95.00
2364 Plate, 16" Torte, 1936-1970; $150.00
2496 Relish, 2-part, 1936-1982; $37.00
2496 Relish, 3-part, 1936-1982; $68.00
2419 Relish, 5-part, 1936-1947; $125.00
2496 Sauce, 6½" Oval, 1936-1944; $120.00
2364 Shaker, Chrome Top "C" (pair) 1950-1982; $68.00
2496 Sugar and Cream, Individual, 1938-1970; $56.00
2440 Sugar and Cream, 1936-1967, 1974-1982; $62.00
2496 Sugar, Cream, Tray, 1947-1970; $65.00
2496 Sweetmeat, 6", 1936-1944; $50.00
2496 Tid Bit, 3-toed, 1938-1982; $48.00
2496 Tray, 8½" Oval, 1936-1944; $68.00
4121 Vase, 5", 1936-1944, 1952-1959; $125.00
4143 Vase, 6", 1952-1955; $130.00
2470 Vase, 10", 1936-1943, 1952-1959; $295.00
2660 Vase, 8" Flip, 1952-1959; $185.00
NA01/790 Table Carafe/Vase, 65 oz. 1982; market
NA01/750 Mini-Carafe/Vase, 10½ oz., 1982; market
NA01/580 Puff Box and Cover, 1982; market
NA01/842 Perfume Bottle and Stopper, 1982; market

Navarre Giftware

Plate Etching No. 327

2496—10 in.
Handled Cake Plate

2496
Cheese and Cracker
Diameter of Plate 11 in.
Diameter of Cheese 5¼ in.
Height 3¼ in.

2400—6 in.
Comport
Height 4½ in.

2496—5½ in.
Comport
Height 4¾ in.

2496
Ice Bucket
Height 4⅜ in. Top Dia. 6½ in.
Chromium Handle and Tongs
Tongs Priced Separately

2496½
Mayonnaise and Plate and
Ladle

2496—3 Part
Candy Box and Cover
Height 2½ in. Width 6¼ in.

2496
3 Part Relish
Length 10 in. Width 7½ in.

2496
2 Part Relish
6 in. Square

2496
8 in. Pickle

2496
Handled Nappy, Fld.
Diameter 5 in.

2496
Handled Nappy, 3 Cor.
Length 4⅝ in.

2496
3 Toed Bon Bon
Diameter 7⅜ in.

2496
3 Toed Tid Bit, Flat
Diameter 8¼ in.

Plate Etching No. 327

2496—Handled Nappy, Reg.
Diameter 4⅜ in.

2496—Handled Nappy, Sq.
4 in. Square

2496—Sweetmeat
6 in. Square

2364—16 in.
Torte Plate

2496—12 in.
Bowl, Flared
Height 3½ in.

2496—10½ in.
Handled Bowl

2496—10 in. Floating Garden
Width 7½ in.

2496
Duo Candlestick
Height 4½ in. Spread 8 in.

NA01/790, Table Carafe/Vase; NA01/750, Mini-Carafe/Vase;
NA01/842, Perfume Bottle and Stopper; NA01/580, Puff Box and Cover

Plate Etching No. 327

2496
Trindle Candlestick
Height 6 in. Spread 8¼ in.

2545—12½ in. "Flame"
Oval Bowl
Height 2⅞ in.

2496—5½ in.
Candlestick

2545—"Flame"
Duo Candlestick
Height 6¾ in. Spread 10¼ in.

2482
Trindle Candlestick
Height 6¾ in. Spread 8½ in.

2470½—10½ in.
Bowl
Height 4 in.

2496—4 in.
Candlestick

2472
Duo Candlestick
Height 5 in. Spread 8¼ in.

332 MAYFLOWER

Plate Etching 332

Stemware is featured in *Fostoria Stemware*, page 92.

Everything about this pattern evokes romance and elegance, from the graceful, flowing lines of the Coronet blank to the delicately etched garlands and cornucopia-shaped basket filled with spring flowers. Mayflower is the only etched pattern to use the 4140 Jug. The 2276 Vanity would be a great addition to any collection.

2560 Bon Bon, 1938-1954; $38.00
2560 Bon Bon, 3-toed, 1938-1954; $38.00
869 Bowl, Finger, 1938-1943; $28.00
2560 Bowl, 5" Fruit, 1938-1943; $28.00
2560 Bowl, 6" Cereal, 1938-1943; $30.00
2560 Bowl, 3-toed Nut, 1938-1944; $40.00
2560 Bowl, 8½" Serving, 1938-1954; $42.00
2560 Bowl, 10" Salad, 1938-1954; $65.00
2430 Bowl, 11", 1938-1942; $68.00
2560 Bowl, 11" Handled, 1938-1954; $75.00
2496 Bowl, 10½" Handled, 1938-1954; $75.00
2560 Bowl, 11½" Crimped, 1938-1954; $68.00
2560 Bowl, 12" Flared, 1938-1954; $65.00
2545 Bowl, 12½" Oval, 1938-1954; $68.00
2560 Bowl, 13" Fruit, 1938-1954; $74.00
2430 Candlestick, 2", (pair) 1938-1942; $65.00
2560½ Candlestick, 4",
    (pair) 1938-1954; $75.00
2545 Candlestick, 4½",
    (pair) 1938-1954; $75.00
2545 Candlestick, Lustre, UD Prisms,
    (pair) 1938-1942; $145.00
2496 Candlestick, Duo, (pair) 1938-1954; $97.00
2545 Candlestick, Duo,
    (pair) 1938-1954; $110.00
2560 Candlestick, Duo,
    (pair) 1938-1954; $110.00
2545 Candelabra, 2-light, B Prisms,
    (pair) 1938-1942; $225.00
2430 Candy Jar and Cover, 1938-1943; $125.00
2560 Celery, 11", 1938-1954; $37.00
2560 Cheese and Cracker, 1938-1944; $125.00
2560 Comport, 6", 1938-1943; $75.00
2560 Cup and Saucer, 1938-1954; $30.00
2560 Ice Bucket, Chrome Handle and Tongs,
    1938-1943; $125.00
2430 Jelly, 7", 1938-1939; $65.00
4140 Jug, 1938, 1943; $565.00
5000 Jug, 1947-1954; $475.00
2560 Lemon, 1938-1944; $32.00

2560 Mayonnaise, Plate, Ladle,
    1938-1954; $68.00
2560 Mayonnaise, 2-part, 2 ladles,
    1938-1943; $76.00
2430 Mint, 5½", 1938-1942; $37.00
2560 Oil, 3½ oz., 1938-1943; $135.00
2560 Olive, 6¾", 1938-1954; $30.00
2560 Pickle, 8¾", 1938-1954; $32.00
2560 Plate, 6", 1938-1954; $12.00
2560 Plate, 7", 1938-1954; $15.00
2560 Plate, 8", 1938-1954; $18.00
2560 Plate, 9", 1938-1954; $45.00
2560 Plate, Cake, 1938-1954; $65.00
2560 Plate, 14" Torte, 1938-1954; $75.00
2560 Relish, 2-part, 1938-1954; $38.00
2560 Relish, 3-part, 1938-1954; $52.00
2560 Relish, 4-part, 1938-1943; $68.00
2560 Relish, 5-part, 1938-1943; $85.00
2560 Salad Set, 4-piece, 1946-1954; $150.00
2586 Sani Cut Server,
    1940-1943; $235.00/market
2560 Shaker, FGT, (pair) 1938-1943; $135.00
2560 Sugar and Cream, 1938-1954; $65.00
2560 Sugar, Cream, Tray, Individual,
    1938-1954; $85.00
2560 Sweetmeat, 1938-1954; $30.00
2560 Tid Bit, 3-toed, 1938-1944; $38.00
2560 Tray, Handled Lunch,
    1938-1939; 1943; $95.00
2560 Tray, Handled Muffin, 1938-1954; $75.00
2276 Vanity Set, 1939-1943; $225.00/market
2430 Vase, 3¾", 1938-1943; $54.00
2560 Vase, 6" Handled, 1939-1943; $125.00
2430 Vase, 8", 1938-1943; $125.00
2545 Vase, 10", 1938-1943; $145.00
5100 Vase, 10", 1938-1943; $145.00
2560 Whip Cream, 1938-1954; $38.00

5000
Footed Jug
Height 9¾ in.
Capacity 3 Pints

2560—6 in.
Plate

2560—7 in.
Plate

2560—8 in.
Plate

2560—9 in.
Plate

2560
Footed Cup

2560
Saucer

2560
Footed Sugar
Height 3½ in.

2560
Footed Cream
Height 4⅛ in. Cap. 7 oz.

2560—10 in.
3 Piece Salad Set
Consisting of:

1/12 Doz. 2560—10 in.
Salad Bowl—Height 4⅛ in.
1/12 Doz. 2560—14 in.
Torte Plate
1/12 Doz. 2560 ¼
Salad Fork and Spoon (Wood

2560—3 Piece
Ind. Sugar and Cream and Tray
Consisting of:
1/12 Doz. 2560½—7½ in.
Sugar and Cream Tray
1/12 Doz. 2560—Ind. Sugar
1/12 Doz. 2560—Ind. Cream

4140—Jug
Height 7½ in. Capacity 60 oz.

869—Finger Bowl

Plate Etching No. 332

2560
Mayonnaise and Plate and Ladle
Height 3½ in.

2560—14 in.
Torte Plate

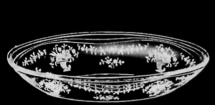

2560—6¾ in.
Olive
2560—8¾ in.
Pickle
2560—11 in.
Celery

2560—2 Part
Relish
Length 6½ in. Width 5¼ in.

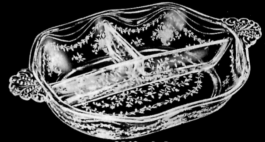

2560—3 Part
Relish
Length 10 in. Width 7¾ in.

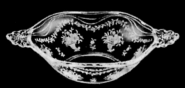

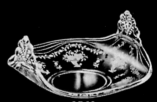

2560
Sweetmeat
Dia. 5½ in. Height 1½ in.

2560
Whip Cream
Diameter 5 in. Height 1¾ in.

2560
Bon Bon
Length 5¾ in. Width 6¼ in.

2560
3 Toed Bon Bon
Dia. 7¼ in. Height 2⅜ in.

2560—10½ in.
Handled Cake Plate

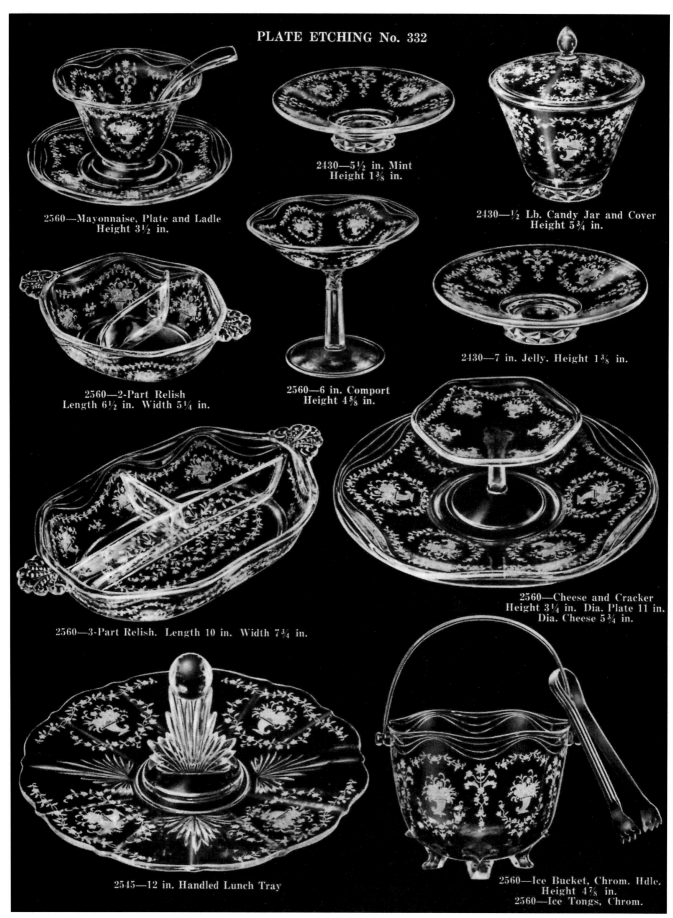

PLATE ETCHING No. 332

2560—Mayonnaise, Plate and Ladle
Height 3½ in.

2430—5½ in. Mint
Height 1⅜ in.

2430—½ Lb. Candy Jar and Cover
Height 5¾ in.

2560—2-Part Relish
Length 6½ in. Width 5¼ in.

2560—6 in. Comport
Height 4⅝ in.

2430—7 in. Jelly. Height 1⅜ in.

2560—3-Part Relish. Length 10 in. Width 7¾ in.

2560—Cheese and Cracker
Height 3¼ in. Dia. Plate 11 in.
Dia. Cheese 5¾ in.

2545—12 in. Handled Lunch Tray

2560—Ice Bucket, Chrom. Hdle.
Height 4⅞ in.
2560—Ice Tongs, Chrom.

PLATE ETCHING No. 332

2560
Duo Candlestick
Height 5⅛ in. Spread 9 in.

2560—11½ in. Bowl, Crimped
Height 3¼ in.

2545—12½ in. "Flame" Oval Bowl
Height 2⅞ in.

2560—10 in. Salad Bowl
Height 4⅛ in.

2560—13 in. Fruit Bowl
Height 2½ in.

2560—12 in. Bowl, Flared
Height 3¼ in.

2545—"Flame" Lustre
Using 8 U. D. P.
Height 7½ in.

PLATE ETCHING No. 332

2545—10 in. Vase

2545—"Flame" Duo Candlestick
Height 6¾ in. Spread 10¼ in.

2545—4½ in. Candlestick

2430—8 in. Vase

2430—3¾ in. Vase

2545—2-Light "Flame" Candelabra
Using 12 "B" Prisms
Height 6¾ in. Spread 11 in.

5100—10 in. Vase

PLATE ETCHING No. 332

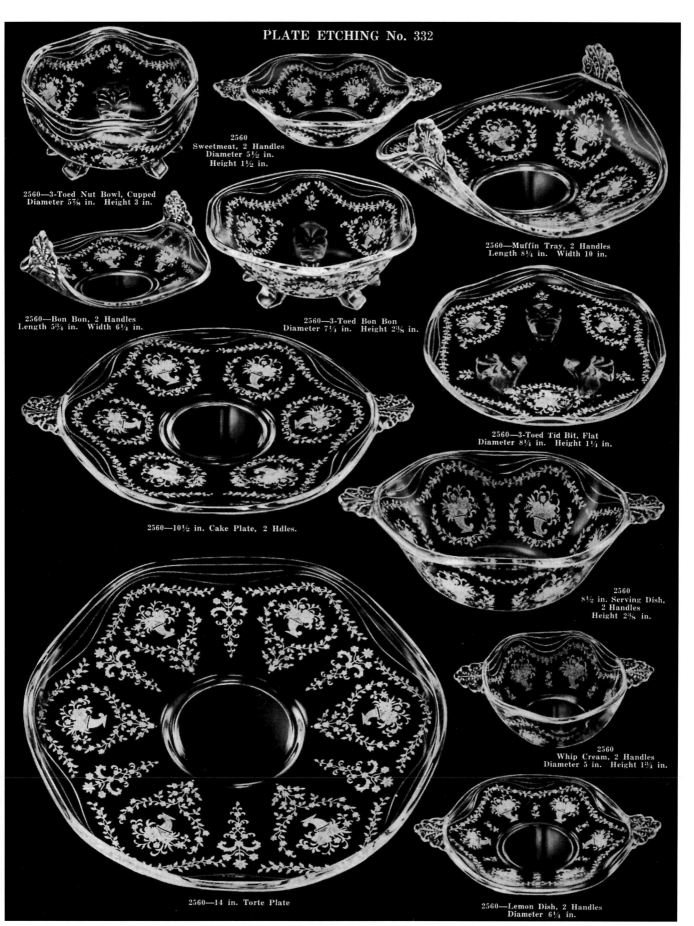

2560
Sweetmeat, 2 Handles
Diameter 5½ in.
Height 1½ in.

2560—3-Toed Nut Bowl, Cupped
Diameter 5⅞ in.   Height 3 in.

2560—Muffin Tray, 2 Handles
Length 8¼ in.   Width 10 in.

2560—Bon Bon, 2 Handles
Length 5¾ in.   Width 6¼ in.

2560—3-Toed Bon Bon
Diameter 7¼ in.   Height 2⅜ in.

2560—3-Toed Tid Bit, Flat
Diameter 8¼ in.   Height 1¼ in.

2560—10½ in. Cake Plate, 2 Hdles.

2560
8½ in. Serving Dish,
2 Handles
Height 2⅜ in.

2560
Whip Cream, 2 Handles
Diameter 5 in.   Height 1¾ in.

2560—14 in. Torte Plate

2560—Lemon Dish, 2 Handles
Diameter 6¼ in.

PLATE ETCHING No. 332

2430—2 in. Candlestick

2430—11 in. Bowl
Height 3 in.

2430—2 in. Candlestick

2560—4½ in. Candlestick

2560—11 in. Handled Bowl
Height 3¼ in.

2560—4½ in. Candlestick

2496—10½ in. Handled Bowl
Height 3⅜ in.

2496—Duo Candlestick
Height 5 in.   Spread 8¼ in.

PLATE ETCHING No. 332

2560—5 in. Fruit
2560—6 in. Cereal

2560—Footed Shaker, F. G. T.
Height 2⅞ in.

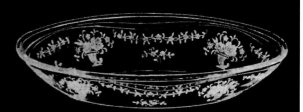

2560—6¾ in. Olive
2560—8¾ in. Pickle
2560—11 in. Celery

2560—4 Part Relish
Length 10 in.
Width 6¾ in.

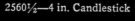

2560½—4 in. Candlestick

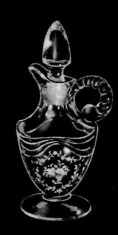

2560—3 oz. Footed Oil & Stopper
Height 4½ in.

2560—2 Part Mayonnaise
with 2 Ladles
Height 3½ in.
Top Diameter 6¾ in.

2560—5 Part Relish
Length 13¼ in.
Width 9⅜ in.

WILLOWMERE

Plate Etching 333

Stemware is featured in *Fostoria Stemware*, page 95.

2560 Bon Bon, 1938-1958; $38.00
2560 Bon Bon, 3-toed, 1938-1958; $38.00
869 Bowl, Finger, 1938-1958; $28.00
2560 Bowl, 5" Fruit, 1938-1943; $28.00
2560 Bowl, 6" Cereal, 1938-1943; $32.00
2560 Bowl, 3-toed Nut, 1938-1944; $40.00
2560 Bowl, 8½" Serving, 1938-1958; $45.00
2560 Bowl, 10" Salad, 1938-1943; $78.00
2560 Bowl, 2-part Salad, 1938; $125.00
2560 Bowl, 11" Handled, 1938-1962; $75.00
2560 Bowl, 11½" Crimped, 1938-1958; $68.00
2560 Bowl, 12", Flared, 1938-1958; $65.00
2560 Bowl, 13" Fruit, 1938-1958; $75.00
2560½ Candlestick, 4", (pair) 1938-1957; $75.00
2560 Candlestick 4½", (pair) 1938-1958; $75.00
2560 Candlestick, Duo, (pair) 1938-1962; $110.00
2560 Celery, 11", 1938-1958; $38.00
2560 Cheese and Cracker, 1938-1944; $125.00
2560 Comport, 6", 1938-1943; $75.00
2560 Cup and Saucer, 1938-1962; $34.00
2560 Ice Bucket, Chrome Handle and Tongs,
    1938-1943; $125.00
5000 Jug, 1938-1957; $495.00
2560 Lemon, 1938-1944; $32.00

2560 Mayonnaise, Plate, Ladle, 1938-1958; $68.00
2560 Mayonnaise, 2-part, 2 Ladles, 1938-1943; $78.00
2560 Oil, 3 oz. and Stopper, 1938-1943; $135.00
2560 Olive, 6¾", 1938-1958; $30.00
2560 Pickle, 8¾", 1938-1958; $34.00
2666 Pitcher, Quart, 1958-1968; $375.00
2560 Plate, 6", 1938-1959; $12.00
2560 Plate, 7", 1938-1967; $16.00
2560 Plate, 8", 1938-1959; $18.00
2560 Plate, 9", 1939-1962; $45.00
2560 Plate, 11½" Cake, 1938-1962; $65.00
2560 Plate, 14" Torte, 1938-1958; $75.00
2560 Relish, 2-part, 1938-1968; $38.00
2560 Relish, 3-part, 1938-1968; $55.00
2560 Relish, 4-part, 1938-1943; $68.00
2560 Relish, 5-part, 1938-1943; $95.00
2560 Salad Set, 3-piece, 1946-1958; $150.00
2586 Sani Cut Server, 1940-1943; $235.00/market
2364 Shaker, Chrome Top "C", (pair) 1950-1968; $95.0(
2560 Shaker, FGT, (pair) 1938-1943; $135.00
2560 Sugar and Cream, 1938-1962; $65.00
2560 Sugar and Cream, Individual, 1938-1958; $65.00
2560 Sugar and Cream Tray, 7½", 1939-1961; $28.00
2560 Sweetmeat, 1938-1958; $30.00

Willowmere Sugar and Cream Tray, Handled Bowl, Cup and Saucer, Two-part Relish

2560 Tid Bit, 3-toed, 1938-1944; $38.00
2560 Tray, Handled Lunch, 1938-1968; $85.00
2560 Tray, Handled Muffin, 1938-1968; $75.00
2276 Vanity Set, 1939-1943; $225.00/market
2560 Vase, 6" Handled, 1939-1943; $135.00
2567 Vase, 7½" 1938-1943; $125.00

2568 Vase, 9", 1938-1943; $135.00
2470 Vase, 10", 1938-1943; $165.00
5100 Vase, 10", 1938-1943; $165.00
2560 Whip Cream, 1938-1958; $37.00

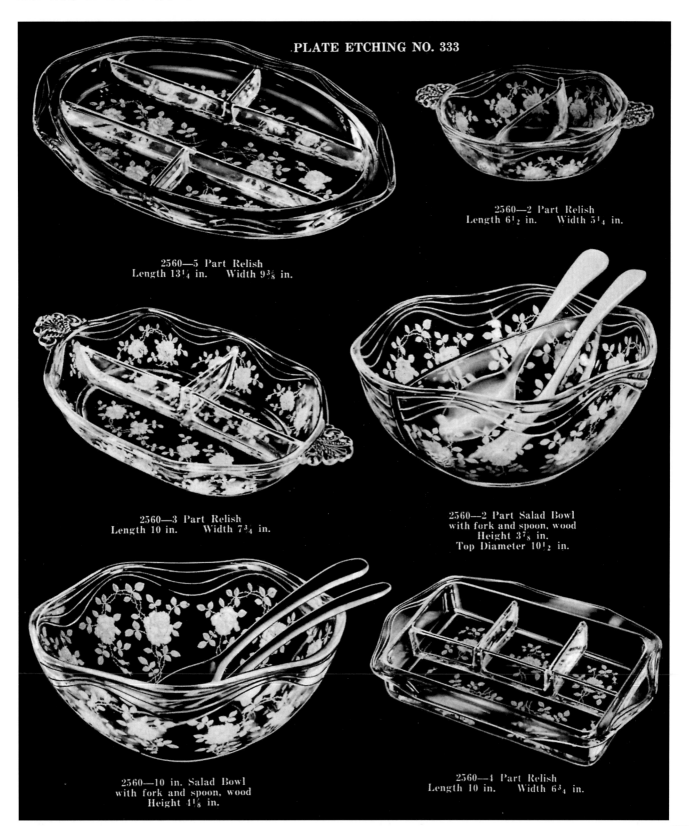

PLATE ETCHING NO. 333

2560—5 Part Relish
Length 13¼ in.   Width 9⅜ in.

2560—2 Part Relish
Length 6½ in.   Width 5¼ in.

2560—3 Part Relish
Length 10 in.   Width 7¾ in.

2560—2 Part Salad Bowl
with fork and spoon, wood
Height 3⅞ in.
Top Diameter 10½ in.

2560—10 in. Salad Bowl
with fork and spoon, wood
Height 4⅛ in.

2560—4 Part Relish
Length 10 in.   Width 6¾ in.

PLATE ETCHING NO. 333

2567—7½ in. Vase

2568—9 in. Vase

2470—10 in. Vase

5100—10 in. Vase

2560—Footed Cup
2560—Saucer
Cup Capacity 5½ oz.

2560
Footed Shaker
F. G. T.
Height 2⅞ in.

2560—Footed Cream
Height 4⅛ in.
Capacity 7 oz.

2560—Individual Sugar
Height 3 in.

2560—Individual Cream
Height 3¼ in.
Capacity 4 oz.

2560—Footed Sugar
Height 3½ in.

5000—7 Footed Jug
Height 9¾ in.   Capacity 3 Pints

Early American Master Etchings

Why would Fostoria introduce three patterns concurrently which used the same pieces and reflected a strong tie to Colonial times? There is no clue offered in catalogs or price lists.

The only insight comes from a June 1939 *Better Homes and Gardens* advertisement which proclaims "At Last! Early American 'Master Etchings' for your loveliest Colonial Settings." Those who ran the Fostoria Glass Company stayed in touch with the design trends of the times, and the move to recover our Colonial past through hard-rock maple furniture, lamps, and mirrors graced with the federal eagle, and hooked and braided rugs, was the motivating force behind those simple Colonial etchings.

Willow, included in this group, reflected another recurring theme in American design history: the Oriental influence.

Because these patterns used the same pieces, samples of each are shown to avoid duplication.

At Last! Early American
"Master-Etchings"
for your loveliest Colonial Settings

When you discover these quaint crystal etchings, you'll exclaim, "Why hasn't this been done before?" Fact is, it never has. *Colonial* "Master-Etchings" are an original Fostoria inspiration.

Every flawless, fragile line of the etcher's craft conspires to weave in glass the charm and romance of provincial settings...a scenic effect as romantic as Old Plymouth ...a motif as piquant as an old-fashioned sampler...and a traditional design as perfectly Early American as the eagle-topped Federal Mirror.

There's truly nothing finer than Fostoria, and nothing so new, so compatible as *Colonial* "Master-Etchings."

• • •

Left to right above: Sampler, Colonial Mirror and Plymouth. All open stock designs at your dealer's. Write for a free copy of "Four Hundred Years from Master Etchers to Master-Etchings." Ask for 39-P. Fostoria Glass Company, Moundsville, W. Va.

"Master-Etchings": by **Fostoria** MADE IN U.S.A.

Better Homes and Gardens,
June 1939

COLONIAL MIRROR

Plate Etching 334
All pieces 1939 – 1943

2574 Bon Bon; $34.00
766 Bowl, Finger; $22.00
2574 Bowl, 8½" Serving; $38.00
6023 Bowl, 9¼" Footed; $45.00
2574 Bowl, 9½" Handled; $48.00
2574 Bowl, 12" Flared; $45.00
2574 Bowl, 13" Fruit; $48.00
2574 Candlestick, 4" (pair); $57.00
2324 Candlestick, 6" (pair); $57.00
2574 Celery, 10½"; $38.00
2574 Comport, 5"; $58.00
6023 Comport, 5"; $58.00
2574 Cup and Saucer; $28.00
2574 Ice Tub; $45.00
2574 Lemon; $18.00
2574 Mayonnaise, Plate, and Ladle; $58.00
2574 Oil, 4½ oz., G.S.; $85.00
2574 Olive, 6"; $20.00

2574 Pickle, 8"; $25.00
6011 Jug; $275.00
2574 Plate, 6"; $12.00
2574 Plate, 7"; $15.00
2574 Plate, 8"; $18.00
2574 Plate, 9"; $42.00
2574 Plate, 10" Cake; $54.00
2574 Plate, 14" Torte; $65.00
2574 Relish, 3-part; $55.00
2574 Shaker, FGT (pair); $85.00
2574 Sugar and Cream; $52.00
2574 Sugar and Cream, Individual; $50.00
2574 Sweetmeat; $34.00
2574 Tray, Handled Muffin; $48.00
2574 Whip Cream; $34.00

766—Finger Bowl

2574—Individual Sugar
Height 2⅞ in.

2574—Individual Cream
Height 3½ in.   Capacity 5¾ oz.

2574—Footed Sugar
Height 3¾ in.

2574—Plate
See Price List for Sizes

6011—Footed Jug
Capacity 53 oz.
Height 8⅞ in.

2574—Footed Cream
Height 4 in.   Capacity 6½ oz.

PLATE ETCHING No. 334

2574—9½ in. Handled Bowl
Height 3⅜ in.

2574—4 in. Candlestick

2574—5 in. Comport
Height 4⅞ in.

2324—6 in. Candlestick

6023—Footed Bowl
Diameter 9¼ in.
Height 4¼ in.

WILLOW

Plate Etching 335

Stemware is featured in *Fostoria Stemware*, pages 93 and 94.

2574 Bon Bon, 1939-1944; $38.00
766 Bowl, Finger, 1939-1943; $25.00
2574 Bowl, 8½" Serving, 1939-1943; $42.00
6023 Bowl, 9½" Footed, 1939-1943; $60.00
2574 Bowl, 9½" Handled, 1939-1944; $57.00
2574 Bowl, 12" Flared, 1939-1944; $52.00
2574 Bowl, 13" Fruit, 1939-1944; $55.00
2574 Candlestick, 4", (pair) 1939-1944; $65.00
2324 Candlestick, 6", (pair) 1939-1943; $65.00
2374 Celery, 10½", 1939-1944; $40.00
2574 Comport, 5", 1939-1943; $60.00
6023 Comport, 5", 1939-1943; $60.00
2574 Cup and Saucer, 1939-1944; $32.00
2574 Ice Tub, 1939-1944; $50.00
6011 Jug, 1939-1943; $315.00
2574 Lemon, 1939-1944; $21.00
2574 Mayonnaise, Plate, Ladle, 1939-1943; $65.00

2574 Oil, 4½ oz. G.S., 1939-1943; $95.00
2574 Olive, 6", 1939-1944; $22.00
2574 Pickle, 8", 1939-1944; $28.00
2574 Plate, 6", 1939-1944; $12.00
2574 Plate, 7", 1939-1944; $16.00
2574 Plate, 8", 1939-1944; $20.00
2574 Plate, 9", 1939-1944; $45.00
2574 Plate, 10" Cake, 1939-1943; $60.00
2574 Plate, 14" Torte, 1939-1944; $75.00
2475 Relish, 3-part, 1939-1944; $58.00
2574 Shaker, FGT, (pair) 1939-1943; $95.00
2574 Sugar and Cream, Individual, 1939-1944; $52.00
2574 Sugar and Cream, 1939-1944; $57.00
2574 Sweetmeat, 1939-1944; $38.00
2574 Tray, Handled Muffin, 1939-1943; $52.00
2574 Whip Cream, 1939-1944; $38.00

Willow Mayonnaise, Plate and Ladle, 9" Plate, 12" Flared Bowl, Cup and Saucer

PLATE ETCHING No. 335

2574—Shaker, F.G.T.
Height 2⅝ in.

2574—4¼ oz. Oil, Ground Stopper
Height 5⅝ in.

2574—Footed Cup
2574—Saucer
Cup Capacity 6 oz.

6023—5 in. Blown Comport
Height 4¾ in.

2574—Whip Cream
Diameter 5 in.
Height 1¾ in.

2574—Bon Bon
Length 5 in.
Width 6⅜ in.

2574—Sweetmeat
Diameter 5¼ in.
Height 1⅛ in.

2574—6 in. Olive
2574—8 in. Pickle
2574—10½ in. Celery

2574—Lemon
Diameter 6½ in.

2574—8½ in. Serving Dish
Height 2½ in.

2574—3 Part Relish
Length 10 in.   Width 7 in.
Height 1¾ in.

PLYMOUTH

Plate Etching 336

Stemware is featured in *Fostoria Stemware*, page 96.

2574 Bon Bon, 1939-1944; $38.00
766 Bowl, Finger, 1939-1943; $25.00
2574 Bowl, 8½" Serving, 1939-1943; $42.00
6023 Bowl, 9½" Footed, 1939-1943; $60.00
2574 Bowl, 9½" Handled, 1939-1944; $57.00
2574 Bowl, 12" Flared, 1939-1944; $52.00
2574 Bowl, 13" Fruit, 1939-1944; $55.00
2574 Candlestick, 4", (pair) 1939-1944; $65.00
2324 Candlestick, 6", (pair) 1939-1943; $65.00
2374 Celery, 10½", 1939-1944; $40.00
2574 Comport, 5", 1939-1943; $60.00
6023 Comport, 5", 1939-1943; $60.00
2574 Cup and Saucer, 1939-1944; $32.00
2574 Ice Tub, 1939-1944; $50.00
6011 Jug, 1939-1943; $315.00
2574 Lemon, 1939-1944; $21.00
2574 Mayonnaise, Plate, Ladle, 1939-1943; $65.00

2574 Oil, 4½ oz. G.S., 1939-1943; $95.00
2574 Olive, 6", 1939-1944; $22.00
2574 Pickle, 8", 1939-1944; $28.00
2574 Plate, 6", 1939-1944; $12.00
2574 Plate, 7", 1939-1944; $16.00
2574 Plate, 8", 1939-1944; $20.00
2574 Plate, 9", 1939-1944; $45.00
2574 Plate, 10" Cake, 1939-1943; $60.00
2574 Plate, 14" Torte, 1939-1944; $75.00
2475 Relish, 3-part, 1939-1944; $58.00
2574 Shaker, FGT, (pair) 1939-1943; $95.00
2574 Sugar and Cream, Individual, 1939-1944; $52.00
2574 Sugar and Cream, 1939-1944; $57.00
2574 Sweetmeat, 1939-1944; $38.00
2574 Tray, Handled Muffin, 1939-1943; $52.00
2574 Whip Cream, 1939-1944; $38.00

PLATE ETCHING No. 336

2574—4 in. Candlestick

2574—9½ in. Handled Bowl
Height 3⅜ in.

2324—6 in. Candlestick

2574—5 in. Comport
Height 4⅞ in.

6023—Footed Bowl
Diameter 9¼ in.
Height 4¼ in.

SAMPLER

Plate Etching 337

1939 – 1943

Stemware is featured in *Fostoria Stemware*, page 96.

2574 Bon Bon; $34.00
766 Bowl, Finger; $22.00
2574 Bowl, 8½" Serving; $38.00
6023 Bowl, 9¼" Footed; $45.00
2574 Bowl, 9½" Handled; $48.00
2574 Bowl, 12" Flared; $45.00
2574 Bowl, 13" Fruit; $48.00
2574 Candlestick, 4" (pair); $57.00
2324 Candlestick, 6" (pair); $57.00
2574 Celery, 10½"; $38.00
2574 Comport, 5"; $58.00
6023 Comport, 5"; $58.00
2574 Cup and Saucer; $28.00
2574 Ice Tub; $45.00
2574 Lemon; $18.00
2574 Mayonnaise, Plate and Ladle; $58.00
2574 Oil, 4½ oz, G.S.; $85.00

2574 Olive, 6"; $20.00
2574 Pickle, 8"; $25.00
6011 Jug; $275.00
2574 Plate, 6"; $12.00
2574 Plate, 7"; $15.00
2574 Plate, 8"; $18.00
2574 Plate, 9"; $42.00
2574 Plate, 10" Cake; $54.00
2574 Plate, 14" Torte; $65.00
2574 Relish, 3-part; $55.00
2574 Shaker, FGT (pair); $85.00
2574 Sugar and Cream; $52.00
2574 Sugar and Cream, Individual; $50.00
2574 Sweetmeat; $34.00
2574 Tray, Handled Muffin; $48.00
2574 Whip Cream; $34.00

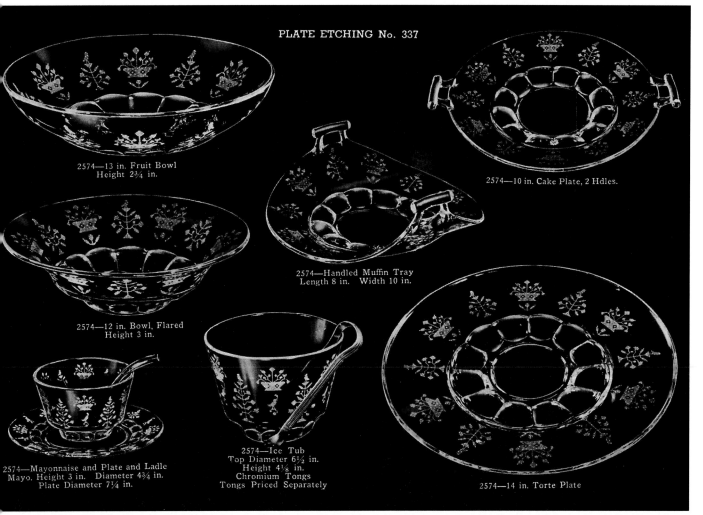

PLATE ETCHING No. 337

2574—13 in. Fruit Bowl
Height 2¾ in.

2574—10 in. Cake Plate, 2 Hdles.

2574—Handled Muffin Tray
Length 8 in. Width 10 in.

2574—12 in. Bowl, Flared
Height 3 in.

2574—Mayonnaise and Plate and Ladle
Mayo. Height 3 in. Diameter 4¾ in.
Plate Diameter 7¼ in.

2574—Ice Tub
Top Diameter 6½ in.
Height 4⅛ in.
Chromium Tongs
Tongs Priced Separately

2574—14 in. Torte Plate

BUTTERCUP

Etching 340

Introduced during World War II, this distinctive pattern survived the war and continued as a favorite of brides for least 20 years. Many brides chose the coordinating Spode "Buttercup" china and Gorham sterling flatware by the sam name. The pieces that did not survive the War are the most difficult to find. The Sani-Cut Syrup, Salad Dressing Bottle, the part Relish and the Blown Cigarette and Ash Tray are among these rare items. The simplicity of the Sonata blank lends itse beautifully to the flowing rhythm of buttercup flowers. For pieces not shown with Buttercup, see the Romance pattern.

No listing was found for the gold encrusted bowl pictured. The decoration may have been done by another comp ny. Stemware is featured in *Fostoria Stemware*, page 100.

2337—Plate
See Price List for Sizes

2364 Ash Tray, Individual, 1941-1943; $38.00
1769 Bowl, Finger, 1941-1943; $34.00
2364 Bowl, 6" Baked Apple, 1941-1943; $45.00
2364 Bowl, 9" Salad, 1941-1959; $58.00
6023 Bowl, 9" Footed, 1941-1943; $95.00
2594 Bowl, 10" Handled, 1941-1959; $125.00
2364 Bowl, 10½" Salad, 1941-1959; $65.00
2364 Bowl, 12" Flared, 1941-1959; $68.00
2364 Bowl, 12" Lily Pond, 1941-1959; $68.00
2364 Bowl, 13" Fruit, 1941-1959; $75.00
2324 Candlestick, 4", (pair) 1941-1959; $42.00
2324 Candlestick, 6", (pair) 1941-1943; $65.00
2594 Candlestick, 5½", (pair) 1941-1959; $75.00
6023 Candlestick, Duo, (pair) 1941-1959; $75.00
2594 Candlestick, Trindle,
    (pair) 1942-1959; $125.00
2364 Candy Jar and Cover, 1941-1943;
    $125.00/market
2350 Celery, 11", 1941-1959; $38.00
2364 Cheese and Cracker, 1941-1957; $87.00
2364 Cigarette Holder, 1941-1943; $75.00
6030 Comport, 5", 1942-1959; $57.00
2364 Comport, 8", 1942-1959; $95.00
2350½ Cup and Saucer, 1941-1959; $30.00
2666 Jug, 1-Quart, 1958-1959; $30.00
6011 Jug, 1941-1957; $425.00
2364 Mayonnaise, Plate, Ladle, 1941-1959; $65.00

2350 Pickle, 8", 1941-1959; $30.00
2337 Plate, 6", 1941-1959; $10.00
2337 Plate, 7", 1941-1959; $14.00
2337 Plate, 8", 1941-1959; $18.00
2337 Plate, 9", 1941-1959; $45.00
2364 Plate, Crescent Salad, 1941-1959; $43.00
2364 Plate, 11" Sandwich, 1941-1959; $45.00
2364 Plate, 14" Torte, 1941-1959; $65.00
2364 Plate, 16" Torte, 1941-1959; $75.00
2364 Relish, 2-part, 1942-1944; $75.00
2364 Relish, 3-part, 1942-1959; $60.00
2083 Salad Dressing Bottle, 1941-1943; $300.00/marke
2364 Salad Set, 9", 1946-1959; $125.00
2364 Salad Set, 10½", 1946-1959; $140.00
2586 Sani-Cut Syrup, 1941-1943; $300.00/market
2364 Shaker, 2¼", (pair) 1942-1959; $75.00
2350½ Sugar and Cream, 1941-1959; $64.00
2364 Tray, Handled Lunch, 1942-1959; $58.00
6021 Vase, 6" Bud, 1942-1943; $95.00
4143 Vase, 6" Footed, 1941-1943; $120.00
4143 Vase, 7½" Footed, 1941-1943; $150.00
2614 Vase, 10", 1942-1943; $195.00

Buttercup 8" Comport, Gold Encrusted Salad Bowl

PLATE ETCHING No. 340

2350—8 in. Pickle
2350—11 in. Celery

2364—Cheese and Cracker
Height 3¼ in.
Plate Diameter 11¼ in.   Cheese Diameter 5¾ in.
Cheese Height 2⅞ in.

2364—Crescent Salad Plate
Length 7¼ in.   Width 4½ in.

2364—Mayonnaise and Plate and Ladle
Mayo. Height 2½ in.
Mayo. Diameter 5 in.
Plate Diameter 6¾ in.

2350½—Footed Cup
2350—Saucer
Cup Capacity 6 oz.

2364—14 in. Torte Plate
2364—16 in. Torte Plate

2364—Salad Set
10½ in. Set Consisting of:
1/12 Doz. 2364—10½ in. Salad Bowl—Height 4 in.
1/12 Doz. 2364—14 in. Torte Plate
9 in. Set Consisting of:
1/12 Doz. 2364—9 in. Salad Bowl—Height 2⅝ in.
1/12 Doz. 2364—11 in. Sandwich Plate

PLATE ETCHING No. 340

2586—Sani-Cut Syrup
Height 5½ in.
Capacity 9 oz.

2364—Candy Jar and Cover, Blown
Height with Cover 4 in.
Top Diameter 3¾ in.

2083—Salad Dressing Bottle
Height 6½ in.   Capacity 7 oz.

2324—6 in. Candlestick

2364—13 in. Fruit Bowl
Height 2¾ in.

2364—9 in. Salad Bowl
Height 2⅝ in.
2364—10½ in. Salad Bowl
Height 4 in.

4143—6 in. Footed Vase
4143—7½ in. Footed Vase

2364—12 in. Bowl Flared
Height 2⅞ in.

PLATE ETCHING No. 340

2350½—Footed Cream
Height 3¼ in.
Capacity 7 oz.

2364—Cigarette
Holder, Blown
Height 2 in.
Top Diameter 1⅝ in.

2350½—Footed Sugar
Height 3⅛ in.

6011—Footed Jug
Capacity 53 oz.
Height 8⅞ in.

2364—12 in. Lily Pond
Height 2¼ in.

2364—Individual
Ash
Tray, Blown
Diameter 2⅝ in.

6023—Duo Candlestick
Height 5½ in.   Spread 6 in.

2324—4 in. Candlestick

6023—9 in. Footed Bowl
Height 4¼ in.

2594—10 in. Handled Bowl
Height 3 in.
Length Overall 13½ in.

2594—5½ in. Candlestick

137

PLATE ETCHING No. 340

2364—3-Pt. Relish
Height 1½ in.   Length 10 in.
Width 7¼ in.

2364—2-Pt. Relish
Height 1¾ in.   Length 6½ in.
Width 5 in.

2364—Shaker
Height 2¼ in.

2364—6 in. Baked Apple
Height 1¼ in.

2364—8 in. Comport

2594—Trindle Candlestick
Height 8 in.
Spread 6½ in.

6030—5 in. Comport

2614—10 in. Vase

2364—Handled Lunch Tray
Diameter 11¼ in.

6021—6 in. Footed Vase

ROMANCE

Plate Etching 341

Romance is another pattern that remained active for a long time. Several pieces were discontinued in 1943 and 1944. Because of the bow and ribbons, Romance is sometimes confused with June. Remember that Romance loops and intertwines a ribbon and a garland of flowers. June's ribbon and garland of flowers are parallel to each other. Most Romance pieces will be on the Sonata blank, whereas June will be on the Fairfax blank.

Stemware is featured in *Fostoria Stemware*, pages 89 and 90.

2364 Ash Tray, 1942-1943; $38.00
766 Bowl, Finger, 1942-1943; $38.00
2364 Bowl, 6" Baked Apple, 1942-1944; $45.00
2364 Bowl, Rim Soup, 1942-1943; $47.00
6023 Bowl, 9¼" Footed, 1942-1943; $95.00
2364 Bowl, 9" Salad, 1942-1968; $58.00
2594 Bowl, 10" Handled, 1942-1957; $125.00
2364 Bowl, 10½" Salad, 1942-1968; $65.00
2596 Bowl, 11" Oblong, 1942-1943; $95.00
2364 Bowl, 12" Flared, 1942-1965; $68.00
2364 Bowl, 12" Lily Pond, 1942-1965; $68.00
2364 Bowl, 13" Fruit, 1942-1965; $75.00
2324 Candlestick, 4", (pair) 1942-1968; $42.00
2596 Candlestick, 5", (pair) 1942-1943; $95.00
2594 Candlestick, 5½", (pair) 1942-1959; $75.00
6023 Candlestick, Duo, (pair) 1942-1965; $75.00
2594 Candlestick, Trindle, (pair) 1942-1959; $125.00
2364 Candy Box and Cover, 1942-1943, $125.00/market
2364 Celery, 11", 1942-1957; $38.00
2364 Cheese and Cracker, 1942-1966; $85.00
2364 Cigarette Holder, 1942-1943; $57.00
6030 Comport, 5", 1942-1943; $57.00
2364 Comport, 8", 1942-1959; $95.00
2350½ Cup and Saucer, 1942-1970; $30.00
4132 Ice Bowl, 1942-1943; $135.00
6011 Jug, 1942-1957; $395.00
2364 Mayonnaise, Plate, Ladle, 1942-1970; $65.00
2364 Pickle, 8", 1942-1958; $30.00
2666 Pitcher, Quart, 1958-1968; $425.00
2337 Plate, 6", 1942-1970; $10.00
2337 Plate, 7", 1942-1974; $14.00
2337 Plate, 8", 1942-1974; $18.00
2337 Plate, 9", 1942-1970; $45.00
2364 Plate, Crescent Salad, 1947-1968; $43.00
2364 Plate, 11" Sandwich, 1942-1970; $45.00
2364 Plate, 14" Torte, 1942-1970; $65.00
2364 Plate, 16" Torte, 1942-1968; $75.00
2364 Relish, 2-part, 1942-1944; $75.00
2364 Relish, 3-part, 1942-1970; $75.00
2364 Salad Set, 9", 3-piece, 1946-1968; $60.00

2364 Salad Set, 10½", 3-piece, 1946-1968; $125.00
2364 Salad Fork and Spoon (Wood), 1942-1968; $25.00
2364 Shaker, FGT, (pair) 1942-1970; $75.00
    Silver Top "C" (pair); $75.00
2350½ Sugar and Cream, 1942-1970; $65.00
2364 Tray, Handled Lunch, 1942-1965; $58.00
4121 Vase, 5", 1942-1943; 1952-1958; $115.00
2619½ Vase, 6" Ground Bottom, 1942-1943; $85.00
4143 Vase, 6" Footed, 1942-1943; 1952-1958; $110.00
6021 Vase, 6" Footed Bud, 1942-1943; 1952-1958; $87.00
2619½ Vase, 7½", 1942-1943; $95.00
4143 Vase, 7½" Footed, 1942-1943; $145.00
2660 Vase, 8" Flip, 1952-1958; $145.00
2619½ Vase, 9½" Ground Bottom, 1942-1943; $145.00
2470 Vase, 10", 1942-1943; 1952-1958; $175.00
2614 Vase, 10", 1942-1943; $200.00

2364—13 in. Fruit Bowl
Height 2¾ in.

2596—11 in. Oblong Shallow Bowl
Height 2 in.

Plate Etching No. 341

2594
Trindle Candlestick
Height 8 in. Spread 6½ in.

2364—12 in.
Lily Pond
Height 2¼ in.

6011—Footed Jug
Height 8⅞ in.   Capacity 53 oz.

2350½—Footed Cup
2350—Saucer

2337—Plate
See Price List for Sizes

2364—12 in.
Bowl, Fld.
Height 2⅞ in.

2364—13 in.
Fruit Bowl
Height 2¾ in.

2350½—Footed Cream
Height 3¼ in.
Capacity 7 oz.

2350½—Footed Sugar
Height 3⅜ in.

2364—9 in.
3 Piece Salad Set
Consisting of:
1 12 Doz. 2364—9 in.
Salad Bowl—Ht. 2⅝ in.
1 12 Doz. 2364—11 in.
Sandwich Plate
1 12 Doz. 2364
Salad Fork and Spoon (Wood)

2364—10½ in.
3 Piece Salad Set (Illustrated)
Consisting of:
1 12 Doz. 2364—10½ in.
Salad Bowl—Ht. 4 in.
1 12 Doz. 2364—14 in.
Torte Plate
1 12 Doz. 2364
Salad Fork and Spoon (Wood)

2364—Shaker
Height 2¼ in.

2594—10 in.
Handled Bowl
Height 3 in.
Length Overall 13½ in.

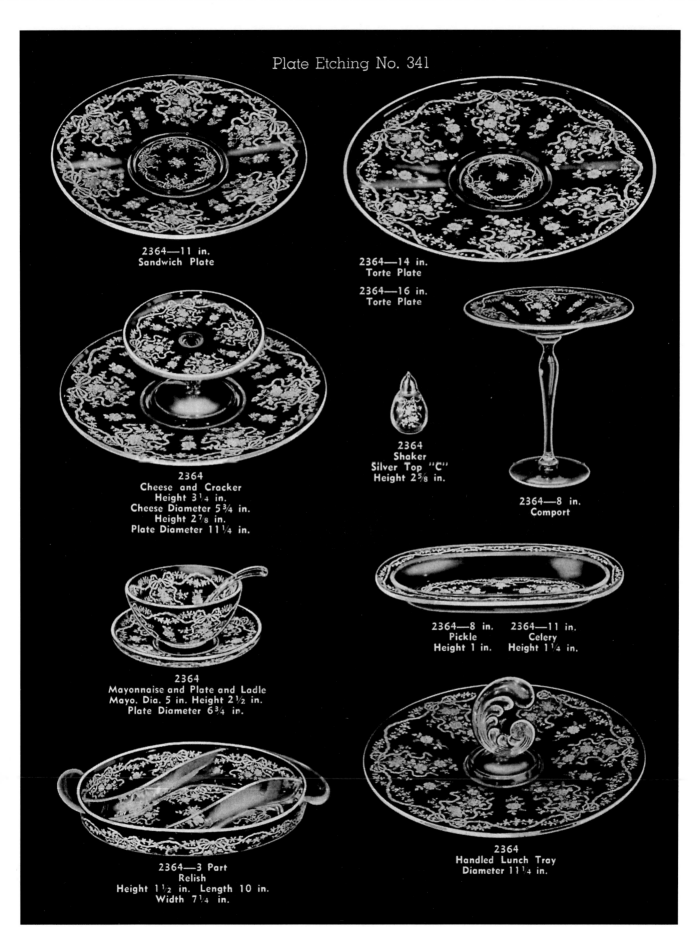

Plate Etching No. 341

2364—11 in.
Sandwich Plate

2364—14 in.
Torte Plate

2364—16 in.
Torte Plate

2364
Cheese and Cracker
Height 3¼ in.
Cheese Diameter 5¾ in.
Height 2⅞ in.
Plate Diameter 11¼ in.

2364
Shaker
Silver Top "C"
Height 2⅝ in.

2364—8 in.
Comport

2364
Mayonnaise and Plate and Ladle
Mayo. Dia. 5 in. Height 2½ in.
Plate Diameter 6¾ in.

2364—8 in.   2364—11 in.
Pickle   Celery
Height 1 in.   Height 1¼ in.

2364—3 Part
Relish
Height 1½ in. Length 10 in.
Width 7¼ in.

2364
Handled Lunch Tray
Diameter 11¼ in.

PLATE ETCHING No. 341

6030—5 in. Comport

2364—8 in. Pickle
Height 1 in.
2364—11 in. Celery
Height 1¼ in.

2364—Cigarette
Holder, Blown
Height 2 in.
Top Diameter 1⅝ in.

2364—8 in. Comport

2364—Individual
Ash Tray
Blown
Diameter 2⅝ in.

4132—Ice Bowl
Height 4¾ in.
Top Diameter 6 in.

2364—6 in. Baked Apple
Height 1¼ in.

2364—8 in. Rim Soup
Height 1¼ in.

2364—Cheese & Cracker
Height 3¼ in.
Cheese Diameter 5¾ in.   Height 2⅞ in.
Plate Diameter 11¼ in.

2364—Candy Box & Cover, Blown
Height with Cover 4 in.
Top Diameter 3¾ in.

2364—14 in. Torte Plate
2364—16 in. Torte Plate

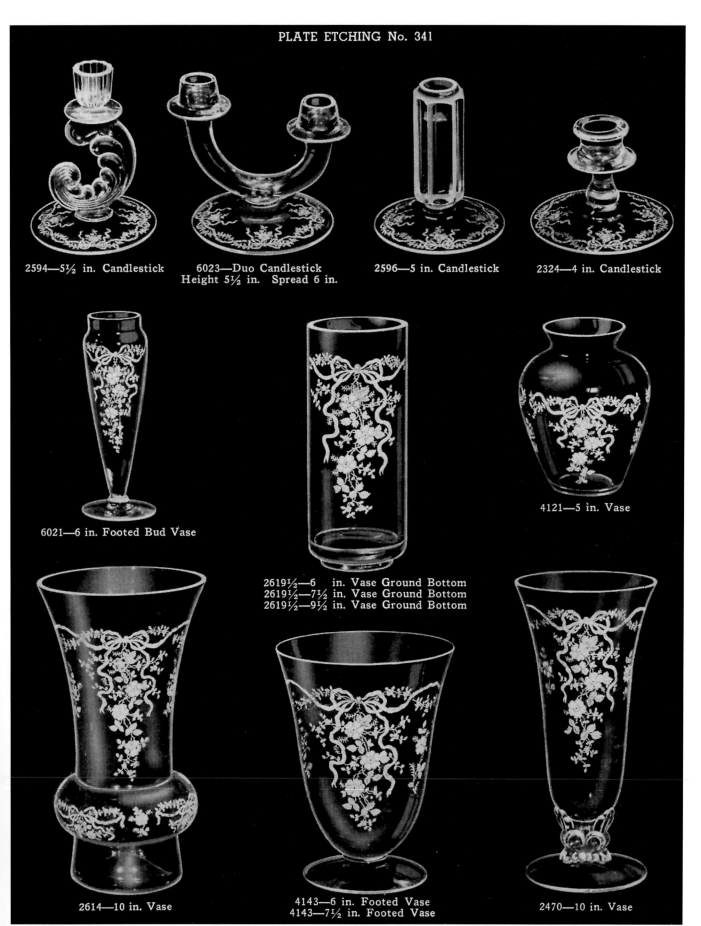

PLATE ETCHING No. 341

2594—5½ in. Candlestick

6023—Duo Candlestick
Height 5½ in.   Spread 6 in.

2596—5 in. Candlestick

2324—4 in. Candlestick

6021—6 in. Footed Bud Vase

2619½—6   in. Vase Ground Bottom
2619½—7½ in. Vase Ground Bottom
2619½—9½ in. Vase Ground Bottom

4121—5 in. Vase

2614—10 in. Vase

4143—6 in. Footed Vase
4143—7½ in. Footed Vase

2470—10 in. Vase

BOUQUET

Plate Etching 342

1949 – 1959 except where noted.
The 3-pint Jug had the shape shown in 1950 – 1952.
The ice lip was changed to the shape more often seen in 1952 (shown with Camelia).
Stemware is featured in *Fostoria Stemware*, page 102.

2630 Basket, Reed Handle; $95.00
2630 Bon Bon, 3 -toed; $30.00
2630 Bowl, Fruit; $22.00
2630 Bowl, Cereal; $26.00
2630 Bowl, 4½" Handled Nappy; $22.00
2630 Bowl, Snack; $28.00
2630 Bowl, 8" Flared; $32.00
2630 Bowl, 8½" Salad; $35.00
2630 Bowl, 9" Lily Pond; $38.00
2630 Bowl, Handled Serving; $44.00
2630 Bowl, Oval Utility; $45.00
2630 Bowl, Oval Vegetable; $38.00
2630 Bowl, 10½" Salad; $50.00
2630 Bowl, 10¾" Footed, Flared; $48.00
2630 Bowl, 11" Rolled Edge; $55.00
2630 Bowl, 11¼" Lily Pond; $54.00
2630 Bowl, 12" Flared; $55.00
2630 Butter and Cover, Oblong; $45.00
2630 Candlestick, 4½" (pair); $48.00
2630 Candlestick, Duo (pair); $58.00
2630 Candlestick, Trindle (pair); $97.00
2630 Candy Jar and Cover; $85.00
2630 Cheese and Cracker; $85.00
2630 Comport; $46.00
2630 Condiment Set, 3-piece; $135.00
2630 Cup and Saucer; $28.00
2630 Ice Bucket, Metal Handle; $135.00
2630 Jug, 3-pint, Ice (1950-1952); $125.00
2630 Jug, (1952-1959); $125.00
2630 Mayonnaise, Plate, Ladle; $47.00
2630 Mayonnaise, 2-part, 2 Ladles; $48.00
2630 Mustard, Cover, and Spoon; $64.00
2630 Oil, DS, 5 oz.; $49.00
2630 Pickle, 8¾"; $20.00
2630 Pitcher, Pint, Cereal; $62.00
2630 Plate, 6"; $10.00
2360 Plate, 7"; $12.00
2360 Plate, 8"; $15.00
2360 Plate, 9"; $24.00
2630 Plate, 10½" Dinner; $40.00
2630 Plate, Crescent Salad; $46.00
2630 Plate, 8" Party, and Cup; $40.00
2630 Plate, Handled Cake; $65.00
2630 Plate, 14" Torte; $65.00
2630 Plate, 16" Torte; $75.00

2630 Platter, 12" Oval; $68.00
2630 Preserve and Cover; $65.00
2630 Relish, 2-part; $27.00
2630 Relish, 3-part; $38.00
2630 Salad Set, 10½", 3-piece; $115.00
2630 Salver; $95.00
2630 Shaker, Chrome Top "B" (pair); $65.00
2630 Sugar and Cream, Regular; $46.00
2630 Sugar and Cream, Individual; $42.00
2630 Sugar/Cream/Tray; $20.00
2630 Tid Bit, 3-toed; $30.00
2630 Tid Bit, 2-tier, Metal Handle; $45.00
2630 Tray, Handled Lunch; $58.00
2630 Tray, Handled Muffin; $65.00
2630 Tray, Handled Utility; $65.00
2630 Tray, 10½" Snack; $45.00
2630 Tricorne, 3-toed; $32.00
4121 Vase, 5", no Optic, 1952-1959; $62.00
2630 Vase, 6" Bud, 1950-1959; $38.00
4143 Vase, 6" Footed, 1952-1955; $67.00
6021 Vase, 6" Footed Bud, 1952-1959; $55.00
2630 Vase, 7½" Handled, 1950-1959; $85.00
5092 Vase, 8" Bud, 1952-1959; $85.00
2660 Vase, 8" Flip, 1952-1959; $85.00
2630 Vase, 8½" Oval, 1950-1959; $85.00
2470 Vase, 10" Footed, 1952-1959; $125.00

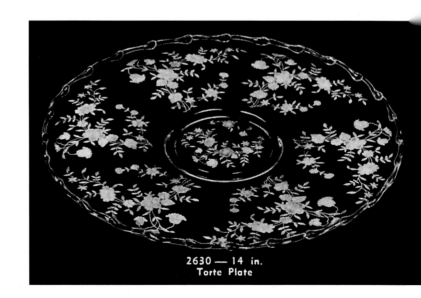

2630 — 14 in.
Torte Plate

Plate Etching No. 342

2630
3 Pint Ice Jug
Height 9½ in.

2630
Pint Cereal Pitcher
Height 6⅛ in.

2630
Mustard, Cover and Spoon
Height 4 in.

2630
Footed Cup
Cup Capacity 6 oz.
2630
Saucer

2630
Candy Jar and Cover
Height 7 in.

2630
Cheese and Cracker
Height 2¾ in.
Plate Diameter—10¾ in.
Cheese Diameter—5⅜ in.
Cheese Height—2½ in.

2630
Handled Cake Plate

2630 — 6 in.
Plate
2630 — 7 in.
Plate
2630 — 8 in.
Plate
2630 — 9 in.
Plate

2630 — 6 in.
Bud Vase

2630
Ice Bucket
Height 4⅞ in. Top Dia. 7⅜ in.
Chromium Handle and Tongs
Tongs priced separately

2630 — 7½ in.
Handled Vase

2630
3 Piece Tid Bit Set
Metal Handle
Height 10¼ in.

2630 — 8½ in.
Oval Vase

HEATHER

Plate Etching 343

1949 – 1971 except as noted.
All pieces were on the 2630 Century blank unless otherwise noted.
The Jug had an ice lip until 1952, the same as Bouquet. Stemware is featured in *Fostoria Stemware*, page 104.

Basket, Reed Handle; $95.00
Bon Bon, 3-toed; $30.00
Bowl, 4½" Handled Nappy; $22.00
Bowl, Fruit; $22.00
Bowl, Cereal; $26.00
Bowl, 8" Flared; $32.00
Bowl, 8½" Salad, 1952-1971; $35.00
Bowl, Snack; $28.00
Bowl, 9" Lily Pond; $1952-1971; $38.00
Bowl, Oval Vegetable; $38.00
Bowl, Oval Utility; $45.00
Bowl, Handled Serving; $44.00
Bowl, 10¾" Footed, Flared; $48.00
Bowl, 11" Footed, Rolled Edge; $55.00
Bowl, 11¼" Lily Pond; $54.00
Bowl, 12" Flared; $55.00
Butter, Oblong and Cover; $45.00
Candlestick, 4½" Single (pair); $48.00
Candlestick, Duo (pair); $68.00
Candlestick, Trindle (pair); $97.00
Candy Jar and Cover; $85.00
Cheese and Cracker; $85.00
Comport; $46.00
Condiment Set; $135.00
Cup and Saucer; $28.00
Ice Bucket, Metal Handle; $85.00
Jug, Ice Lip, 1950-1952; $175.00
Jug, 1952-1959; $175.00
Mayonnaise, Plate, Ladle; $48.00
Mayonnaise, 2-part, 2 spoons; $48.00
Mustard, Cover, Spoon; $46.00
Oil, 5 oz. D.S.; $54.00
Pickle, 8¾"; $20.00
Pitcher, Pint, Cereal; $62.00
Plate, 6"; $10.00

Plate, 7"; $12.00
Plate, 8"; $15.00
Plate, 9"; $24.00
Plate 10½"; $40.00
Plate, Crescent Salad; $46.00
Plate, Party and Cup; $40.00
Plate, Handled Cake; $65.00
Plate, 14" Torte; $65.00
Plate, 16" Torte; $75.00
Platter, 12" Oval; $68.00
Preserve and Cover, Footed; $65.00
Relish, 2-part; $27.00
Relish, 3-part; $38.00
Salad Set, 10½", 3-pc.; $125.00
Salver, Cake; $95.00
Shaker, Chrome Top "B" (pair); $65.00
Sugar and Cream; $48.00
Sugar and Cream, Individual; $45.00
Sugar, Cream, Tray; $20.00
Tid Bit, 3-toed; $30.00
Tid Bit, 3-piece set; $47.00
Tray, 10½" Snack; $45.00
Tray, Handled Muffin; $65.00
Tray, Handled Utility; $65.00
Tray, Handled Lunch; $58.00
Tricorne, 3-toed; $32.00
4121 Vase, 5", Blown, 1952-1959; $62.00
Vase, 6" Bud, 1950-1959; $42.00
6021 Vase, 6" Footed Bud, Blown, 1952-1959; $58.00
4143 Vase, 6" Footed, Blown, 1952-1955; $67.00
Vase, 7½" Handled, 1950-1959; $85.00
2660 Vase, 8" Flip, Blown, 1952-1959; $92.00
5092 Vase, 8" Footed, Blown, 1952-1959; $95.00
Vase, 8½" Oval, 1950-1959; $87.00
2470 Vase, 10" Footed, Blown, 1952-1959; $125.00

2630 — 6 in. Plate
2630 — 7 in. Plate
2630 — 8 in. Plate
2630 — 9 in. Plate

2630
Handled Cake Plate

2630
Footed Cup
Cup Capacity 6 oz.
2630
Saucer

Plate Etching No. 343

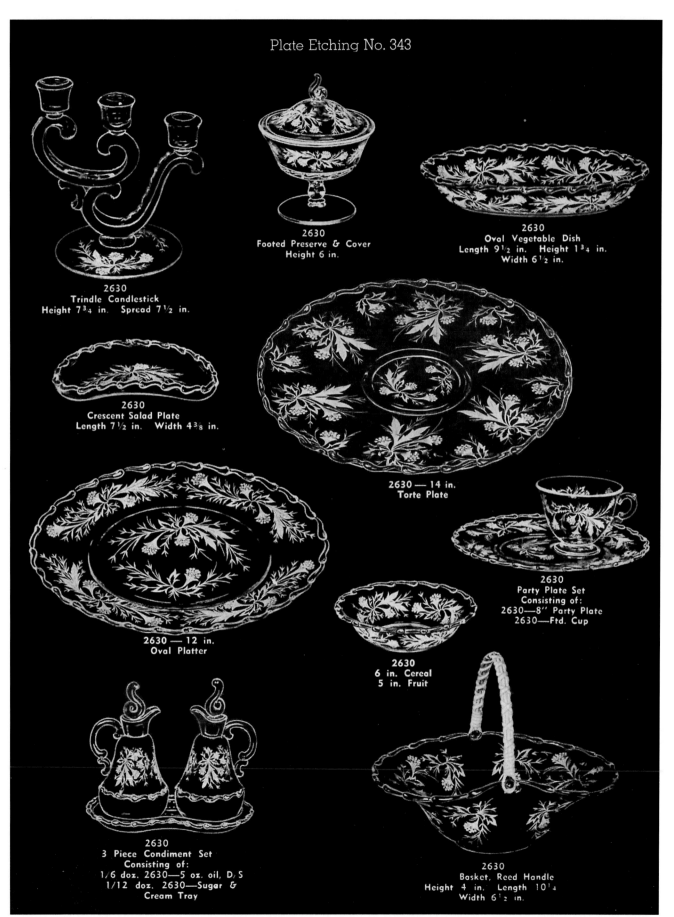

2630
Trindle Candlestick
Height 7¾ in.   Spread 7½ in.

2630
Footed Preserve & Cover
Height 6 in.

2630
Oval Vegetable Dish
Length 9½ in.   Height 1¾ in.
Width 6½ in.

2630
Crescent Salad Plate
Length 7½ in.   Width 4⅜ in.

2630 — 14 in.
Torte Plate

2630
Party Plate Set
Consisting of:
2630—8″ Party Plate
2630—Ftd. Cup

2630 — 12 in.
Oval Platter

2630
6 in. Cereal
5 in. Fruit

2630
3 Piece Condiment Set
Consisting of:
1/6 doz. 2630—5 oz. oil, D/S
1/12 doz. 2630—Sugar &
Cream Tray

2630
Basket, Reed Handle
Height 4 in.   Length 10¼
Width 6½ in.

CAMELIA

Plate Etching 344

All pieces are on the 2630 Century blank except where noted.
Stemware is featured in *Fostoria Stemware*, page 103.

Basket, Reed Handle, 1952-1959; $95.00
Bon Bon, 3-toed, 1952-1965; $30.00
Bowl, 4½" Nappy, 1952-1965; $22.00
Bowl, Fruit, 1952-1965; $22.00
Bowl, Cereal, 1952-1965; $26.00
Bowl, Snack, 1952-1965; $28.00
Bowl, 8" Flared, 1952-1965; $32.00
Bowl, 8½" Salad, 1952-1965; $35.00
Bowl, 9" Lily Pond, 1952-1965; $38.00
Bowl 10½" Salad, 1952-1965; $50.00
Bowl, Handled Serving, 1952-1965; $44.00
Bowl, Oval Vegetable, 1952-1965; $38.00
Bowl, Oval Utility, 1952-1965; $45.00
Bowl, 10¾" Footed, 1952-1965; $48.00
Bowl, 11" Rolled Edge, Footed, 1952-1965; $55.00
Bowl, 11¼" Lily Pond, 1952-1965; $54.00
Bowl, 12" Flared, 1952-1965; $55.00
Butter, Oblong, 1952-1965; $45.00
Candlestick, 4½", (pair) 1952-1965; $48.00
Candlestick, Duo, (pair) 1952-1965; $68.00
Candlestick, Trindle, (pair) 1952-1965; $110.00
Candy Jar and Cover, 1952-1965; $85.00
Cheese and Cracker, 1952-1965; $85.00
Comport, 4¾", 1952-1965; $46.00
Condiment Set, 3-piece, 1952-1965; $135.00
Cup and Saucer, 1952-1965; $28.00
Ice Bucket, Metal Handle, 1952-1965; $85.00
Jug, 3-pint Ice, 1952-1965; $165.00
Mayonnaise, Plate, Ladle, 1952-1965; $47.00
Mayonnaise, 2-part, 2 ladles, 1952-1965; $47.00
Mustard, Cover, Spoon, 1952-1965; $42.00
Oil, D.S., 5 oz., 1952-1965; $54.00
Pickle, 8¾", 1952-1965; $20.00
Pitcher, 1-pint Cereal, 1952-1965; $62.00
Plate, 6", 1952-1965; $10.00
Plate, 7", 1952-1965; $12.00

Plate, 8", 1952-1965; $15.00
Plate, 9", 1952-1965; $24.00
Plate, 10½", 1952-1965; $40.00
Plate, Crescent Salad, 1952-1965; $46.00
Plate, 8" Party and Cup, 1952-1959; $40.00
Plate, Handled Cake, 1952-1965; $65.00
Plate, 14" Torte, 1952-1965; $65.00
Plate, 16" Torte, 1952-1965; $75.00
Platter, 12" Oval, 1952-1965; $68.00
Preserve, Footed and Cover, 1952-1965; $65.00
Relish, 2-part, 1952-1965; $27.00
Relish, 3-part, 1952-1965; $38.00
Salad Set, 10½", 1952-1965; $115.00
Salver, 1952-1965; $95.00
Shaker, Chrome Top "B", (pair) 1952-1965; $65.00
Sugar and Cream, 1952-1965; $46.00
Sugar and Cream, Individual, 1952-1965; $42.00
Sugar and Cream Set, Individual, 1952-1965; $62.00
Tidbit, 3-toed, 1952-1965; $30.00
Tidbit Set, 3-piece, 1952-1965; $45.00
Tray, Handled Lunch, 1952-1965; $58.00
Tray, Handled Muffin, 1952-1965; $65.00
Tray, 10½" Snack, 1952-1965; $45.00
Tray, Handled Utility, 1952-1965; $65.00
Tricorne, 3-toed, 1952-1965; $32.00
Vase, 6" Bud, 1952-1965; $38.00
Vase, 7½" Handled, 1952-1959; $85.00
Vase, 8½" Oval, 1952-1959; $85.00
4121 Vase, 5", 1952-1959; $62.00
4143 Vase, 6" Footed, 1952-1955; $67.00
6021 Vase, 6" Footed Bud, 1952-1959; $55.00
2660 Vase, 8" Flip, 1952-1959; $85.00
5092 Vase, 8" Footed Bud, 1952-1959; $85.00
2470 Vase, 10" Footed, 1952-1959; $125.00
2657 Vase, 10½" Footed, 1952-1957; $175.00

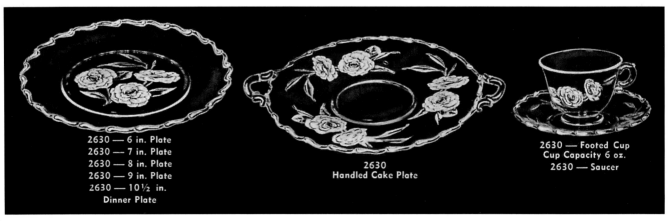

2630 — 6 in. Plate
2630 — 7 in. Plate
2630 — 8 in. Plate
2630 — 9 in. Plate
2630 — 10½ in. Dinner Plate

2630
Handled Cake Plate

2630 — Footed Cup
Cup Capacity 6 oz.
2630 — Saucer

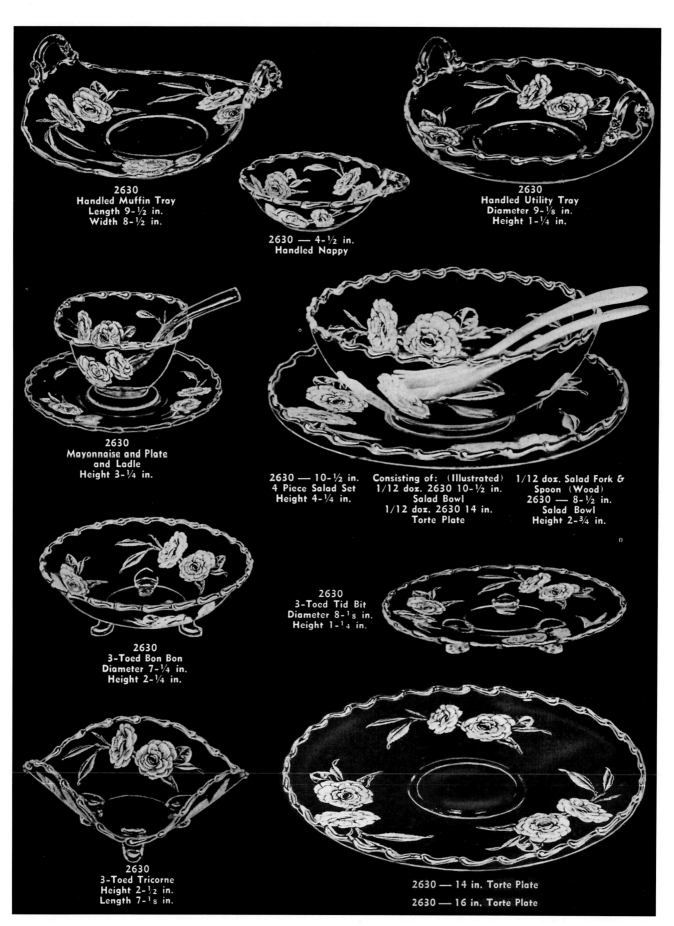

2630
Handled Muffin Tray
Length 9-½ in.
Width 8-½ in.

2630 — 4-½ in.
Handled Nappy

2630
Handled Utility Tray
Diameter 9-⅛ in.
Height 1-¼ in.

2630
Mayonnaise and Plate
and Ladle
Height 3-¼ in.

2630 — 10-½ in.
4 Piece Salad Set
Height 4-¼ in.

Consisting of: (Illustrated)
1/12 doz. 2630 10-½ in.
Salad Bowl
1/12 doz. 2630 14 in.
Torte Plate

1/12 doz. Salad Fork &
Spoon (Wood)
2630 — 8-½ in.
Salad Bowl
Height 2-¾ in.

2630
3-Toed Bon Bon
Diameter 7-¼ in.
Height 2-¼ in.

2630
3-Toed Tid Bit
Diameter 8-⅛ in.
Height 1-¼ in.

2630
3-Toed Tricorne
Height 2-½ in.
Length 7-⅛ in.

2630 — 14 in. Torte Plate
2630 — 16 in. Torte Plate

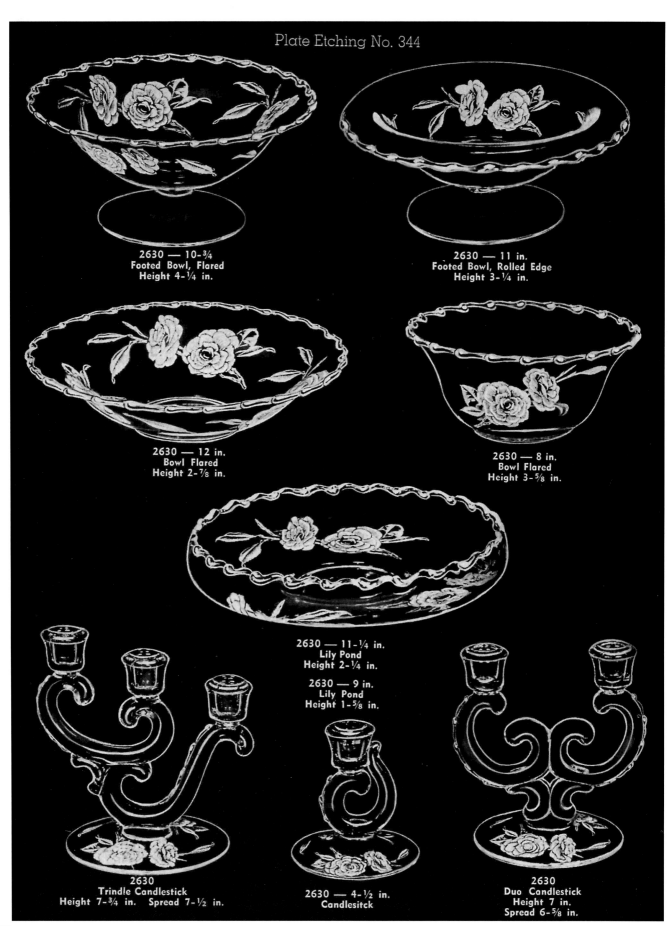

Plate Etching No. 344

2630 — 10-¾
Footed Bowl, Flared
Height 4-¼ in.

2630 — 11 in.
Footed Bowl, Rolled Edge
Height 3-¼ in.

2630 — 12 in.
Bowl Flared
Height 2-⅞ in.

2630 — 8 in.
Bowl Flared
Height 3-⅝ in.

2630 — 11-¼ in.
Lily Pond
Height 2-¼ in.

2630 — 9 in.
Lily Pond
Height 1-⅝ in.

2630
Trindle Candlestick
Height 7-¾ in.   Spread 7-½ in.

2630 — 4-½ in.
Candlesitck

2630
Duo Candlestick
Height 7 in.
Spread 6-⅝ in.

Plate Etching No. 344

2630
3 Pint Ice Jug
Height 7-1/8 in.

2630
Mustard, Cover and Spoon
Height 4 in.

2630
Pint Cereal Pitcher
Height 6-1/8 in.

2630
Ice Bucket
Height 4-7/8 in.   Top Dia. 7-3/8 in.
Chromium Handle and Tongs
Tongs priced separately

2630
Candy Jar and Cover
Height 7 in.

2630
3 Piece Tid Bit Set
Metal Handle
Height 10-1/4 in.

2630
2-part Mayonnaise
and 2 Ladles
Height 3-3/8 in.

2630
Snack Bowl
Height 3-1/2 in.

2630 — 10-1/2 in.
Snack Tray

2630
Cheese and Cracker
Height 2-3/4 in.
Plate Diameter—10-3/4 in.
Cheese Diameter—5-3/8 in.
Cheese Height—2-1/2 in.

151

Plate Etching No. 344

2470 — 10 in.
Footed Vase

4143 — 6 in.
Footed Vase

2657 — 10½ in.
Footed Vase

5092 — 8 in.
Footed Bud Vase

2630 — 6 in.
Bud Vase

6021 — 6 in.
Footed Bud Vase

4121 — 5 in.
Vase

2630 — 8½ in.
Oval Vase

2660 — 8 in.
Flip Vase

2630 — 7½ in.
Handled Vase

STARFLOWER

Plate Etching 345
1952 – 1957 unless noted.
Stemware is featured in *Fostoria Stemware*, page 105.

2630 Basket, Reed Handle; $85.00
2630 Bon Bon; $30.00
2630 Bowl, 4½" Handled Nappy, $18.00
2630 Bowl, Fruit; $18.00
2630 Bowl, Cereal; $20.00
2630 Bowl, Snack; $25.00
2630 Bowl, 8" Flared; $30.00
2630 Bowl, 8½" Salad; $32.00
2630 Bowl, Handled Serving; $40.00
2630 Bowl, Oval Vegetable; $35.00
2630 Bowl, Oval Utility; $40.00
2630 Bowl, 9" Lily Pond; $35.00
2630 Bowl, 10½" Salad; $47.00
2630 Bowl, 10¾" Footed, Flared; $45.00
2630 Bowl, 11" Rolled Edge; $50.00
2630 Bowl, 11¼" Lily Pond; $50.00
2630 Bowl, 12" Flared; $50.00
2630 Butter and Cover, Oblong; $45.00
2630 Candlestick, 4½" (pair); $45.00
2630 Candlestick, Duo (pair); $64.00
2630 Candlestick, Trindle; $85.00
2630 Candy Jar and Cover; $80.00
2630 Cheese and Cracker; $75.00
2630 Comport, 4⅜"; $40.00
2630 Condiment Set, 3-piece; $125.00
2630 Cup and Saucer; $26.00
2630 Ice Bucket, Metal Handle; $75.00
2630 Jug, 3-Pint Ice; $115.00
2630 Mayonnaise, Plate, Ladle; $45.00
2630 Mayonnaise, 2-part, 2 spoons; $45.00
2630 Mustard, Cover, Spoon; $40.00
2630 Oil, 5 oz. D.S.; $48.00
2630 Pickle, 8¾"; $20.00
2630 Pitcher, Pint, Cereal; $57.00
2630 Plate, 6"; $8.00

2630 Plate, 7"; $10.00
2630 Plate, 8"; $12.50
2630 Plate, 9"; $18.00
2630 Plate, 10½" Dinner; $40.00
2630 Plate, Crescent Salad; $40.00
2630 Plate, Party, and Cup; $35.00
2630 Plate, Handled Cake; $55.00
2630 Plate 14" Torte; $60.00
2630 Plate, 16" Torte; $65.00
2630 Platter, 12" Oval; $60. 00
2630 Preserve and Cover, Footed; $58.00
2630 Relish, 2-part; $20.00
2630 Relish, 3-part; $32.00
2630 Salad Set, 4-piece; $95.00
2630 Salver; $85.00
2630 Shaker, Chrome Top "B" (pair); $55.00
2630 Sugar and Cream; $40.00
2630 Sugar, Cream, Individual, and Tray; $52.00
2630 Tid Bit, 3-toed; $30.00
2630 Tid Bit, 3-piece; $40.00
2630 Tray, Handled Muffin; $55.00
2630 Tray, Handled Utility; $55.00
2630 Tray, Handled Lunch; $52.00
2630 Tray, 10½" Snack; $40.00
2630 Tricorne, 3-toed; $30.00
4121 Vase, 5"; $60.00
2630 Vase, 6" Bud; $38.00
4143 Vase, 6" Footed, 1952-1955; $58.00
6021 Vase, 6" Footed Bud; $55.00
2630 Vase, 7½" Handled; $75.00
2660 Vase, 8" Flip; $75.00
5092 Vase, 8" Footed Bud; $75.00
2630 Vase, 8½" Oval; $75.00
2470 Vase, 10" Footed; $95.00
2657 Vase, 10½" Footed; $145.00

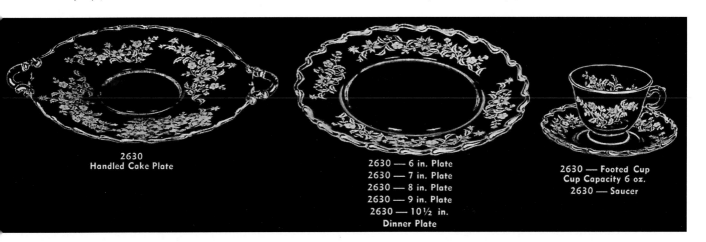

2630
Handled Cake Plate

2630 — 6 in. Plate
2630 — 7 in. Plate
2630 — 8 in. Plate
2630 — 9 in. Plate
2630 — 10½ in.
Dinner Plate

2630 — Footed Cup
Cup Capacity 6 oz.
2630 — Saucer

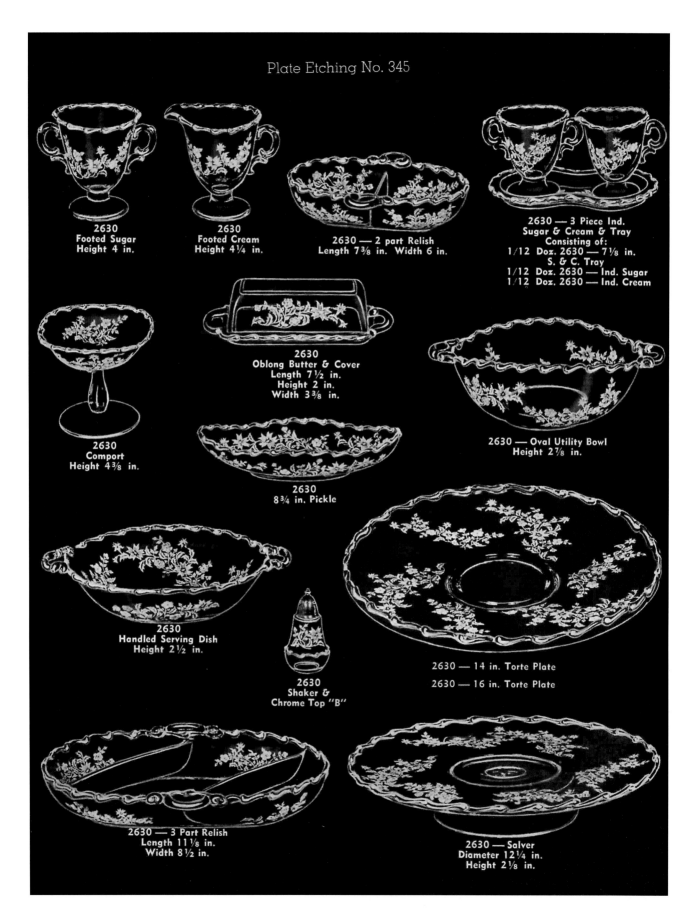

Plate Etching No. 345

2630
Footed Sugar
Height 4 in.

2630
Footed Cream
Height 4¼ in.

2630 — 2 part Relish
Length 7⅜ in. Width 6 in.

2630 — 3 Piece Ind.
Sugar & Cream & Tray
Consisting of:
1/12 Doz. 2630 — 7⅛ in.
S. & C. Tray
1/12 Doz. 2630 — Ind. Sugar
1/12 Doz. 2630 — Ind. Cream

2630
Comport
Height 4⅜ in.

2630
Oblong Butter & Cover
Length 7½ in.
Height 2 in.
Width 3⅜ in.

2630 — Oval Utility Bowl
Height 2⅞ in.

2630
8¾ in. Pickle

2630
Handled Serving Dish
Height 2½ in.

2630
Shaker &
Chrome Top "B"

2630 — 14 in. Torte Plate
2630 — 16 in. Torte Plate

2630 — 3 Part Relish
Length 11⅛ in.
Width 8½ in.

2630 — Salver
Diameter 12¼ in.
Height 2⅛ in.

THISTLE

Plate Etching 346

1953 – 1956

The 7" plate was available through the matching service through 1965.
Stemware is featured in *Fostoria Stemware*, page 107.

2666 Bon Bon; $30.00
2666 Bowl, Individual Salad/Dessert; $20.00
2666 Bowl, 8¼" Oval; $30.00
2666 Bowl, 9" Salad; $38.00
2666 Bowl, 11" Salad; $45.00
2666 Butter Pat; $18.00
2666 Candle, Flora (pair); $44.00
2666 Celery; $22.00
2666 Cup and Saucer; $25.00
2666 Mayonnaise, Plate, Ladle; $47.00
2666 Pickle; $22.00
2666 Pitcher, Pint; $42.00
2666 Pitcher, Quart; $85.00
2666 Pitcher, 3-Pint; $110.00
2666 Plate, 7"; $8.00

2666 Plate, Canape, 7⅜"; $10.00
2666 Plate, 10"; $24.00
2666 Plate 10" Snack; $24.00
2666 Plate, 14" Serving; $38.00
2666 Relish, 2-part; $32.00
2666 Relish, 3-part; $38.00
2666 Salad Set, 11", 4-piece; $87.00
2364 Shaker, Large, Chrome Top "C" (pair); $65.00
2666 Sugar and Cream; $52.00
2666 Sugar and Cream, Individual; $48.00
2666 Sugar and Cream Tray; $15.00
6021 Vase, 6" Footed Bud; $54.00
2660 Vase, 8" Flip; $80.00
2470 Vase, 10"; $95.00

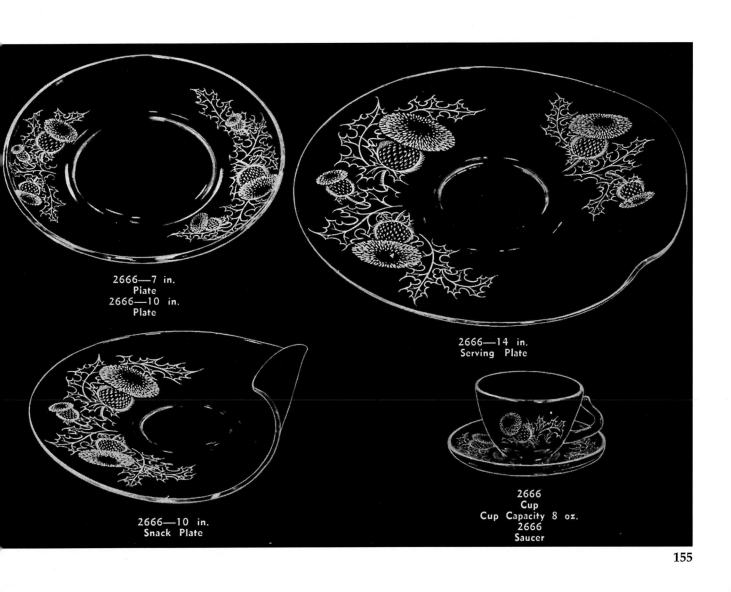

2666—7 in.
Plate
2666—10 in.
Plate

2666—14 in.
Serving Plate

2666—10 in.
Snack Plate

2666
Cup
Cup Capacity 8 oz.
2666
Saucer

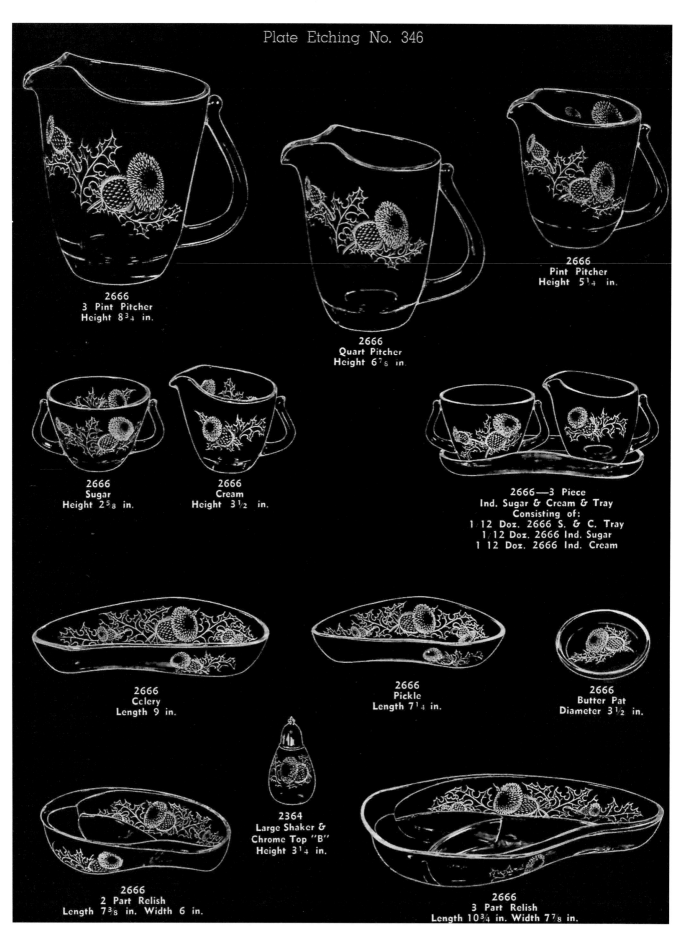

Plate Etching No. 346

2666
3 Pint Pitcher
Height 8³₄ in.

2666
Quart Pitcher
Height 6⁷₈ in.

2666
Pint Pitcher
Height 5¹₄ in.

2666
Sugar
Height 2⁵₈ in.

2666
Cream
Height 3¹₂ in.

2666—3 Piece
Ind. Sugar & Cream & Tray
Consisting of:
1/12 Doz. 2666 S. & C. Tray
1/12 Doz. 2666 Ind. Sugar
1/12 Doz. 2666 Ind. Cream

2666
Celery
Length 9 in.

2666
Pickle
Length 7¹₄ in.

2666
Butter Pat
Diameter 3¹₂ in.

2364
Large Shaker &
Chrome Top "B"
Height 3¹₄ in.

2666
2 Part Relish
Length 7³₈ in. Width 6 in.

2666
3 Part Relish
Length 10³₄ in. Width 7⁷₈ in.

Plate Etching No. 346

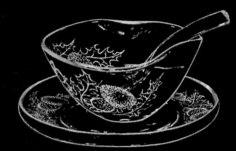

2666
Mayonnaise and Plate
and Ladle
Height 3¹⁄₄ in.

2666—9 in.
Salad Bowl
Height 2³⁄₄ in.

2666—11 in.
4 Pc. Salad Set
Height 4⁷⁄₈ in.
Consisting of:
1 12 Doz. 2666—11 in. Salad Bowl
1 12 Doz. 2666—14 in. Serving Plate
1 12 Doz. 2666—Salad Fork & Spoon
(Wood)

2666
Ind. Salad Dessert
Height 2¹⁄₄ in.

2666
Bon Bon
Diameter 6⁷⁄₈ in.
Height 3 in.

2666
Canape Plate
Diameter 7³⁄₈ in.
Height 2 in.

Plate Etching No. 346

2666
Flora—Candle
Diameter 6 in.

2666
Oval Bowl
Diameter 8¼ in.
Height 3¼ in.

6021—6 in .
Footed Bud Vase

2470—10 in.
Footed Vase

2660—8 in.
Flip Vase

CRYSTAL PRINTS

Crystal Prints were introduced in the mid 1950s using the same process as plate etchings except that the design was more delicate and not as heavily etched. Four dinnerware services employed Crystal Print designs. Several stemware lines featured Crystal Prints, but as they did not also offer dinnerware, they are included in *Fostoria Stemware* only.

Sylvan and Skyflower used the same pieces from the Contour pattern, and Lacy Leaf and Milkweed used the same pieces from the Century pattern; thus, as we did with the previous etchings which had similar pieces, we are showing catalog pages from all four patterns, but not any pattern in its entirety. Values will be the same for the two patterns with common pieces.

SYLVAN

Crystal Print 1
1955 – 1965
Stemware is featured in *Fostoria Stemware*, page 110.

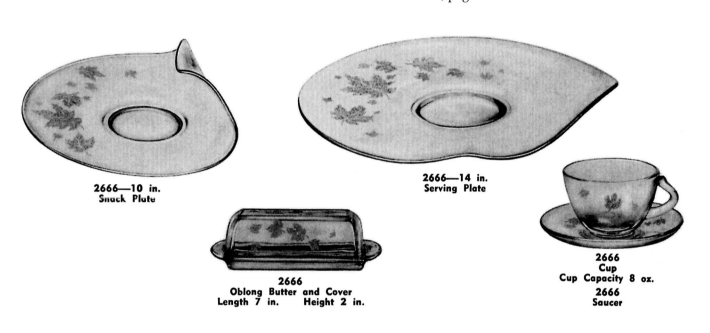

2666—10 in.
Snack Plate

2666—14 in.
Serving Plate

2666
Oblong Butter and Cover
Length 7 in.   Height 2 in.

2666
Cup
Cup Capacity 8 oz.
2666
Saucer

SKYFLOWER

Crystal Print 2
1955 – 1958
Stemware is featured in *Fostoria Stemware*, page 110.

2666 Bon Bon; $18.00
2666 Bowl, Oval; $22.00
2666 Butter and Cover, Oblong; $34.00
2666 Candle, Flora (pair); $32.00
2666 Celery; $16.00
2666 Cup and Saucer; $20.00
2666 Mayonnaise, Plate, Ladle; $36.00
2666 Plate, 7"; $9.00
2666 Plate, 10"; $18.00
2666 Plate, Canape; $18.00

2666 Plate, 10" Snack; $20.00
2666 Plate, 14" Serving; $32.00
2685 Preserve, Handled; $22.00
2666 Relish, 2-part; $20.00
2666 Relish, 3-part; $26.00
2685 Salver; $45.00
2364 Shaker, Large, Chrome Top "B" (pair); $45.00
2666 Sugar and Cream; $40.00
2666 Sugar and Cream, Individual, and Tray; $48.00

Crystal Print No. 2

2666
Sugar
Height 2⅝ in.

2666
Cream
Height 3½ in.

2666 — 3 Piece
Ind. Sugar & Cream & Tray
Consisting of:
1/12 doz. 2666 S.&C. Tray
1/12 doz. 2666 Ind. Sugar
1/12 doz. 2666 Ind. Cream

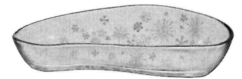

2685
Handled Preserve
Length 6½ in.

2666
Celery
Length 9 in.

2666
2 Part Relish
Length 7⅜ in.   Width 6 in.

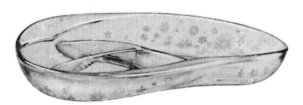

2666
3 Part Relish
Length 10¾ in.   Width 7⅞ in.

2685
Salver
Diameter 12¼ in.   Height 2½ in.

2364
Large Shaker
Chrome Top "B"
Height 3¼ in.

2666
Mayonnaise and Plate
and Ladle
Height 3¼ in.

2666
Bon Bon
Diameter 6⅞ in.
Height 3 in.

2666
Canape Plate
Diameter 7⅜ in.
Height 2 in.

2666
Oval Bowl
Diameter 8¼ in.
Height 3¼ in.

2666
Flora Candle
Diameter 6 in.

LACY LEAF

Crystal Print 6

1957 – 1958

See Milkweed, page 162, for pieces.

Crystal Print No. 6

2630
3 Pint Ice Jug
Height 7 1/8 in.

2630
14 in. Torte Plate

2630
Footed Sugar
Height 4 in.

Footed Cream
Height 4 1/4 in.

2630—3 Piece Ind.
Sugar & Cream & Tray

2630
Handled Cake Plate

2630
Oblong Butter & Cover
Length 7 1/2 in. Width 2 in.
Height 2 in.

2630
Shaker & Chrome Top "B"

2630
8 3/4 in. Pickle

2630
3 Part Relish
Length 11 1/8 in. Width 8 1/2 in.

2630
2 Part Relish
Length 7 3/8 in. Width 6 in.

MILKWEED

Crystal Print 7

1957 – 1958

2630 Bon Bon, 3-toed; $18.00
2630 Bowl, 10½" Salad; $38.00
2630 Bowl, 12" Flared; $38.00
2630 Butter and Cover, Oblong; $35.00
2630 Candlestick, 4½" (pair); $44.00
2630 Candlestick, Duo (pair); $68.00
2630 Jug, 3-pint Ice; $94.00
2630 Lily Pond, 9"; $32.00
2630 Mayonnaise, Plate and Ladle; $37.00
2630 Nappy, 4½" Handled; $14.00
2630 Pickle, 8¾"; $15.00

2630 Plate, Handled Cake; $45.00
2630 Relish, 2-part; $20.00
2630 Relish, 3-part; $30.00
2630 Salad Set, 4-piece; $95.00
2630 Shaker, Chrome Top "B" (pair); $35.00
2630 Sugar and Cream; $40.00
2630 Sugar and Cream, Individual, and Tray; $48.00
2630 Tidbit, 3-toed; $20.00
2630 Torte, 14"; $48.00
2630 Tray, Handled Lunch; $54.00
2630 Tricorne, 3-toed; $20.00

Crystal Print No. 7

2630
Handled Lunch Tray
Diameter 11¼ in.

2630
Mayonnaise and Plate
and Ladle
Height 3¼ in.

2630
3 Toed Bon Bon
Diameter 7¼ in.
Height 2¼ in.

2630
3-Toed Tricorne
Height 2½ in.
Length 7⅛ in.

2630—10½ in.
4 Piece Salad Set
Height 4¼ in.
Consisting of:
1/12 Doz. 2630
10½ in Salad Bowl
1/12 Doz. 2630
14 in. Torte Plate
1/12 Doz. Salad Fork
& Spoon (Wood)

2630
3-Toed Tid Bit
Diameter 8⅛ in.
Height 1¼ in.

2630—9 in.
Lily Pond
Height 1⅝ in.

2630
4½ in. Handled Nappy

2630—4½ in.
Candlestick

2630—12 in.
Bowl Flared
Height 2⅞ in.

2630
Duo Candlestick
Height 7 in. Spread 6⅝ in.

CUTTINGS

743 Heraldry

776 Laurel

787 Pilgrim

801 Brighton

802 Wentworth

815 Holly

823 Sprite

826 Minuet

827 Rose

833 Bridal Wreath

834 Nosegay

835 Pine

836 Ingrid

837 Fostoria Wheat

839 Plume

840 Circlet

841 Spray

842 Regal

843 Crest

851 Stardust

852 Gossamer

855 Kimberly

856 Moonbeam

CUTTINGS

Before World War II, cuttings were used primarily on stemware, and a few complimentary pieces such as console sets, plates and the occasional jug or decanter. Cut patterns introduced during the war often had a cup and saucer, but only included an 8" plate, making them more luncheon services rather than formal dinner services. Heraldry, Laurel, Holly, Sprite, Minuet, Rose, and Bridal Wreath fall into this category. In the 1950s a new kind of dinner service was offered in three cut patterns, Pine, the second Wheat cutting (Fostoria Wheat), and Spray. To the cup and saucer and 8" luncheon plate was added a 10" snack plate. The snack plate was from the Contour pattern, with the left side of the plate curving up and back on itself, nearly forming a kind of handle. Without a doubt, the snack plate was not intended to replace the elegant Fairfax or Lafayette dinner plates, but reflected the trend toward more casual dining popular after the war. After 1960, even the luncheon service was dropped, and patterns included stemware with one or two sizes of plates and sometimes a dessert/finger bowl.

The Holly pattern is a good example of what was happening to tableware patterns during this period. Introduced in 1942, Holly was nearly a complete dinner service, lacking only the dinner plate, and offering a respectable number of serving pieces. By 1944, the pattern had been reduced to Candlesticks, Mayonnaise, Plate and Ladle, Pickle, Pitcher, Plates, Relishes, Shakers, Sugar and Creams, and Handled Lunch Tray. By 1976, nothing was left but stemware.

HERALDRY

Cutting 743

For pieces in the initial introduction of Heraldry, see *Fostoria Tableware: 1923 – 1944*.
Stemware is featured in *Fostoria Stemware*, pages 83 and 84.

4185 Bowl, Dessert/Finger, 1962-1969; $22.00
2364 Bowl, 9" Salad, 1953-1969; $38.00
2364 Bowl, 12" Flared, 1953-1969; $45.00
2364 Bowl, 12" Lily Pond, 1953-1965; $45.00
2324 Candlestick, 4", (pair) 1953-1969; $40.00
6023 Candlestick, Duo, (pair) 1953-1965; $45.00
2666 Cup and 2350 Saucer, 1953-1969; $22.00
2364 Mayonnaise, Plate, Ladle, 1953-1969; $42.00
2666 Pitcher, Pint, 1953-1969; $40.00
2666 Pitcher, Quart, 1953-1969; $75.00
2666 Pitcher, 3-Pint, 1953-1969; $85.00
2337 Plate, 6", 1935-1968; $6.00

2337 Plate, 7", 1935-1969; $8.00
2337 Plate, 8", 1935-1969; $14.00
2364 Plate, 11" Sandwich, 1953-1969; $28.00
2364 Plate, 14" Torte, 1953-1969; $35.00
2364 Relish, 2-part, 1953-1969; $28.00
2364 Relish, 3-part, 1953-1969; $34.00
3264 Shaker, Chrome Top "C", (pair) 1953-1969; $55.00
2666 Sugar and Cream, 1953-1969; $35.00
2666 Sugar and Cream, Individual, 1953-1969; $35.00
2666 Sugar and Cream Tray, 1953-1969; $14.00
2364 Tray, Handled Lunch, 1953-1965; $38.00

Cutting No. 743
Gray Cutting

2666
Cup
Cup Capacity 8 oz.
2350
Saucer

2364
Shaker
Chrome Top "C"
Height 2⅝ in.

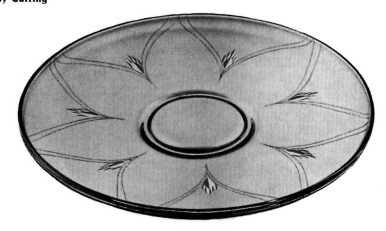

2364
14 in. Torte Plate

2364
11 in. Sandwich Plate

2666
Sugar
Height 2⅝ in.

2666
Cream
Height 3½ in.

2666
3 Piece Ind. Sugar & Cream & Tray
Consisting of:
1/12 doz. 2666—S. & C. Tray
1/12 doz. 2666—Ind. Sugar
1/12 doz. 2666—Ind. Cream

2364
Handled Lunch Tray
Diameter 11¼ in.

Cutting No. 743
Gray Cutting

2364
2 Part Relish
Length 8 ¼ in.
Width 5 in.

2364
9 in. Salad Bowl
Height 2 ⅝ in.

2364
Mayonnaise and Plate and Ladle
Mayo. Diameter 5 in.
Height 2 ½ in.
Plate Diameter 6 ¾ in.

2364
3 Part Relish
Length 10 in.
Width 7 ¼ in.

2364
12 in. Bowl, Flared
Height 2 ⅞ in.

6023
Duo Candlestick
Height 5 ½ in. Spread 6 in.

2324
4 in. Candlestick

2364
12 in. Lily Pond
Height 2 ¼ in.

LAUREL

Cutting 776
1939 – 1943 except where noted.

Two stemware blanks were used and are featured in *Fostoria Stemware*, pages 89 – 91. Stemware in Rondel, Blank 6019, was made the same years as the serving pieces; stemware in Sceptre, Blank 6017, was made 1938 – 1959 with matchings through 1977.

4148 Ash Tray, Individual, 1940-1943; $20.00
2574 Bon Bon; $32.00
755 Bowl, Finger; $18.00
2574 Bowl, Serving Dish; $34.00
6023 Bowl, Footed; $42.00
2574 Bowl 9½" Handled; $38.00
2527 Candelabra, 2-light, UDP (pair); $135.00
2574 Candlestick, 4" (pair); $58.00
2324 Candlestick, 6", (pair) 1940-1943; $65.00
2574 Celery; $30.00
4148 Cigarette Holder, 2¼", 1940-1943; $35.00
2574 Comport, 5"; $35.00
2451 Ice Dish; $22.00
2451 Ice Dish Liner (not cut); $15.00
2574 Ice Tub and 2510 Chrome Tongs; $48.00
6011 Jug; $295.00
2574 Lemon; $28.00
2574 Mayonnaise, Plate, Ladle; $37.00
2574 Olive; $18.00
2574 Pickle; $23.00
2337 Plate, 6"; $6.00
2337 Plate, 7"; $8.00
2337 Plate, 8"; $10.00
2574 Plate, 14" Torte, $52.00
2574 Plate, Cake, $48.00

2574 Relish, 3-part; $34.00
2586 Sani-Cut Syrup, 1940-1943; $275.00
2574 Sugar and Cream; $37.00
2574 Sugar and Cream, Individual; $35.00
2574 Sweetmeat; $20.00
2574 Whip Cream; $20.00

2337
6 in. Plate
2337
7 in. Plate
2337
8 in. Plate

Laurel Candlestick and Sugar

PILGRIM

Cutting 787

1939 – 1943 unless otherwise noted.

Stemware was made through 1951 and is featured in *Fostoria Stemware*, pages 93 and 94.

2574 Bon Bon; $30.00
766 Bowl, Finger; $22.00
2574 Bowl, 8½" Serving; $34.00
2574 Bowl, 9½" Handled; $38.00
6023 Bowl, Footed; $48.00
2574 Bowl, 12" Flared; $48.00
2574 Bowl, 13" Fruit; $52.00
2574 Candlestick, 4" (pair); $58.00
2324 Candlestick, 6" (pair); $65.00
2574 Celery, 10½"; $30.00
2574 Comport, 5"; $35.00
6023 Comport, 5"; $35.00
2574 Cup and Saucer; $28.00
2574 Ice Tub and Tongs; $48.00
6011 Jug; $275.00
2574 Lemon; $28.00
2574 Mayonnaise, Plate, Ladle; $38.00
2574 Oil, 4½ oz., G.S.; $54.00

2574 Olive, 6"; $18.00
2574 Pickle, 8"; $23.00
2574 Plate, 6", 1939-1941; $6.00
2574 Plate, 7", 1939-1951; $8.00
2574 Plate, 8", 1939-1951; $12.00
2574 Plate, 9", 1939-1942; $28.00
2574 Plate, 10" Cake; $40.00
2574 Plate, 14" Torte; $52.00
2574 Relish, 3-part; $37.00
2586 Sani-Cut Server, 1940-1943; $275.00
2574 Sugar and Cream, Individual; $35.00
2574 Sugar and Cream; $37.00
2574 Sweetmeat; $22.00
2567 Vase, 6"; $68.00
2567 Vase, 7½"; $75.00
2567 Vase, 8½", 1939-1942; $85.00
2574 Whip Cream; $24.00

BRIGHTON

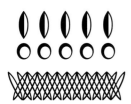

Cutting 801

1940 – 1943

Brighton and Wentworth patterns offered the pieces listed below.

WENTWORTH

Cutting 802

1940 – 1954

Stemware is featured in *Fostoria Stemware*, pages 93 and 94.

766 Bowl, Finger; $22.00
2574 Bowl, 9½" Handled; $38.00
2574 Candlestick, Duo (pair); $87.00
6023 Comport, 5"; $35.00
6011 Jug; $250.00
2337 Plate, 7"; $8.00
2337 Plate, 8"; $10.00

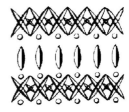

HOLLY

Cutting 815

Stemware is featured in *Fostoria Stemware*, page 100.

2364 Ash Tray, Individual, 1942-1943; $20.00
1769 Bowl, Dessert/Finger, 1942-1943; $32.00
2364 Bowl, 5" Fruit, 1942-1943; $20.00
2364 Bowl, 6" Baked Apple, 1942-1943; $20.00
2364 Bowl, 8" Rimmed Soup, 1942-1943; $30.00
2364 Bowl, 9" Salad, 1942-1943; 1950-1970; $52.00
6023 Bowl, 9" Footed, 1942-1943; $64.00
2364 Bowl, 10½" Salad, 1942-1943; $30.00
2364 Bowl, 12" Flared, 1942-1943; 1950-1970; $55.00
2364 Bowl, 12" Lily Pond, 1942-1943; 1950-1965; $55.00
2364 Bowl, 13" Fruit, 1942-1943; 1950-1965; $58.00
2324 Candlestick, 4", 1942-1943;
    (pair) 1950-1970; $38.00
2324 Candlestick, 6", (pair) 1942-1943; $68.00
6023 Candlestick, Duo, (pair) 1941-1943;
    1950-1965; $54.00
2364 Celery, 11", 1942-1943; $32.00
2364 Cheese and Cracker, 1942-1943; $68.00
2364 Cigarette, 1942-1943; $35.00
2364 Comport, 8", 1942-1943; $47.00
6030 Comport, 5", 1942-1943; $40.00
2350½ Cup and 2350 Saucer, 1943; 1950-1970; $28.00
6011 Jug, 1941-1943; 1952-1957; $295.00
2364 Mayonnaise, Plate, and Ladle,

1942-1943; 1950-1970; $52.00
2364 Pickle, 8", 1942-1943; 1950-1970; $20.00
2666 Pitcher, Quart, 1958-1970; $195.00
2337 Plate, 6", 1941-1970; $12.00
2337 Plate, 7", 1941-1975; $15.00
2337 Plate, 8", 1941-1975; $18.00
2364 Plate, 11", 1942-1943; 1950-1970; $34.00
2374 Plate, 14", 1942-1943; 1950-1970; $50.00
2364 Plate, 16" Torte, 1942-1943; $65.00
2364 Relish, 2-part, 1942-1943; 1950-1970; $34.00
2364 Relish, 3-part, 1942-1943; 1950-1970; $45.00
2364 Salad Set, 4-piece, 1942-1943; $125.00
2364 Shaker, FGT, (pair) 1942-1943; $58.00
2364 Shaker, Chrome Top "C", (pair) 1950-1970; $47.00
2364 Shaker, Large, Chrome Top "B", 1953-1970; $65.00
2350½ Sugar and Cream, 1942-1943; 1950-1970; $45.00
2666 Sugar and Cream, Individual, 1953-1970; $42.00
2666 Sugar and Cream Tray, no etching,
    1953-1970; $15.00
2364 Tray, Handled Lunch, 1942-1943;
    1950-1965; $45.00
2619½ Vase, 6" Ground Bottom, 1942-1943; $75.00
2619½ Vase, 7½" Ground Bottom, 1942-1943; $85.00
2619½ Vase, 9½" Ground Bottom, 1942-1943; $95.00

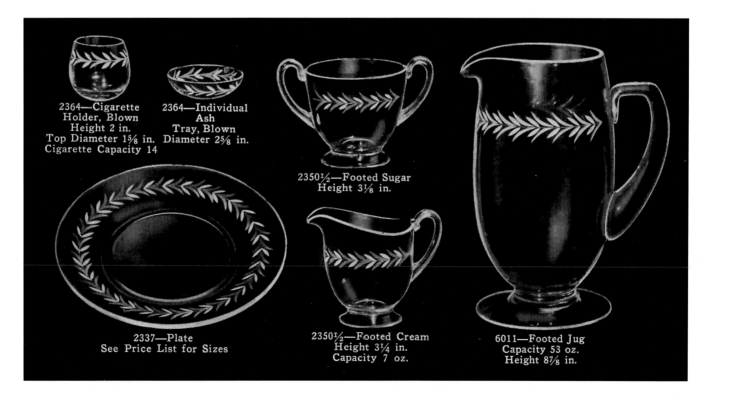

2364—Cigarette Holder, Blown
Height 2 in.
Top Diameter 1⅝ in.
Cigarette Capacity 14

2364—Individual Ash Tray, Blown
Diameter 2⅝ in.

2350½—Footed Sugar
Height 3⅛ in.

2337—Plate
See Price List for Sizes

2350½—Footed Cream
Height 3¼ in.
Capacity 7 oz.

6011—Footed Jug
Capacity 53 oz.
Height 8⅞ in.

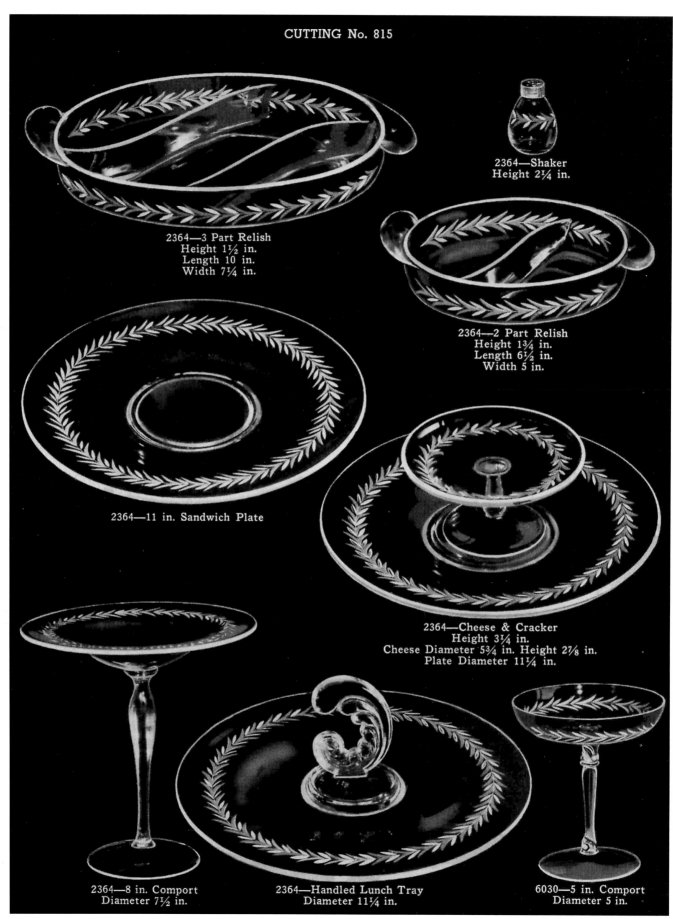

CUTTING No. 815

2364—Shaker
Height 2¼ in.

2364—3 Part Relish
Height 1½ in.
Length 10 in.
Width 7¼ in.

2364—2 Part Relish
Height 1¾ in.
Length 6½ in.
Width 5 in.

2364—11 in. Sandwich Plate

2364—Cheese & Cracker
Height 3¼ in.
Cheese Diameter 5¾ in. Height 2⅞ in.
Plate Diameter 11¼ in.

2364—8 in. Comport
Diameter 7½ in.

2364—Handled Lunch Tray
Diameter 11¼ in.

6030—5 in. Comport
Diameter 5 in.

CUTTING No. 815

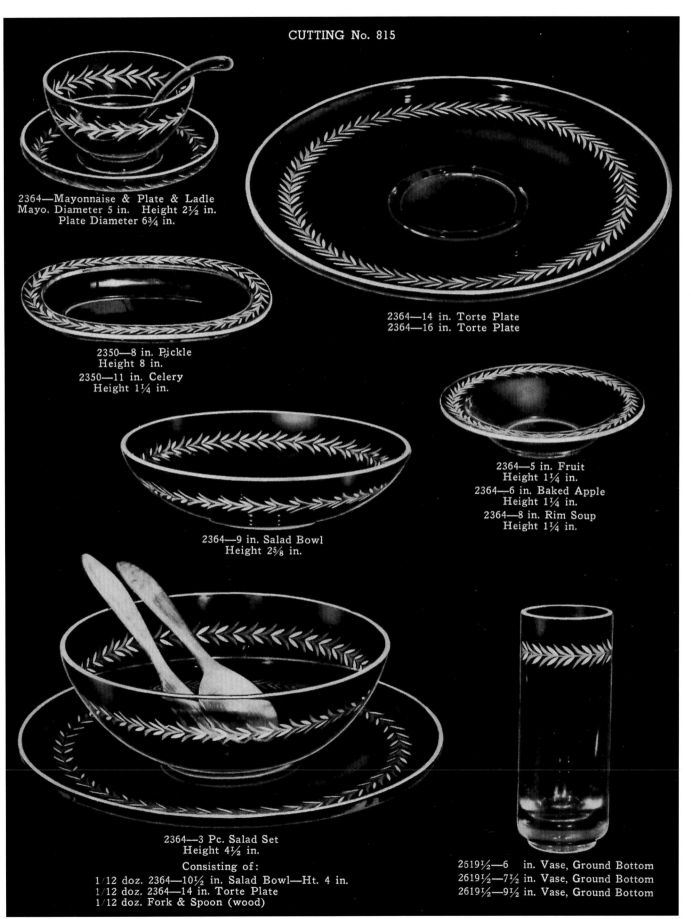

2364—Mayonnaise & Plate & Ladle
Mayo. Diameter 5 in.   Height 2½ in.
Plate Diameter 6¾ in.

2364—14 in. Torte Plate
2364—16 in. Torte Plate

2350—8 in. Pickle
Height 8 in.
2350—11 in. Celery
Height 1¼ in.

2364—5 in. Fruit
Height 1¼ in.
2364—6 in. Baked Apple
Height 1¼ in.
2364—8 in. Rim Soup
Height 1¼ in.

2364—9 in. Salad Bowl
Height 2⅝ in.

2364—3 Pc. Salad Set
Height 4½ in.
Consisting of:
1/12 doz. 2364—10½ in. Salad Bowl—Ht. 4 in.
1/12 doz. 2364—14 in. Torte Plate
1/12 doz. Fork & Spoon (wood)

2619½—6   in. Vase, Ground Bottom
2619½—7½ in. Vase, Ground Bottom
2619½—9½ in. Vase, Ground Bottom

CUTTING No. 815

6023—9 in. Footed Bowl
Height 4¼ in.

6023—Duo Candlestick
Height 5½ in.   Spread 6 in.

2364—12 in. Bowl, Fld.
Height 2⅞ in.

2364—13 in. Fruit Bowl
Height 2¾ in.

2324—4 in. Candlestick

2364—12 in. Lily Pond
Height 2¼ in.

2364—6 in. Candlestick

Cutting No. 815
Combination Gray & Rock Crystal

2350½
Footed Cup
2350
Saucer

2364
8 in. Pickle
Height 1 in.

2350½
Footed Cream
Height 3¼ in.
Capacity 7 oz.

2666
3 Piece Ind. Sugar & Cream & Tray
Consisting of:
1/12 doz. 2666—S. & C. Tray (not cut)
1/12 doz. 2666—Ind. Sugar
1/12 doz. 2666—Ind. Cream

2350½
Footed Sugar
Height 3⅛ in.

2364
Large Shaker
Chrome Top "B"
Height 3¼ in.

2364
3 Part Relish
Length 10 in.
Width 7¼ in.

2364
Shaker
Chrome Top "C"
Height 2⅝ in.

2364
2 Part Relish
Length 8¼ in.
Width 5 in.

SPRITE
Cutting 823

1950 – 1968 unless otherwise noted.
Stemware is featured in *Fostoria Stemware*, page 102.

2630 Bon Bon, 3-toed; $28.00
2630 Bowl, 10¾" Footed, Flared; $48.00
2630 Candle, Duo (pair); $68.00
2630 Candle, Trindle (pair); $85.00
2630 Comport; $30.00
2630 Cup and Saucer; $24.00
6011 Jug, 1952-1957; $250.00
2630 Mayonnaise, Plate, Ladle; $47.00
2666 Pitcher, Quart, 1958-1968; $165.00

2337 Plate, 7"; $10.00
2337 Plate, 8"; $12.00
2630 Plate, Handled Cake; $38.00
2630 Plate, 14" Torte; $54.00
2630 Relish, 2-part; $30.00
2630 Shaker, Large, Chrome
     Top "B" (pair); $54.00
2630 Sugar and Cream; $38.00

Cutting No. 823
Combination Gray & Rock Crystal

2630
Footed Sugar
Height 4 in.

2630
Footed Cream
Height 4¼ in.

2630
2 Part Relish
Length 7⅜ in. Width 6 in.

2630
Comport
Height 4⅜ in.

2630
Shaker
Chrome Top "B"
Height 3¼ in.

2630
3-Toed Bon Bon
Diameter 7¼ in.
Height 2¼ in.

2630
Duo Candlestick
Height 7 in. Spread 6⅝ in.

2630
Mayonnaise and Plate and Ladle
Height 3¼ in.

2630
10¾ in. Footed Bowl, Flared
Height 4¼ in.

2630
Trindle Candlestick
Height 7¾ in. Spread 7½ in.

MINUET

Cutting 826

1950 – 1958

Stemware is featured in *Fostoria Stemware*, page 96.

2574 Bowl, 12" Flared; $48.00
2574 Candlestick, Duo (pair); $65.00
2574 Cup and Saucer; $28.00
2574 Mayonnaise, Plate, Ladle; $47.00
2574 Plate, 7"; $12.00
2574 Plate, 8"; $14.00

2574 Plate, 10" Handled Cake; $45.00
2574 Plate, 14" Torte; $55.00
2574 Relish, 3-part; $36.00
2574 Shaker, Chrome Top "B" (pair); $58.00
2574 Sugar and Cream; $42.00

2574
7 in. Plate
2574
8 in. Plate

2574
14 in. Torte Plate

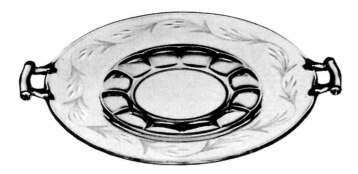

2574
10 in. Handled Cake Plate

2574
Footed Cup
Cup Capacity 6 oz.
2574
Saucer

Cutting No. 826
Rock Crystal

2574
Footed Sugar
Height 3¾ in.

2574
Footed Cream
Height 4 in. Capacity 7 oz.

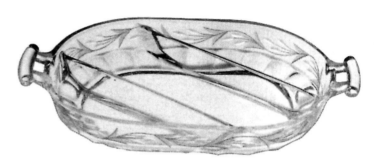

2574
3 Part Relish
Length 10 in. Width 7 in.
Height 1¾ in.

2574
Shaker
Chrome Top "B"
Height 3¼ in.

2574
Mayonnaise and Plate and Ladle
Mayo. Height 3 in.
Mayo. Diameter 4¾ in.
Plate Diameter 7¼ in.

2574
Duo Candlestick
Height 5¼ in. Spread 8½ in.

2574
12 in. Bowl, Flared
Height 3 in.

ROSE

Cutting 827
1952 – 1970 unless otherwise noted.
Stemware was made 1951 – 1973 and is featured in *Fostoria Stemware*, page 103.

4185 Bowl, Finger/Dessert, 1962-1973; $35.00
2666 Bowl, Individual Salad/Dessert; $30.00
2666 Bowl, 11" Salad; $48.00
2666 Celery; $36.00
2666 Cup and Saucer; $36.00
6011 Jug, 1952-1957; $325.00
2666 Mayonnaise, Plate, Ladle; $57.00
2666 Pickle, 1952-1965; $28.00
2666 Pitcher, Quart, 1958-1970; $195.00
2337 Plate, 7", 1951-1973; $12.00

2337 Plate, 8", 1951-1973; $15.00
2666 Plate, 14" Serving; $68.00
2666 Relish, 2-part; $35.00
2666 Relish, 3-part; $47.00
2666 Salad Set; $125.00
2364 Shaker, Chrome Top "C" (pair); $54.00
2666 Sugar and Cream; $45.00
2666 Sugar and Cream,
    Individual and Tray; $65.00

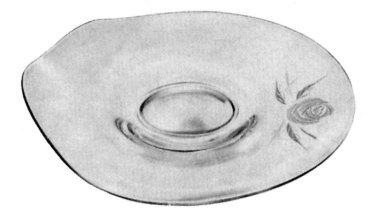

**2666
14 in. Serving Plate**

**6011
Footed Jug
Capacity 53 oz.
Height 8 7/8 in.**

Rose 4185 Finger Bowl, 2666 Quart Pitcher

**2337
7 in. Plate
2337
8 in. Plate**

Cutting No. 827
Combination Gray and Rock Crystal

2666
Sugar
Height 2⅝ in.

2666
Cream
Height 3½ in.

2666
3 Piece Ind. Sugar & Cream & Tray
Consisting of:
1/12 doz. 2666—S. & C. Tray
1/12 doz. 2666—Ind. Sugar
1/12 doz. 2666—Ind. Cream

2364
Shaker
Chrome Top "C"
Height 2⅝ in.

2666
Pickle
Length 7¼ in.

2666
Celery
Length 9 in.

2666
Ind. Salad/Dessert
Height 2¼ in.

2666
2 Part Relish
Length 7⅜ in. Width 6 in.

2666
3 Part Relish
Length 10¾ in. Width 7⅞ in.

2666
Cup
Cup Capacity 8 oz.
2666
Saucer

2666
Mayonnaise and Plate and Ladle
Height 3¼ in.

2666
4 Pc. Salad Set
Height 4⅞ in.
Consisting of:
1/12 doz. 2666—Salad Bowl
1/12 doz. 2666—14 in.
Serving Plate
1/12 doz. 2666—Salad Fork &
Spoon (Wood)

BRIDAL WREATH

Cutting 833

1952 – 1965 except where noted.
Stemware is featured in *Fostoria Stemware*, page 105.

2630 Bon Bon; $28.00
2630 Bowl, 10½" Salad; $48.00
2630 Bowl, 10¾" Footed, Flared; $48.00
2630 Bowl, 11¼" Lily Pond; $54.00
2630 Candlestick, 4½" (pair); $44.00
2630 Candlestick, Duo (pair); $68.00
2630 Cup and Saucer; $24.00
6011 Jug, 1952-1957; $250.00
2630 Mayonnaise, Plate, Ladle; $47.00
2666 Pitcher, Quart, 1958-1965; $165.00
2337 Plate, 7"; $10.00

2337 Plate, 8"; $12.00
2630 Plate, Cake; $42.00
2630 Plate, 14" Torte; $54.00
2630 Relish, 2-part; $30.00
2630 Relish, 3-part; $38.00
2630 Salad Set, 4-piece; $110.00
2630 Shaker, Chrome Top "B"(pair); $54.00
2630 Sugar and Cream; $38.00
2630 Sugar and Cream,
     Individual, and Tray; $45.00
2630 Tray, Handled Lunch; $52.00

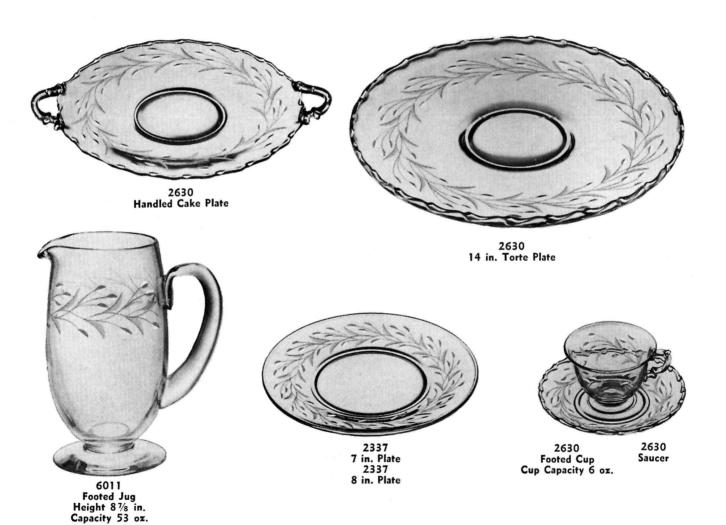

2630
Handled Cake Plate

2630
14 in. Torte Plate

6011
Footed Jug
Height 8⅞ in.
Capacity 53 oz.

2337
7 in. Plate
2337
8 in. Plate

2630
Footed Cup
Cup Capacity 6 oz.

2630
Saucer

Cutting No. 833
Combination Gray and Rock Crystal

2630
Footed Sugar
Height 4 in.

2630
Footed Cream
Height 4¼ in.

2630
3 Piece Ind. Sugar & Cream & Tray
Consisting of:
1/12 Doz. 2630—7⅛ in.
S. & C. Tray
1/12 Doz. 2630—Ind. Sugar
1/12 Doz. 2630—Ind. Cream

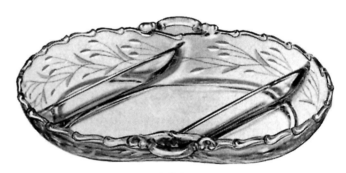

2630
2 Part Relish
Length 7⅜ in.
Width 6 in.

2630
Shaker
Chrome Top "B"
Height 3¼ in.

2630
3 Part Relish
Length 11⅛ in.
Width 8½ in.

2630
Handled Lunch Tray
Diameter 11¼ in.

2630
Mayonnaise and Plate and Ladle
Height 3¼ in.

Cutting No. 833
Combination Gray and Rock Crystal

2630
3-Toed Bon Bon
Diameter 7¼ in.
Height 2¼ in.

2630
10½ in. 4 Piece Salad Set
Height 4¼ in.
Consisting of:
1/12 doz. 2630—10½ in.
Salad Bowl
1/12 doz. 2630—14 in.
Torte Plate
1/12 doz. Salad Fork &
Spoon (Wood)

2630
10¾ in. Footed Bowl, Flared
Height 4¼ in.

2630
4½ in. Candlestick

2630
11¼ in. Lily Pond
Height 2¼ in.

2630
Duo Candlestick
Height 7 in. Spread 6⅝ in.

NOSEGAY

Cutting 834

1953 – 1970 unless otherwise noted.
Stemware is featured in *Fostoria Stemware*, page 106.

4185 Bowl, Finger/Dessert, 1962-1972; $24.00
2666 Bowl, Oval; $38.00
2666 Candle, Flora (pair); $48.00
2364 Mayonnaise, Plate, Ladle; $47.00
2337 Plate, 7"; $10.00
2337 Plate, 8"; $12.00
2666 Plate, 10" Snack; $22.00

2364 Plate, 14" Torte; $35.00
2666 Relish, 2-part; $30.00
2666 Relish, 3-part; $37.00
2364 Shaker, Large, Chrome
    Top "B" (pair); $48.00
2666 Sugar and Cream; $42.00
2666 Sugar and Cream Tray; $20.00

Cutting No. 834
Rock Crystal

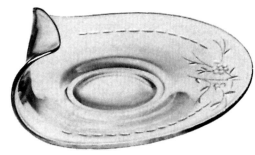

2666
10 in. Snack Plate

2666
Cream
Height 3 ½ in.

2666
Sugar
Height 2 ⅝ in.

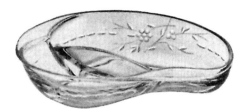

2666
2 Part Relish
Length 7 ⅜ in. Width 6 in.

2666
3 Part Relish
Length 10 ¾ in. Width 7 ⅞ in.

2364
Mayonnaise and Plate and Ladle
Mayo. Height 2 ½ in.
Mayo. Diameter 5 in.
Plate Diameter 6 ¾ in.

2364
Large Shaker
Chrome Top "B"
Height 3 ¼ in.

PINE

Cutting 835
Stemware is featured in *Fostoria Stemware*, page 107.

2666 Bon Bon, 1953-1965; $26.00
4185 Bowl, Finger/Dessert, 1962-1972; $24.00
2666 Bowl, Oval, 1953-1965; $38.00
2666 Bowl, 10½" Salad, 1956-1970; $45.00
2666 Butter and Cover, Oblong,
    1956-1970; $47.00
2666 Candle, Flora, (pair) 1953-1965; $48.00
2666 Cup and Saucer, 1956-1970; $25.00
2666 Mayonnaise, Plate, Ladle
    1953-1970; $47.00
2666 Pitcher, Quart, 1956-1970; $145.00
2337 Plate, 7", 1953-1972; $10.00

2337 Plate, 8", 1953-1972; $12.00
2666 Plate, 10" Snack, 1953-1970; $22.00
2666 Plate, 14" Serving, 1953-1970; $36.00
2666 Relish, 2-part, 1953-1970; $30.00
2666 Relish, 3-part, 1953-1970; $37.00
2666 Salad Set, 4-piece, 1956-1970; $95.00
2685 Salver, 1956-1965; $75.00
2364 Shaker, Large, Chrome Top "B", (pair)
    1953-1970; $55.00
2666 Sugar and Cream, 1953-1970; $45.00
2666 Sugar and Cream, Individual, and Tray
    1953-1970; $55.00

2666
Mayonnaise and Plate and Ladle
Height 3¼ in.

2364
Large Shaker
Chrome Top "B"
Height 3¼ in.

2666
Bon Bon
Diameter 6⅞ in.
Height 3 in.

2666
Oval Bowl
Diameter 8¼ in.
Height 3¼ in.

2666
Flora-Candle
Diameter 6 in.

INGRID

Cutting 836

1953 – 1965

This pattern is similar to Ingrid Cutting 794 (see *Fostoria Tableware: 1924 – 1943*).
Stemware is featured in *Fostoria Stemware*, page 107.

2666 Bowl, Oval; $38.00
2666 Candle, Flora (pair); $48.00
2364 Mayonnaise, Plate, Ladle; $47.00
2337 Plate, 7"; $10.00
2337 Plate, 8"; $12.00
2666 Plate, 10" Snack; $24.00
2364 Plate, 14" Torte; $35.00

2364 Relish, 2-part; $30.00
2364 Relish, 3-part; $38.00
2364 Shaker, Large, Chrome
    Top "B" (pair); $48.00
2666 Sugar and Cream; $45.00
2666 Sugar and Cream, Individual
    and Tray; $55.00

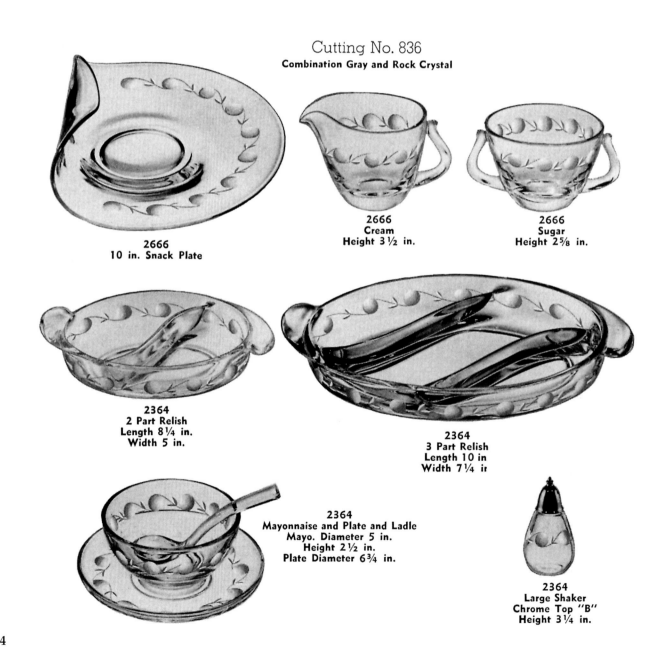

Cutting No. 836
Combination Gray and Rock Crystal

2666
10 in. Snack Plate

2666
Cream
Height 3 ½ in.

2666
Sugar
Height 2 ⅝ in.

2364
2 Part Relish
Length 8 ¼ in.
Width 5 in.

2364
3 Part Relish
Length 10 in
Width 7 ¼ ir

2364
Mayonnaise and Plate and Ladle
Mayo. Diameter 5 in.
Height 2 ½ in.
Plate Diameter 6 ¾ in.

2364
Large Shaker
Chrome Top "B"
Height 3 ¼ in.

FOSTORIA WHEAT

Cutting 837

This pattern is similar to Wheat Cutting 760 (see *Fostoria Tableware: 1924 – 1943*).
Stemware is featured in *Fostoria Stemware*, page 106.

2666 Bon Bon, 1956-1970; $26.00
4185 Bowl, Dessert/Finger, 1962-1973; $24.00
2666 Bowl, Oval, 1953-1965; $38.00
2666 Bowl, 10½" Salad, 1956-1970; $45.00
2666 Butter and Cover, Oblong, 1956-1970; $48.00
2666 Candle, Flora, 1953-1965 (pair); $48.00
2666 Cup and Saucer, 1956-1970; $25.00
2666 Mayonnaise, Plate, Ladle, 1953-1970; $48.00
2666 Pitcher, Quart, 1953-1970; $150.00
2337 Plate, 7", 1953-1970; $10.00
2337 Plate, 8", 1953-1970; $12.00

2666 Plate, 10" Snack, 1953-1970; $24.00
2666 Plate, 14" Serving, 1953-1970; $35.00
2666 Relish, 2-part, 1953-1970; $30.00
2666 Relish, 3-part, 1953-1970; $38.00
2666 Salad Set, 4-piece, 1956-1970; $95.00
2685 Salver, 1956-1965; $75.00
2364 Shaker, Large, Chrome Top "B", (pair)
    1953-1970; $55.00
2666 Sugar and Cream, 1953-1970; $45.00
2666 Sugar and Cream, Individual ,
    and Tray, 1953-1970; $55.00

Cutting No. 837
Combination Gray and Rock Crystal

2666
Oblong Butter and Cover
Length 7 in. Height 2

2666
Cup
Cup Capacity 8 oz.

2666
Saucer

2685
Salver
Diameter 12¼ in.
Height 2½ in.

2666
Quart Pitcher
Height 6⅞ in.

PLUME

Cutting 839
1955 – 1957
Stemware was made through 1960 and is featured in *Fostoria Stemware*, page 106.

2666 Bowl, Oval; $38.00
2666 Candle, Flora (pair); $48.00
2666 Mayonnaise, Plate, Ladle; $47.00
2337 Plate, 7"; $10.00
2337 Plate, 8"; $12.00
2666 Plate, Canape; $22.00
2666 Plate, 10" Snack; $24.00
2666 Plate, 14" Serving; $35.00
2666 Relish, 2-part; $30.00
2666 Relish, 3-part; $38.00
2364 Shaker, Large, Chrome
    Top "B" (pair); $55.00
2666 Sugar and Cream; $45.00
2666 Sugar and Cream, Individual,
    and Tray; $55.00

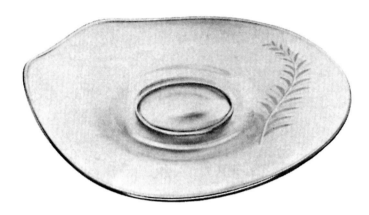

**2666—14 in.
Serving Plate**

CIRCLET

Cutting 840
1955 – 1965
Stemware is featured in *Fostoria Stemware*, page 108.

**2666
Oval Bowl
Diameter 8¼ in.
Height 3¼ in.**

2666 Bowl, Oval; $38.00
2666 Candle, Flora (pair); $48.00
2666 Mayonnaise, Plate, Ladle; $47.00
2337 Plate, 7"; $10.00
2337 Plate, 8"; $12.00
2666 Plate, Canape; $22.00
2666 Plate, 10" Snack; $24.00
2666 Plate, 14" Serving; $35.00
2666 Relish, 2-part; $30.00
2666 Relish, 3-part; $38.00
2364 Shaker, Large, Chrome
    Top "B" (pair); $55.00
2666 Sugar and Cream; $45.00
2666 Sugar and Cream, Individual
    and Tray; $55.00

SPRAY

Cutting 841

Stemware is featured in *Fostoria Stemware*, page 108.

4185 Bowl, Dessert/Finger, 1962-1972; $24.00
2666 Bowl, 8¼" Oval, 1954-1965; $38.00
2666 Bowl, 10½" Salad, 1956-1970; $45.00
2666 Butter and Cover, Oblong, 1956-1970; $48.00
2666 Candle, Flora, (pair) 1954-1965; $48.00
2666 Cup and Saucer, 1956-1970; $24.00
2666 Mayonnaise, Plate, Ladle, 1954-1970; $48.00
2666 Pitcher, Quart, 1956-1970; $155.00
2337 Plate, 7", 1954-1972; $10.00
2337 Plate, 8", 1954-1872; $12.00
2666 Plate, Canape, 1954-1965; $22.00
2666 Plate, 10" Snack, 1954-1970; $24.00
2666 Plate, 14" Serving, 1954-1970; $36.00
2666 Relish, 2-part, 1954-1970; $30.00
2666 Relish, 3-part, 1954-1970; $38.00
2666 Salad Set, 4-piece, 1956-1970; $95.00
2685 Salver, 1956-1965; $75.00
2364 Shaker, Large, Chrome Top "B",
    (pair) 1954-1970; $55.00
2666 Sugar and Cream, 1954-1970; $45.00
2666 Sugar and Cream, Individual, and Tray,
    1954-1970; $55.00

2666
Quart Pitcher
Height 6⅞ in.

REGAL

Cutting 842
1955 – 1958
Stemware is featured in *Fostoria Stemware*, page 110.

2691 Ash Tray, Individual; $18.00
2666 Bowl, Oval; $38.00
2666 Candle, Flora (pair); $48.00
2691 Cigarette Holder, Individual; $22.00
2337 Plate, 7"; $10.00
2337 Plate, 8"; $12.00
2364 Plate, 11" Sandwich; $24.00
2364 Plate, 14" Torte; $34.00
691 Preserve, Handled; $22.00

2691 Sauce Bowl, Plate, Ladle; $45.00
2691 Server, 2-part; $30.00
2691 Server, 3-part; $38.00
2691 Shaker, Chrome Top "A" (pair); $48.00
2691 Sugar and Cover; $26.00
2691 Sugar and Cream; $35.00
2691 Sugar and Cream, Individual and Tray; $45.00

Cutting No. 842
Gray Cutting

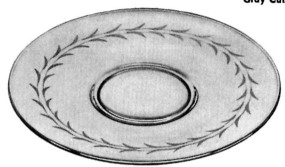

2364—11 in.
Sandwich Plate

2691
Sugar and Cream and Tray
Consisting of:
1/12 doz. 2691 Sugar and Cream and Tray
1/12 doz. 2691 Sugar and Cover
1/12 doz. 2691 Cream

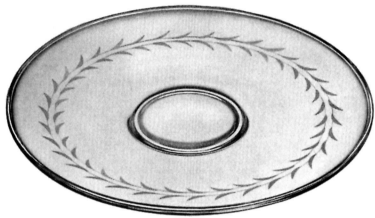

2364—14 in.
Torte Plate

2691
2 Part Server
Height 1½ in. Width 6⅜ in.

2691
Sauce Bowl and Plate and Ladle
Height 2¾ in.

2691
Handled Preserve
Width 4 in.

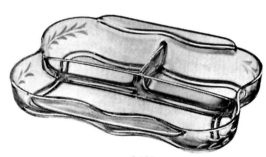

2691
3 Part Server
Length 9¾ in. Width 7½ in.
Height 1½ in.

2666
Flora—Candle
Diameter 6 in.

2691
Individual
Cigarette Holder
Height 2½ in.

2691
Individual Ash Tray
Diameter 2⅝ in.

2666
Oval Bowl
Diameter 8¼ in.
Height 3¼ in.

CREST

Cutting 843

1955 – 1962
Stemware is featured in *Fostoria Stemware*, page 110.

2691 Ash Tray, Individual; $18.00
2666 Bowl, Oval; $38.00
2666 Candle, Flora (pair); $48.00
2691 Cigarette Holder, Individual; $22.00
2337 Plate, 7"; $10.00
2337 Plate, 8"; $12.00
2364 Plate, 11" Sandwich; $24.00
2364 Plate, 14" Torte; $35.00
2691 Preserve, Handled; $22.00
2691 Sauce Bowl, Plate, Ladle; $45.00
2691 Server, 2-part; $30.00
2691 Server, 3-part; $38.00
2691 Shaker, Chrome Top "A" (pair); $48.00
2691 Sugar and Cover; $24.00
2691 Sugar and Cream; $35.00
2691 Sugar and Cream, Individual
    and Tray; $45.00

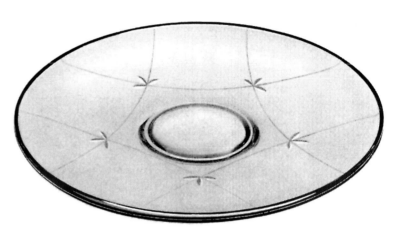

**2364—14 in.
Torte Plate**

STARDUST

Cutting 851

1957 – 1968
Stemware is featured in *Fostoria Stemware*, page 113.

**2666/136
Bon Bon
Diameter 6⅞ in.
Height 3 in.**

2666 Bon Bon; $28.00
4185 Bowl, Dessert/Finger; $24.00
2337 Plate, 7"; $10.00
2337 Plate, 8"; $12.00
2364 Plate, 14" Torte; $36.00
2364 Relish, 2-part; $30.00
2364 Relish, 3-part; $37.00
2666 Sugar and Cream; $45.00

GOSSAMER

Cutting 852
1957 – 1962
Stemware is featured in *Fostoria Stemware*, page 113.

2666 Bon Bon; $28.00
2337 Plate, 7"; $10.00
2337 Plate, 8"; $12.00
2364 Plate, 14" Torte; $35.00
2364 Relish, 2-part; $30.00
2364 Relish, 3-part; $38.00
2666 Sugar and Cream; $45.00

2337
7 in. Plate

2337
8 in. Plate

KIMBERLY

Cutting 855
1957 – 1965
Stemware is featured in *Fostoria Stemware*, page 114.

2574/622
3 Part Relish
Length 10 in. Width 7 in.
Height 1¾ in.

2574 Plate, 7"; $10.00
2574 Plate, 8"; $12.00
2574 Plate, 14" Torte; $36.00
2574 Relish, 3-part; $38.00
2574 Sugar and Cream; $45.00

MOONBEAM

Cutting 856
1957 – 1965
Stemware is featured in *Fostoria Stemware*, page 114.

2337 Plate, 7"; $10.00
2337 Plate, 8"; $12.00
2574 Plate, 7"; $12.00
2574 Plate, 8"; $14.00
2574 Plate, 14" Torte; $38.00
2574 Relish, 3-part; $40.00
2574 Sugar and Cream; $48.00

2574/679
Footed Sugar
Height 3¾ in.

2574/681
Footed Cream
Height 4 in.
Capacity 7 oz.

DECORATIONS

514 Gold Lace
515 Richlieu
526 Snow Drop
618 Simplicity
619 Florin
Platinum and Gold Bands
625 Reflection
626 Wedding Ring
635 Legacy
653 Sheffield
627 Mardi Gras
631 Highlighted Blue Spray
632 Burnished Gold Highlights
633 Shell Pearl

DECORATIONS

Few elaborate decorations were produced after 1943. As tableware patterns became simpler, so did the decorations. Most often pieces were adorned with a gold or platinum band on the rim. Accessory tableware was interchangeable among several stemware lines.

Iridescence was used to create Shell Pearl, Coral Pearl, and Firelight. Silver Mist appeared extensively on crystal and color. Mardi Gras was the only departure from the conventional decorations of this period. Using Milk glass as the base, multi-colored cullet was applied to the molten glass, creating a confetti appearance.

GOLD LACE

Decoration 514
1943 – 1949
All-over etching with Gold edge

Italian Lace was renamed Gold Lace in 1943. Although Fostoria consistently used the same description for the pattern, we have found a sugar and cream, pictured below, whose design seems more like a silkscreen print in gold than an etching. The design is similar otherwise.

2496 Bowl, 12" Flared; $48.00
2545 Bowl, 12½" Oval; $54.00
2545 Candlestick, 4½" (pair); $65.00
2545 Candlestick, Duo (pair); $87.00
2496 Candlestick, 5½" (pair): $68.00
2496 Candlestick, Duo (pair); $85.00
2496 Candy Box and Cover; $95.00
2496 Celery; $30.00
2496 Cheese and Cracker; $75.00
2496 Comport, 5½"; $37.00
2496 Ice Bucket, Gold Handle; $68.00
2496 Mayonnaise, 2-part; $40.00
2496½ Mayonnaise, Plate, Ladle; $55.00

2496 Nappy, Handled Flared; $24.00
2496 Nappy, Handled Square; $24.00
2496 Nappy, Handled 3-cornered; $24.00
2496 Pickle; $24.00
2496 Plate, 10" Cake; $52.00
2496 Plate, 14" Torte; $65.00
2496 Relish, 2-part; $35.00
2496 Relish, 3-part; $50.00
2496 Sauce Dish and Tray; $58.00
2496 Sugar and Cream; $55.00
2496 Sweetmeat; $32.00
2467 Vase, 7½"; $65.00
2545 Vase, 10"; $95.00

Gold Lace Cream and Sugar

RICHLIEU

Decoration 515
1938 – 1939
Gold filled etching
Stemware is featured in *Fostoria Stemware*, pages 87 and 88.

Richlieu is the last of the elaborate gold encrusted decorations. Made for only two years just before World War II, one would expect it to be in short supply. We looked long and hard before finally locating two pieces of stemware. The Handled Cake surfaced in Texas. This is truly an elegant pattern, one worthy of serious consideration as a collectible.

2560 Bon Bon, 2 handled; $45.00
2560 Bon Bon, 3-toed; $45.00
869 Bowl, Finger; $38.00
2430 Bowl, 11"; $75.00
2560 Bowl, 11½" Crimped; $95.00
2560 Bowl, 12" Flared; $85.00
2560 Bowl, 13" Fruit; $110.00
2430 Candlestick, 2" (pair); $65.00
2560 Candlestick, 4½" (pair); $95.00
2560 Candlestick, Duo (pair); $125.00
2430 Candy Jar and Cover; $95.00
2560 Cheese and Cracker; $95.00
2560 Comport, 6"; $75.00
2560 Ice Bucket, Gold Handle and
    Tongs; $125.00
2430 Jelly, 7"; $38.00
5000 Jug; $595.00/market

2560 Lemon; $45.00
2560 Mayonnaise, Plate, Ladle; $85.00
2430 Mint, 5½"; $38.00
2337 Plate, 7"; $30.00
2337 Plate, 8"; $35.00
2560 Plate, Handled Cake; $85.00
2560 Plate, 14" Torte; $95.00
2560 Relish, 2-part; $45.00
2560 Relish, 3-part; $68.00
2560 Sugar and Cream; $75.00
2560 Sugar and Cream, Individual; $70.00
2560 Sweetmeat; $38.00
2467 Vase, 7½"; $125.00
2430 Vase, 8"; $135.00
2545 Vase, 10"; $175.00
5100 Vase, 10"; $175.00
2560 Whip Cream; $45.00

Richlieu Goblet and Champagne, Handled Cake

SNOW DROP

1955 – 1956

No description for this pattern is given in price guides, and no pictures are to be found in catalogs. For an estimated value, add ten percent to prices for pieces in the Decorator Pattern.

2691 Ash Tray, Individual
2691 Cigarette Holder, Individual
2691 Cup and Saucer, Demitasse
2691 Sauce Bowl, Plate, Ladle
2691 Server, 2-part

2691 Server, 3-part
2691 Sugar and Cream
2691 Sugar and Cover
2691 Sugar and Cream Tray

SIMPLICITY

Decoration 618

Stemware is featured in *Fostoria Stemware*, pages 89 and 90.
Pieces have a plain gold band on the rim.

766 Bowl, Finger, 1938-1943; $18.00
2364 Bowl, 10½" Salad, 1940-1967; $35.00
6023 Bowl, Footed, 1940-1943; $65.00
2364 Bowl, 13" Fruit, 1942-1965; $58.00
6023 Candlestick, Duo, (pair) 1940-1965; $64.00
2324 Candlestick, 4" (pair); $35.00
2527 Candelabra, 2-light,
    (pair) 1940-1943; $125.00
2350 Celery, 1942-1944; $25.00
2364 Cheese and Cracker, 1942-1943; $48.00
2350½ Cup and 2350 Saucer,
    1938-1967; $26.00
6011 Jug, 1938-1943; $150.00

2364 Lily Pond, 12", 1942-1965; $50.00
2364 Mayonnaise, Plate, and Ladle,
    1942-1967; $58.00
2350 Pickle, 1942-1944; $22.00
2337 Plate, 6", 1938-1967; $9.00
2337 Plate, 7", 1938-1967; $12.00
2337 Plate, 8", 1938-1967; $15.00
2350 Plate, 10", 1938-1943; $30.00
2350½ Sugar and Cream, 1942-1967; $45.00
2364 Torte, 14", 1940-1967; $45.00
4143 Vase, 6" Footed, 1940-1943; $55.00
4143 Vase, 7½" Footed, 1940-1943; $65.00

FLORIN

Decoration 619

1940 – 1942
Crystal with ¾" Gold Band
Stemware is featured in *Fostoria Stemware*, page 98.

4021 Bowl, Finger, $18.00
6023 Bowl, 9" Footed; $65.00
2364 Bowl, 101/2" Salad; $35.00
2527 Candelabra,
    2-light UDP (pair); $125.00
6023 Candlestick, Duo (pair); $64.00
6011 Jug; $150.00

2337 Plate, 6"; $9.00
2337 Plate, 7"; $12.00
2337 Plate, 8"; $15.00
2364 Plate, 14" Torte; $45.00
4143 Vase, 6" Footed; $55.00
4143 Vase, 7½" Footed; $65.00

GOLD AND PLATINUM BANDS

Fostoria advertised that even though all the pieces decorated with Gold and Platinum Bands were not listed with every pattern, the pieces were usable with any pattern employing the same decoration. The following lists include the pieces made with Gold and Platinum Bands and their coordinating patterns.

Gold Band Decoration

Coordinated with Anniversary, Aurora, Classic Gold, Rehearsal, Richmond, and Vermeil stemware.

4185 Bowl, Dessert/Finger; $18.00
2785 Bowl, 10" Footed; $35.00
2364 Bowl, 10½" Salad; $35.00
2364 Bowl, 12" Lily Pond; $50.00
2364 Bowl, 13" Fruit; $58.00
2324 Candlestick, 4" (pair); $35.00
6023 Candlestick, Duo (pair); $64.00
2350½ Cup and Saucer; $26.00
2364 Mayonnaise, Plate, Spoon; $58.00

2337 Plate, 6"; $9.00
2337 Plate, 7"; $12.00
2337 Plate, 8", $15.00
2364 Plate, 14" Torte; $45.00
2785 Relish, 2-part; $30.00
2785 Relish, 4-part; $35.00
2785 Relish, 5-part; $42.00
2350½ Sugar and Cream; $45.00
2785 Sugar and Cream; $45.00

Platinum Band Decoration

Coordinated with Announcement, Beloved, Candlelight, Engagement, Invitation, Legacy, Reflection, Sheffield, Trousseau, and Wedding Ring stemware.

4185 Bowl, Dessert/Finger; $18.00
2364 Bowl, 9" Salad; $32.00
2785 Bowl, 10" Footed; $35.00
2324 Candlestick, 4" (pair); $35.00
2666 Cup and Saucer; $26.00
2364 Mayonnaise, Plate, Ladle; $58.00
2337 Plate, 7"; $9.00
2337 Plate, 8"; $12.00

2785 Relish, 2-part; $32.00
2785 Relish, 4-part; $35.00
2785 Relish, 5-part; $42.00
2666 Sugar and Cream; $40.00
2666 Sugar and Cream, Individual; $35.00
2666 Sugar and Cream, Individual, and
　　Tray; $45.00
2785 Sugar and Cream; $40.00

REFLECTION

Decoration 625
1952 – 1971

Reflection through Legacy had a platinum band decoration and offered the pieces listed below. Stemware is featured in *Fostoria Stemware*, pages 102, 106, and 112 respectively.

WEDDING RING

Decoration 626
1953 – 1975

LEGACY

Decoration 635
1956 – 1967

2364 Bowl, 9" Salad; $32.00
2324 Candlestick, 4" (pair); $35.00
2666 Cup and Saucer; $26.00
2364 Mayonnaise, Plate and Ladle; $58.00
2337 Plate, 7"; $9.00

2337 Plate, 8"; $12.00
2666 Sugar and Cream; $40.00
2666 Sugar and Cream, Individual; $35.00
2666 Tray, Individual Sugar and Cream; $10.00

SHEFFIELD

Decoration 653
Platinum band on rim.

4185/495 Bowl, Dessert/Finger,
   1961-1973; $18.00
2364/195 Bowl, 9" Salad, 1961-1970; $32.00
2785/224 Bowl, 10" Footed, 1971-1972; $35.00
2324/315 Candlestick, 4",
   (pair) 1961-1970; $35.00
2666/396 Cup and Saucer, 1961-1970; $26.00
2364/477 Mayonnaise, Plate and Ladle,
   1961-1970; $58.00
2337/549 Plate, 7", 1961-1982; $9.00

2337/549 Plate, 8", 1961-1982; $12.00
2785/620 Relish, 2-part, 1971-1972; $32.00
2785/643 Relish, 4-part, 1971-1972; $35.00
2785/644 Relish, 5-part, 1971-1972; $42.00
2666/677 Sugar and Cream, 1961-1970; $40.00
2666/686 Sugar and Cream, Individual,
   1961-1970; $35.00
2666 Tray, Individual Sugar and Cream,
   1961-1970; $10.00

Reflection Design—Dec. 625
Wedding Ring Design—Dec. 626
Legacy Design—Dec. 635

2666—3 Piece
Ind. Sugar & Cream & Tray
Consisting of:
1/12 Doz. 2666 S. & C. & Tray
1/12 Doz. 2666 Ind. Sugar
1/12 Doz. 2666 Ind. Cream

2666
Cup

2666
Saucer

2364
Mayonnaise & Plate & Ladle
Mayonnaise Diameter 5 in.
Height 2½ in.
Plate Diameter 6¾ in.

2666
Sugar
Height 2⅝ in.

2666
Cream
Height 3½ in.

2324
4 in. Candlestick

2364
9 in. Salad Bowl
Height 2⅝ in.

MARDI GRAS

Decoration 627

Milk Glass with colored glass added, 1954 – 1957.

2677 Ash Tray; $30.00
2666 Bowl, Ribbon; $48.00
2618 Cigarette Box and Cover; $75.00
2666 Comport; $48.00
2666 Sweetmeat; $45.00
2666 Tid Bit; $55.00
2619 Vase, 6"; $67.00
4116 Vase, 6"; $75.00
2619 Vase, 9½"; $125.00

Mardi Gras Cigarette Box Cover, Tid Bit, and Ash Tray

HIGHLIGHTED BLUE SPRAY

Decoration 631

July 1953 – 1957
Blue enamel spray on Milk Glass

BURNISHED GOLD HIGHLIGHTS

Decoration 632

July 1953 – 1957
Burnished Gold on Milk Glass

2513 Candy Jar and Cover; $125.00
2519 Cologne and Stopper; $125.00

2519 Puff and Cover; $125.00

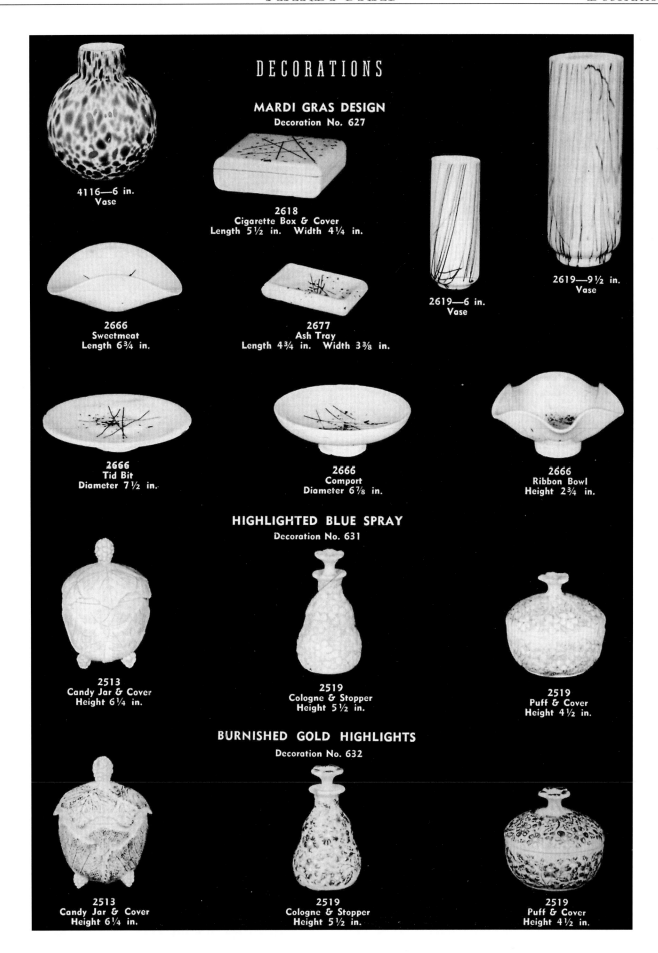

DECORATIONS

MARDI GRAS DESIGN
Decoration No. 627

4116—6 in.
Vase

2618
Cigarette Box & Cover
Length 5½ in.   Width 4¼ in.

2666
Sweetmeat
Length 6¾ in.

2677
Ash Tray
Length 4¾ in.   Width 3⅜ in.

2619—6 in.
Vase

2619—9½ in.
Vase

2666
Tid Bit
Diameter 7½ in.

2666
Comport
Diameter 6⅞ in.

2666
Ribbon Bowl
Height 2¾ in.

HIGHLIGHTED BLUE SPRAY
Decoration No. 631

2513
Candy Jar & Cover
Height 6¼ in.

2519
Cologne & Stopper
Height 5½ in.

2519
Puff & Cover
Height 4½ in.

BURNISHED GOLD HIGHLIGHTS
Decoration No. 632

2513
Candy Jar & Cover
Height 6¼ in.

2519
Cologne & Stopper
Height 5½ in.

2519
Puff & Cover
Height 4½ in.

Mardi Gras Footed Swung Vase; a whimsey

SHELL PEARL

Decoration 633

1955 – 1970
Mother of Pearl on Crystal
Stemware is featured in *Fostoria Stemware*, page 108.

    Although Fostoria did not offer the Mother of Pearl decoration on tableware other than plates with Firelight an Coral Pearl, it stands to reason that Shell Pearl pieces could also be used with those patterns.

2666 Bowl, Oval; $45.00
2666 Candle, Flora (pair); $48.00
2666 Mayonnaise, Plate, Ladle; $55.00
2337 Plate, 7" (Loop Optic); $15.00
2666 Plate, Canape; $30.00
2666 Plate, 10" Snack; $30.00
2666 Plate, 14" Serving; $58.00

2666 Relish, 2-part; $35.00
2666 Relish, 3-part; $40.00
2364 Shaker, Large, Chrome Top "B"
    (pair); $60.00
2666 Sugar and Cream; $45.00
2666 Sugar and Cream, Individual,
    and Tray; $40.00

MILK GLASS

1229 Frisco
1704 Winburn
2620 Betsy Ross/ Fruit and Flowers Decoration
2675 Randolph
2678 Monroe
2694 Arlington
2710 Daisy and Button
2711 Diamond Sunburst
2712 Berry
2713 Vintage
Miscellaneous Pieces
Jenny Lind

MILK GLASS

Fostoria milk glass covers two main periods. The early period began in the late 1890s and lasted until around 1915. This turn-of-the-century white opaque glass was called Opal Glass or Opal Ware. Pieces often had enough transluscence to seem to have an orange fire in them when held up to a bright light. Fostoria used this Opal Ware for an extensive assortment of hand painted and decorated lamps and vases. Other items made were vanity sets, trinket boxes and trays, and many novelty items. Since the early period precedes 1924, it is not included in this book or in *Fostoria Tableware: 1924 – 1943*.

The second period of milk glass began in July of 1953 with the introduction of the 1513 Candy and Cover and two pieces of 2519 offered with Blue Spray and Burnished Gold Decorations. In 1953 and 1954 several other patterns and a group of miscellaneous pieces were shown and continued to be made in white through 1965. The aqua and peach colors were made from 1957 through 1959. Fostoria was quite proud of its milk glass and placed an "Authentic Milk Glass" sticker on each piece. Unusual for any glass company are the blown milk glass pieces, such as the Jenny Lind tumblers, cologne flask and pitcher, and the stemware in the Vintage pattern.

All milk glass catalog pages are shown at the end of the section, and where possible, we have included photographs of actual pieces in the aqua and peach colors.

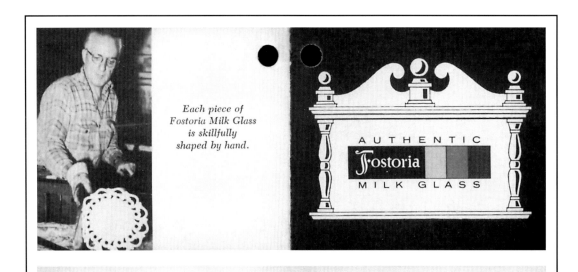

Each piece of Fostoria Milk Glass is skillfully shaped by hand.

AUTHENTIC
Fostoria
MILK GLASS

This is a Wedding Bowl . . . handmade by Fostoria craftsmen

The name "Wedding Bowl" is derived from olden days when, as the story goes, it was a tradition to display a bowl at wedding receptions for gifts of money. This was to help the newlyweds set up housekeeping.

Today, many brides save a piece of their wedding cake as a memento. The cake goes into the wedding bowl as a wish is made. The bowl supposedly makes it come true.

These bowls have many decorative uses . . . as table centerpieces, dish gardens, candy dishes and so forth. When used in pairs, they make delightful mantle decorations.

Fostoria Milk Glass is made by hand . . . just like the antique originals

That's why Fostoria Milk Glass has the fine quality and porcelain-like finish collectors prize — the wonderful mellow look you see in museum pieces.

1229 FRISCO

White Milk Glass, 1954 – 1965
Aqua and Peach Milk Glass, 1957 – 1959

Frisco dates back to the early 1900s when it was offered as a pressed crystal pattern with a number of pieces. Only five shapes were chosen for production in milk glass, and all were made in white and colors except the toothpick. The 6" Bud Vase was used in the Heirloom pattern and was made in ruby from 1961 – 1970, and for a short time in 1982.

Candy Jar and Cover, 6½"; $40.00
    Aqua, $46.00
    Peach, $46.00
Spoon Holder, 3⅞"; $32.00
    Aqua, $40.00
    Peach, $40.00
Toothpick, 2¼"; $24.00

Vase, 6" Bud; $18.00
    Aqua, $24.00
    Peach, $24.00
Vase, 10" Swung; $35.00
    Aqua, $40.00
    Peach, $40.00

Peach 6" Frisco Bud Vases, Aqua 6" Bud Vase, 10" Vase, Peach Candy Jar and Cover

1704 WINBURN

Milk Glass

The 1704 Rosby pattern made in Crystal early in this century was renamed Winburn when offered in milk glas
Of the 15 pieces made, eight were made in aqua and peach. This was the only pattern that offered a punch bowl and cup
The set may be seen on display in the Fostoria Glass Museum in Moundsville, West Virginia, an elegant sight indeed. Th
Shakers were available with either chrome or glass tops. The Pickle Jar was used for the Fruit and Flowers Decoration (se
Fruit and Flowers Decoration).

Butter and Cover, Round
    White, 1954-1965; $65.00
Cracker Jar and Cover
    White, 1954-1960; $65.00
Jelly, 3-cornered
    White, 1954-1965; $18.00
    Aqua, 1957-1959; $22.00
    Peach, 1957-1959; $22.00
Jelly, Oblong
    White, 1954-1965; $18.00
    Aqua, 1957-1959; $22.00
    Peach, 1957-1959; $22.00
Jelly, Square
    White, 1954-1965; $18.00
    Aqua, 1957-1959; $22.00
    Peach, 1957-1959; $22.00
Jug, ½-Gallon Ice
    White, 1954-1965; $77.00
Nappy, 3-cornered, handled
    White, 1954-1965; $18.00
    Aqua, 1957-1959; $22.00
    Peach, 1957-1959; $22.00

Nappy, Square, Handled
    White, 1954-1965; $18.00
    Aqua, 1957-1959; $22.00
    Peach, 1957-1959; $22.00
Oil and Stopper
    White, 1954-1965; $47.00
Punch Bowl and Foot, 16" (Plastic ladle and
    hooks)
    White, 1955-1965; $250.00
Punch Cup
    White, 1955-1965; $16.00
Pickle Jar and Cover
    White, 1954-1959; $48.00
Shaker, FGT or Chrome Top "D" (pair)
    White, 1954-1960; $38.00
    Aqua, 1957-1959; $45.00
    Peach, 1957-1959; $45.00
Sugar and Cover, and Cream
    White, 1954-1965; $65.00
    Aqua, 1957-1959; $85.00
    Peach, 1957-1959; $85.00

Aqua Winburn Square Jelly, 3-cornered Jelly, Shakers, Berry Vase, Footed Jelly

Aqua Betsy Ross Basket and Candlestick Holders

2620 BETSY ROSS

White, Aqua and Peach Milk Glass
Stemware is featured in *Fostoria Stemware*, page 48.

FRUIT AND FLOWERS

Decoration 523
1955 – 1958
Enamel decoration on Milk Glass

Wistar (2620) was introduced right before World War II and made in crystal only. Pieces offered in milk glass were renamed Betsy Ross. Most of the Fruit and Flowers decorations were put on the Betsy Ross Plate; however, the Pickle Jar and Cover was borrowed from the Winburn pattern. The most difficult piece to find in this pattern is the chimney for the Hurricane Lamp since it was so easily broken. The hand decorated plates would make a fine addition to any kitchen reminiscent of the 1950s.

Basket, 11½"
  White, 1954-1965; $37.00
  Peach, 1957-1959; $54.00
  Aqua, 1957-1959; $54.00
Bowl, 8½" Cupped,
  White, 1954-1965; $24.00
Bowl, 10½" Flared,
  White, 1954-1965; $32.00
Bowl, 10¾" Fruit,
  White, 1954-1958; $32.00
Candlestick, 3" (pair)
  White, 1954-1965; $30.00
  Peach, 1957-1959; $40.00
  Aqua, 1957-1959; $40.00
Hurricane Lamp, Crystal Chimney
  White, 1954-1960; $45.00
  Peach, 1957-1959; $55.00
  Aqua, 1957-1959; $55.00
Nappy, Handled Square
  White, 1954-1963; $18.00

Nappy, 3-cornered
  White, 1954-1958; $18.00
Plate, 8"
  White, 1954-1958; $18.00
  Fruit and Flowers Decoration,
   1955-1958
  Apple; $25.00
  Peach; $25.00
  Grape; $25.00
  Pear; $25.00
  Raspberry; $25.00
  Cherry; $25.00
Sugar and Cream
  White, 1954-1960; $35.00
1704 Pickle Jar and Cover
  Fruit and Flowers Decoration,
  1955-1958
  Daisy; $65.00
  Redbud; $65.00

Peach 2513 Crimped Bowl, Aqua 2513 Candy Jar and Cover

Peach Winburn Sugar and Cover, White Oil and Stopper,
Peach Hen and Nest, Cream, Colony Candy and Cover, Oblong Jelly

2675 RANDOLPH

White, Aqua, and Peach Milk Glass

Randolph was a new creation and the only milk glass pattern that might qualify as a dinner service, having a tumbler, cup and saucer, and 9" plate. The Hurricane Lamp in this pattern is the most elusive since the shade was so easily broken.

Ash Tray, 1954-1961; $20.00
Bowl, 10" Footed and Cover, 1954-1961; $67.00
Bowl, 10" Shallow, Footed, 1956-1965; $40.00
    Aqua, 1957-1959; $47.00
    Peach, 1957-1959; $47.00
Candleholder, 1½", (pair) 1955-1965; $30.00
    Aqua, 1957-1959; $38.00
    Peach, 1957-1959; $38.00
Candleholder, 6", (pair) 1955-1965; $48.00
    Aqua, 1957-1959; $57.00
    Peach, 1957-1959; $57.00
Cigarette Box and Cover, 1954-1961; $45.00
Cup and Saucer, 1955-1961; $24.00
Egg Cup, 4½", 1955-1962; $26.00
Egg Plate, 1955-1961; $55.00
Hurricane Lamp, 1½" Candle and Shade,
    1956-1961; $65.00
Nappy, 6" Square, 1955-1965; $22.00
    Aqua, 1957-1959; $26.00
    Peach, 1957-1959; $26.00
Nappy, 5⅜" Cupped, 1955-1965; $22.00
    Aqua, 1957-1959; $26.00

Peach, 1957-1959; $26.00
Nappy, 5" Oblong, 1955-1965; $22.00
    Aqua, 1957-1959; $26.00
    Peach, 1957-1959; $26.00
Nappy, 6", 1955-1965; $22.00
Plate, 9", 1955-1965; $22.00
Plate, 12½" Buffet, 1956-1965; $35.00
    Aqua, 1957-1959; $45.00
    Peach, 1957-1959; $45.00
Preserve, Footed and Cover, 1954-1965; $42.00
    Aqua, 1957-1959; $48.00
    Peach, 1957-1959; $48.00
Shaker, Chrome Top "A",
    (pair) 1955-1965; $48.00
Sugar and Cover, and Cream,
    1955-1965; $55.00
    Aqua, 1957-1959; $65.00
    Peach, 1957-1959; $65.00
Tray, 7", 1955-1961; $22.00
Tumbler, 9 oz. Footed, 1955-1965; $22.00
Urn and Cover, 1954-1961; $64.00

*Aqua Randolph 6" Candleholders, Preserve and Cover,
Sugar and Cover and Cream, Square Nappy, 1½" Candleholders*

2678 MONROE

Milk Glass, 1954 – 1965

Made in white only, Monroe was a newly created pattern. Because of the delicate open work, it is difficult to find a perfect piece. Instead one is apt to find stretch marks. The salver shown below exhibits a couple of tiny indentations that could be misconstrued as being cracks, however, we feel the piece came from the factory that way. These pieces are so extraordinary in design that a few "character" flaws should not matter to most collectors.

Bowl, Shallow Fruit; $48.00
Bowl, Banana; $85.00
Bowl, Footed Fruit; $85.00
Salver; $85.00

Monroe Salver, Banana Bowl, Shallow Fruit

ANTIQUE PURPOSE: Early American sugar jar and cover.
MODERN USES: Flower bowl, snack bowl, ivy planter.

New ways to enjoy
Fostoria authentic milk glass

Don't just collect Fostoria Milk Glass — use it! After all, Fostoria Milk Glass is made by hand, just like the antique originals. Not only does it have the porcelain-like authentic look collectors prize, but it is just as *functional* as its years-ago counterparts — and often in exciting new ways. May we send you our catalog? (Prices begin at only $1.35.) Fostoria Glass Company, Moundsville, West Virginia.

Authentic Milk Glass
with Fashion Flair

The American Home, April 1959

2694 ARLINGTON

White, Aqua, and Peach Milk Glass

Although Arlington had 18 pieces, only three were offered in colors. The ash trays could be confused with the Randolph pattern. The shape and size are the clues.

Ash Tray, 7"
White, 1954-1962; $15.00
Aqua, 1957-1959; $20.00
Peach, 1957-1959; $20.00
Ash Tray, 9"
White, 1957-1960; $20.00
Aqua, 1957-1959; $26.00
Peach, 1957-1959; $26.00
Banana Stand
White, 1954-1959; $78.00
Bowl, Lace
White, 1954-1963; $75.00
Candleholder, Duo (pair)
White, 1957-1959; $75.00
Compote, Belled
White, 1954-1965; $75.00
Compote and Cover, Flared
White, 1954-1965; $85.00
Compote, Flared
White, 1954-1965; $75.00
Compote, Square
White, 1954-1965; $75.00

Marmalade, Cover and Crystal Spoon
White, 1957; $40.00
Mustard, Cover and Crystal Spoon
White, 1957-1959; $24.00
Oil and Stopper
White, 1957-1962; $35.00
Pepper Mill
White, 1954-1960; $40.00
Salver
White, 1954-1959; $75.00
Shaker (pair)
White, 1954-1960; $35.00
Shaker and Pepper Mill Set
White, 1954-1960; $75.00
Spoonholder
White, 1954-1959; $42.00
Aqua, 1957-1959; $54.00
Peach, 1957-1959; $54.00
Spoonholder and Cover
White, 1954-1959; $48.00
Syrup, Dripcut
White, 1957-1960; $55.00

White Arlington Duo Candleholder, Mustard, Cover, and Spoon; Peach 7" Ash Tray; White Spoonholder and Cover

2710 DAISY AND BUTTON

White, Aqua, and Peach Milk Glass

Many companies made a Daisy and Button pattern. The handles on the Fostoria version are distinctive. Later the Sugar and Cream were offered as part of the lead crystal gift items.

Butter and Cover,
    White, 1958-1965; $46.00
Nappy, 3-cornered
    White, 1957-1965; $18.00
    Aqua, 1957-1959; $22.00
    Peach, 1957-1959; $22.00
Nappy, Square
    White, 1957-1965; $18.00
    Aqua, 1957-1959; $22.00

Peach, 1957-1959; $22.00
Sugar and Cream, Individual
    White, 1957-1965; $45.00
    Aqua, 1957-1959; $55.00
    Peach, 1957-1959; $55.00
Sugar and Cream Tray
    White, 1957-1965; $20.00
    Aqua, 1957-1959; $25.00
    Peach, 1957-1959; $25.00

Peach Daisy and Button Sugar and Cream on Tray, Aqua Hen and Nest,
3-cornered Nappy, Diamond Sunburst Sugar and Cream,

2711 DIAMOND SUNBURST

White, Aqua, and Peach Milk Glass

There are only a few pieces in Diamond Sunburst. Though made for a very short time, pieces in any of the three colors make wonderful gifts.

Candy and Cover, Footed
    White, 1957-1960; $42.00
    Aqua, 1957-1959; $48.00
    Peach, 1957-1959; $48.00
Planter
    White, 1957-1960; $35.00

    Aqua, 1957-1959; $40.00
    Peach, 1957-1959; $40.00
Sugar and Cream
    White, 1957-1965; $45.00
    Aqua, 1957-1959; $55.00
    Peach, 1957-1959; $55.00

Peach Randolph Shakers, Square Nappy, Cupped Nappy; Aqua Violet Bowl, Pansy Basket

2712 BERRY

White, Aqua, and Peach Milk Glass

Berry was created by Fostoria especially to be made in milk glass. The aqua and peach colors are outstanding. For an attractive dessert, we recommend the 8" Plate and the 4½" Berry Bowl filled with your most delicious concoction.

Bowl, 4½" Berry
    White, 1958-1965; $18.00
    Aqua, 1958-1959; $22.00
    Peach, 1958-1959; $22.00
Bowl, 6½" Shallow
    White, 1958-1965; $22.00
Bowl, 7½" Cupped
    White, 1958-1965; $32.00
    Aqua, 1958-1959; $40.00
    Peach, 1958-1959; $40.00
Bowl, 8" Berry
    White, 1958-1965; $32.00
    Aqua, 1958-1959; $40.00
    Peach, 1958-1959; $40.00
Candle, Flora (pair)
    White, 1958-1965; $44.00
Candy and Cover
    White, 1958-1965; $38.00
Jelly, Footed
    White, 1957-1965; $18.00
    Aqua, 1957-1959; $22.00
    Peach, 1957-1959; $22.00
Nappy, 4½" 3-cornered

    White, 1958-1965; $18.00
    Aqua, 1958-1959; $22.00
    Peach, 1958-1959; $22.00
Nappy, 4½" Oblong
    White, 1958-1965; $18.00
    Aqua, 1958-1959; $22.00
    Peach, 1958-1959; $22.00
Plate, 8"
    White, 1958-1960; $20.00
    Aqua, 1958-1959; $24.00
    Peach, 1958-1959; $24.00
Sugar and Cream, Individual
    White, 1957-1965; $45.00
    Aqua, 1957-1959; $55.00
    Peach, 1957-1959; $55.00
Sugar and Cream Tray
    White, 1957-1965; $20.00
    Aqua, 1957-1959; $25.00
    Peach, 1957-1959; $25.00
Vase, 8" Bud
    White, 1957-1965; $42.00
    Aqua, 1957-1959; $48.00
    Peach, 1957-1959; $48.00

Peach Berry Sugar and Cream on Tray, 8" Berry Bowl, 4½" Berry Bowl and Plate, Bud Vase

VINTAGE

Milk Glass

The Vintage design is unique in the way it utilizes a cluster of grapes flanked by two large grape leaves. In order to fully appreciate this pattern, one must see the delicately blown stemware. The Leaf Tray differs from one made by another company in that the handle creates an oval with no points of glass inside. Stemware is featured in *Fostoria Stemware*, page 49.

Bowl, Wedding and Cover
    White, 1958-1965; $58.00
Bowl, 4½" Berry
    White, 1958-1965; $20.00
    Aqua, 1958-1959; $24.00
    Peach, 1958-1959; $24.00
Bowl, 8" Berry
    White, 1958-1965; $38.00
    Aqua, 1958-1959; $45.00
    Peach, 1958-1959; $45.00
Bowl, 8" Crimped
    White, 1958-1965; $42.00
    Aqua, 1958-1959; $48.00
    Peach, 1958-1959; $48.00
Bread Tray
    White, 1958-1960; $65.00
Butter, Oblong and Cover
    White, 1958-1965; $65.00
Candleholder, Leaf (pair)
    White, 1958-1965; $54.00
Candleholder, 4" (pair)
    White, 1958-1965; $54.00
Candy Jar and Cover

White, 1958-1965; $45.00
Nappy, 4" Crimped
    White, 1958-1965; $20.00
    Aqua, 1958-1959; $24.00
    Peach, 1958-1959; $24.00
Nappy, 4" Square
    White, 1958-1965; $20.00
    Aqua, 1958-1959; $24.00
    Peach, 1958-1959; $24.00
Plate, 8"
    White, 1958-1965; $20.00
    Aqua, 1958-1959; $24.00
    Peach, 1958-1959; $24.00
Planter
    White, 1958-1965; $35.00
Shaker, Chrome Top A (pair)
    White, 1958-1965; $45.00
Sugar, Cream, Tray
    White, 1958-1965; $68.00
    Aqua, 1958-1959; $87.00
    Peach, 1958-1959; $87.00
Leaf Tray
    White, 1958-1965; $30.00

Peach Sugar and Cream and Tray; White Vintage Bread Tray, Blown Goblet; White Leaf Tray

MISCELLANEOUS PIECES

600 Vase, 6½" Cupped
  White, 1957-1959; $67.00
  Aqua, 1957-1959; $75.00
  Peach, 1957-1959; $75.00
1121 Compote, 6¾"
  White, 1957-1965; $58.00
1121 Compote, 5¾"
  White, 1957-1965; $48.00
1200 Bowl, 4" Rose
  White, 1957-1965; $35.00
  Aqua, 1957-1959; $45.00
  Peach, 1957-1959; $45.00
1200 Bowl, Crimped
  White, 1957-1965; $35.00
  Aqua, 1957-1959; $45.00
  Peach, 1957-1959; $45.00
1200 Spoonholder
  White, 1957-1965; $35.00
  Aqua, 1957-1959; $45.00
  Peach, 1957-1959; $45.00
1200 Vase, 8½" Celery
  White, 1957-1965; $35.00
  Aqua, 1957-1959; $46.00
  Peach, 1957-1959; $46.00

1300 Bowl, 5" Rose
  White, 1957-1960; $35.00
  Aqua, 1957-1959; $45.00
  Peach, 1957-1959; $45.00
1300 Planter Vase
  White, 1957-1959; $38.00
  Aqua, 1957-1959; $45.00
  Peach, 1957-1959; $45.00
1886 Pin Box and Cover
  White, 1957-1962; $65.00
  Aqua, 1957-1959; $75.00
  Peach, 1957-1959; $75.00
1886 Pin Tray
  White, 1957-1960; $34.00
  Aqua, 1957-1959; $38.00
  Peach, 1957-1959; $38.00
1886 Puff and Cover
  White, 1957-1959; $65.00
  Aqua, 1957-1959; $75.00
  Peach, 1957-1959; $75.00
2493 Beer Mug
  White, 1954-1959; $45.00
2513 Bowl, Crimped
  White, 1954-1965; $32.00

Peach 1200 Crimped Bowl; Aqua 1300 Planter Vase, 1200 Rose Bowl

Aqua, 1957-1959; $38.00
Peach, 1957-1959; $38.00
2513 Candy Jar and Cover, Maple Leaf
White, 1954-1965; $38.00
Aqua, 1957-1959; $45.00
Peach, 1957-1959; $45.00
2519 Cologne and Stopper
White, 1954-1962; $58.00
2519 Puff and Cover
White, 1954-1958; $58.00
2521 Bird
White, 1954-1958; $25.00
2589 Deer
White, 1954-1958; $42.00
2589½ Deer
White, 1954-1958; $40.00
2595 Sleigh, 3"
White, 1954-1958; $38.00
2595 Sleigh, 4½"
1954-1958; $42.00
2595 Sleigh, 6"
White, 1954-1958; $54.00
2676 Hen and Nest
White, 1954-1965; $125.00
Aqua, 1957-1959; $145.00
Peach, 1957-1959; $145.00

2676 Hen and Nest, Decorated
White, 1954-1965; $135.00
2679 Puff and Cover
White, 1954-1960; $65.00
2680 Stagecoach and Cover
White, 1954-1958; $125.00
2682 Fish Nappy
White, 1954-1960; $42.00
2693 Urn and Cover, Footed (see Garden
Club Items)
White, 1956-1965; $68.00
2700 Basket, Pansy
White, 1957-1960; $18.00
Aqua, 1957-1959; $22.00
Peach, 1957-1959; $22.00
2700 Bowl, Violet
White, 1957-1962; $18.00
Aqua, 1957-1959; $22.00
Peach, 1957-1959; $22.00
2714 Crocus Pot and Cover
White, 1957-1965; $78.00
2720 Trivet
White, 1958-1960; $54.00
4165 Santa Claus, Decorated
White, 1955 (six months only); market

Aqua 1886 Pin Box and Cover; Decorated White Hen and Nest,
Colony Low Comport and Cover, White Deer, 2521 Bird

JENNY LIND

White Milk Glass, 1954 – 1965 except where noted.
Aqua and Peach Milk Glass, 1957 – 1959
Blown tumblers are featured in *Fostoria Stemware*, page 149.

The Jenny Lind pattern has attracted many collectors. The Victorian elegance of the design would suggest that it came from an earlier time, perhaps from the Civil War era or the 1880s. However, it was not shown by Fostoria until 1903, and was not called Jenny Lind until its reintroduction in 1954.

The pattern did not have its own line number as did most patterns. Instead, each piece was individually numbered in sequence. The early pieces were called Opal glass and were available decorated in Rouge, Green, and Burnt Orange with other colors having been seen. The colors were painted on the surface, and the beads outlining the medallion and ribbon were painted gold. Refiring the piece fused the colors into the glass, but after a while the colors showed wear. Early pieces have been seen with a bubble of clear glass over a portrait or picture in the oval medallion.

Other pieces may have been made in the early period. We have a 9" tray that we have not found listed unless it was the 825 Pen Tray. The number 825 is missing from the later period, indicating that the Pen Tray was not made then. Number 834, originally assigned to the Cracker Jar, was given to the Pitcher, followed by 835 for the Tumbler.

One wonders why Fostoria waited until 1954 to call this line after the famed Swedish singer. Jenny Lind was famous the world over before she died in London in 1887, the year the Fostoria Glass Company was founded. She had toured the United States from 1850 – 1852, receiving wide acclaim and many honors. In 1894 a bust of the singer was unveiled in Westminster Abbey, an honor reserved for only the most noted.

All Jenny Lind pieces were made in White, Aqua, and Peach. The Aqua and Peach are not seen as often as the White, and usually carry a higher price. In 1960 the Pitcher was included in the Garden Center Items and made in other colors at that time. The Pitcher, Cologne Flask, and the Tumbler were the only pieces of this line that were blown. All others were pressed.

Continually experimenting, Fostoria sampled other colors for Jenny Lind pieces, but none were listed as production items. We have seen boxes and trays in Amber, Ruby, Light Green, Dark Green, some with an iridescent finish, and some with a frosted finish reminiscent of Silver Mist.

Jenny Lind Tumblers in Aqua, White, and Peach; Aqua Pitcher

824 Comb and Brush Tray
   White, $85.00
   Aqua, $125.00
   Peach, $125.00
826 Pin Tray
   White, $34.00
   Aqua, $45.00
   Peach, $45.00
827 Cologne Flask and Stopper
   White, $125.00
   Aqua, $165.00
   Peach, $150.00
828 Pin Box and Cover
   White, $54.00
   Aqua, $65.00
   Peach, $65.00
829 Puff and Cover
   White, $58.00
   Aqua, $75.00
   Peach, $70.00
830 Pomade and Cover
   White, $62.00

   Aqua, $78.00
   Peach, $78.00
831 Handkerchief Box and Cover
   White, $65.00
   Aqua, $89.00
   Peach, $89.00
832 Glove Box and Cover
   White, $125.00
   Aqua, $175.00
   Peach, $195.00
833 Jewel Box and Cover
   White, $56.00
   Aqua, $67.00
   Peach, $67.00
834 Pitcher, Blown (see Garden Center Items)
   White, 1955-1965; $125.00
   Aqua, $175.00
   Peach, $165.00
835 Tumbler, Blown
   White, 1955-1965; $50.00
   Aqua, $75.00
   Peach, $68.00

Aqua Cologne Flask, Glove Box, Square Handkerchief Box, Pin Tray

Peach Handkerchief Box, Cologne Flask,
Puff Box, Comb and Brush Tray,

White Pin Box,
Old Tray, Jewel Box, Pomade

2675—9 in.
Plate

2678
Footed Fruit Bowl
Diameter 10 in.
Height 6½ in.

2675
Footed Cup
Cup Capacity 6 oz.

2675
Saucer

2675—9 oz.
Footed Tumbler
Height 5¼ in.

2678
Shallow Fruit Bowl
Length 10½ in. Width 7½ in.

2682
Fish Nappy
Length 9½ in.
Width 6 in.

2675
Egg Cup
Height 4½ in

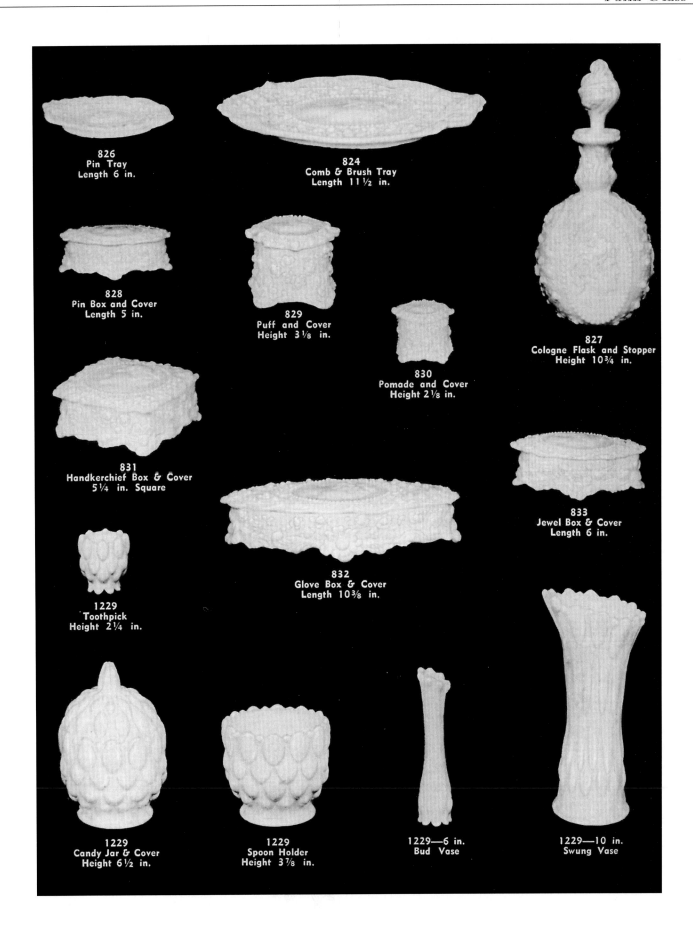

826
Pin Tray
Length 6 in.

824
Comb & Brush Tray
Length 11½ in.

828
Pin Box and Cover
Length 5 in.

829
Puff and Cover
Height 3⅛ in.

830
Pomade and Cover
Height 2⅛ in.

827
Cologne Flask and Stopper
Height 10¾ in.

831
Handkerchief Box & Cover
5¼ in. Square

833
Jewel Box & Cover
Length 6 in.

832
Glove Box & Cover
Length 10⅜ in.

1229
Toothpick
Height 2¼ in.

1229
Candy Jar & Cover
Height 6½ in.

1229
Spoon Holder
Height 3⅞ in.

1229—6 in.
Bud Vase

1229—10 in.
Swung Vase

FRUIT AND FLOWERS
Decoration No. 523
Enamel Decoration on Milk Glass

2620—8 in.
Plate
Apple

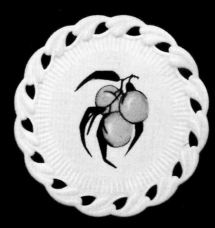

2620—8 in.
Plate
Peach

2620—8 in.
Plate
Grape

2620—8 in.
Plate
Pear

2620—8 in.
Plate
Cherry

2620—8 in.
Plate
Raspberry

1704
Pickle Jar and Cover
Daisey
Height 4¾ in.

1704
Pickle Jar and Cover
Redbud
Height 4¾ in.

1704
½ Gallon Ice Jug
Height 8 in.

1704
Water (ill.)
Height 4⅜ in.
Capacity 7 oz.

1704
Ice Tea
Height 5¼ in.
Capacity 10½ oz.

1704
Sugar and Cover
Height 6⅞ in.

1704
Cream
Height 4½ in.

1704
Pickle Jar and Cover
Height 4¾ in.

1704
Butter and Cover

1704
Cracker Jar and Cover
Height 8¾ in.

1704
Jelly, 3 Cornered
Height 3⅛ in.

1704
Handled Nappy, 3 Cornered

1704
Handled Nappy, Square

1704
Jelly, Oblong
Height 4 in.

1704
Jelly, Square
Height 3¼ in.

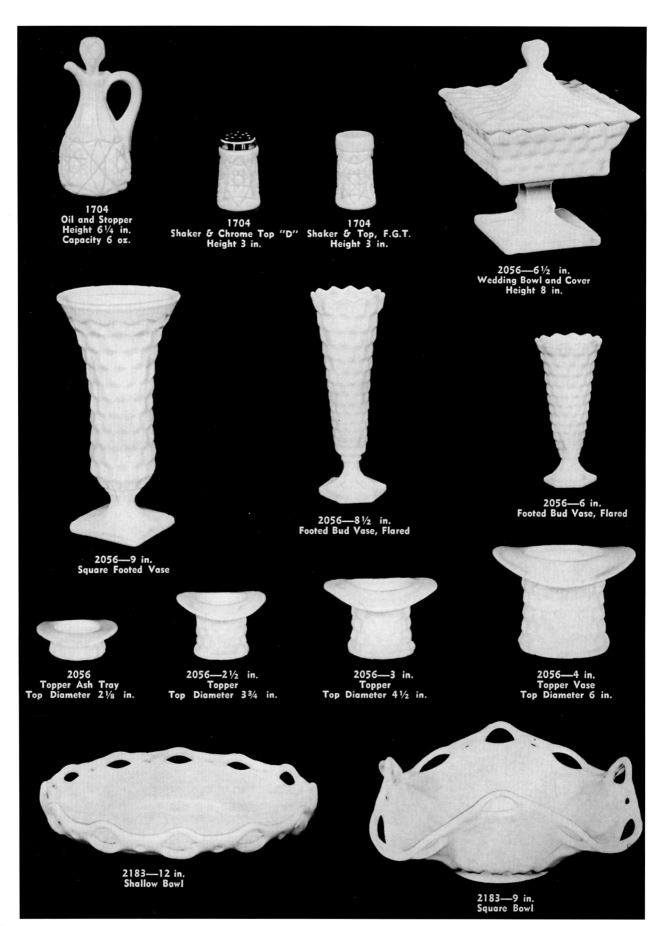

1704
Oil and Stopper
Height 6¼ in.
Capacity 6 oz.

1704
Shaker & Chrome Top "D"
Height 3 in.

1704
Shaker & Top, F.G.T.
Height 3 in.

2056—6½ in.
Wedding Bowl and Cover
Height 8 in.

2056—9 in.
Square Footed Vase

2056—8½ in.
Footed Bud Vase, Flared

2056—6 in.
Footed Bud Vase, Flared

2056
Topper Ash Tray
Top Diameter 2⅛ in.

2056—2½ in.
Topper
Top Diameter 3¾ in.

2056—3 in.
Topper
Top Diameter 4½ in.

2056—4 in.
Topper Vase
Top Diameter 6 in.

2183—12 in.
Shallow Bowl

2183—9 in.
Square Bowl

2412
Oblong Butter and Cover
Length 7½ in.   Height 2 in.
Width 3½ in.

2412
Candy Box and Cover
Height 4 in.   Diameter 6½ in.

2412
Low Comport and Cover
Height 6⅜ in.

2513
Candy Jar and Cover
Height 6 in.

2519
Cologne and Stopper
Height 5½ in.

2519
Puff and Cover
Height 4⅜ in.

2595—3 in. Sleigh
Height 1¾ in.   Width 2⅛ in.

2595—4¼ in. Sleigh
Height 2¼ in.   Width 3⅛ in.

2595—6 in. Sleigh
Height 3⅜ in.   Width 4⅜ in.

2589
Deer
Height 4⅜ in.

2589½
Deer
Height 2½ in.

2521
Bird

2620
Goblet
Height 6 in.
Capacity 9 oz.

2620
Sherbet
Height 4 in.
Capacity 4⅛ in.

2620
Ice Tea
Height 5¼ in.
Capacity 12 oz.

2620
Juice
Height 3⅝ in.
Capacity 5 oz.

2620—8 in.
Plate

2620
Handled Nappy, 3 Cornered
Length 4½ in.

2620
Handled Nappy, Square
Width 4 in.

2620
Footed Sugar
Height 3¾ in.

2620
Footed Cream
Height 4 in.

2620—8½ in.
Bowl, Cupped

2620—10½ in.
Bowl, Flared

2620—10¾ in.
Fruit Bowl

2620—11½ in.
Basket

2620
Candlestick
Height 3 in.

2620
Hurricane Lamp, Complete
Height 9⅞ in.
Consisting of:
1/12 Dz. 2620 Candlestick
1/12 Dz. 2620 Hurricane Lamp Chimney

2675
Footed Preserve & Cover
Height 5⅝ in.

2675
Footed Urn & Cover
Height 8 in.

2675
Ash Tray
3½ in. square.

2675
Cigarette Box & Cover
Length 6⅜ in.
Width 4¾ in.

2676
Hen and Nest
Length 7¼ in.

2675—10 in.
Footed Bowl & Cover

2676
Hen and Nest (Decorated)
Length 7¼ in.

2678
Banana Bowl
Height 7 in.
Length 10¾ in.

2678
Salver
Height 4½ in.
Diameter 11¼ in.

2680
Stagecoach & Cover
Height 5⅜ in.

2679
Puff & Cover
Height 4⅝ in.

2183
Candleholder
Height 2¾ in.

2493
Beer Mug
Height 5⅝ in.
Capacity 14 oz.

2183
Hurricane Lamp Complete
Height 11¼ in.
Consisting of:
1/12 Dz. 2183—Candleholder
1/12 Dz. 2183—Hurricane Lamp Chimney

2675—6 in.
Nappy

2675
Footed Sugar and Cover
Height 5¾ in.

2675
Footed Cream
Height 3⅝ in.

2675—7 in.
Tray

2675
Nappy, Cupped
Diameter 5⅜ in.

2675—6 in.
Nappy, Square

2675
Nappy, Oblong
Width 5 in.

2675—1½ in.
Candleholder

835
Jenny Lind Tumbler
Height 4½ in.

1704—5½ oz.
Punch Cup
Height 2¼ in.
Top Diameter 3½ in.

2675—6 in.
Candleholder

1704—16 in.
Punch Bowl
Capacity 2¾ gal.
Height including foot—14 in.

2675
Egg Plate
Length 12 in.   Width 9½ in.

2675
Shaker & Chrome Top "A"
Height 3½ in.

834
Jenny Lind Pitcher
Height 8¼ in.

2675—10 in.
Shallow Footed Bowl

2693
Footed Urn & Cover
Height 8½ in.

2675—12½ in.
Footed Buffet Plate

2675
Hurricane Lamp Complete
Height 14¾ in.
Consisting of:
1/12 doz. 2675
Hurricane Lamp Base
1 12 doz. 2675
Hurricane Lamp Chimney

2694
7 in. Ash Tray
2694
9 in. Ash Tray

2694
Spoonholder and Cover
Height 7½ in.

2694
Comport Flared and Cover
Height 11½ in.

2694
Compote, Square
Height 9½ in.

2694
Compote, Belled
Height 8 in.

2694
Lace Bowl
Height 7 in.
Diameter 11½ in.

2694
Banana Stand
Height 7 in.
Width 13 in.

2694
Mustard and Cover
and Spoon
Height 3¾ in.

2694
Salver
Height 5 in.
Diameter 13½ in.

2694
Dripcut Syrup
Height 5¼ in.
Capacity 8½ oz.

2694
Salt Shaker
Height 5½ in.

2694
Pepper Mill
Height 6¼ in.

2694
Duo Candleholder
Height 5¼ in., Spread 8½ in.

2694
Marmalade and Cover
and Spoon
Height 5⅞ in.

2694
Oil and Stopper
Height 6⅝ in.
Capacity 5 oz.

600/767—6½ in.
Cupped Vase

1121/388—6¾ in.
Compote

1121/389—5¾ in.
Compote

1200/677
Spoon Holder
Height 4¼ in.

1200/146—4 in.
Rose Bowl

1200/792—8½ in.
Celery Vase

1200/155
Crimped Bowl
Height 3½ in.

1300/751
Planter Vase
Height 4¼ in.

1300/149—5 in.
Rose Bowl

1886/580
Puff and Cover
Height 3 in.

1886/544
Pin Tray
Length 5½ in.

1886/281
Pin Box and Cover
Length 4⅝ in.

2513/155
Crimped Bowl
Height 3½ in.

2700/743
Pansy Basket
Width 4¾ in.

2700/747
Violet Bowl
Height 2⅜ in.

Milk Glass

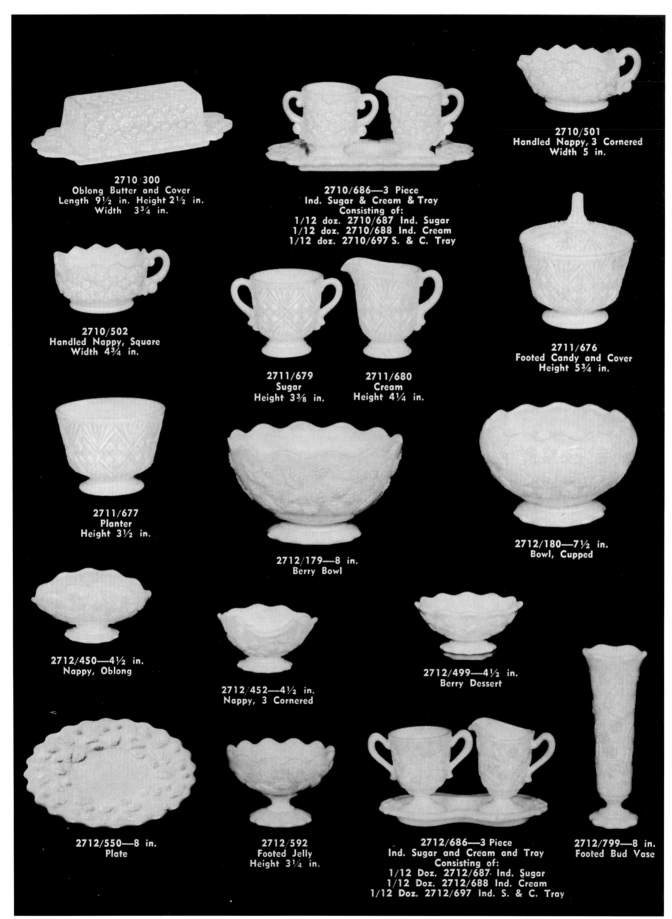

2710/300
Oblong Butter and Cover
Length 9½ in. Height 2½ in.
Width 3¾ in.

2710/686—3 Piece
Ind. Sugar & Cream & Tray
Consisting of:
1/12 doz. 2710/687 Ind. Sugar
1/12 doz. 2710/688 Ind. Cream
1/12 doz. 2710/697 S. & C. Tray

2710/501
Handled Nappy, 3 Cornered
Width 5 in.

2710/502
Handled Nappy, Square
Width 4¾ in.

2711/679
Sugar
Height 3⅜ in.

2711/680
Cream
Height 4¼ in.

2711/676
Footed Candy and Cover
Height 5¾ in.

2711/677
Planter
Height 3½ in.

2712/179—8 in.
Berry Bowl

2712/180—7½ in.
Bowl, Cupped

2712/450—4½ in.
Nappy, Oblong

2712/452—4½ in.
Nappy, 3 Cornered

2712/499—4½ in.
Berry Dessert

2712/550—8 in.
Plate

2712/592
Footed Jelly
Height 3¼ in.

2712/686—3 Piece
Ind. Sugar and Cream and Tray
Consisting of:
1/12 Doz. 2712/687 Ind. Sugar
1/12 Doz. 2712/688 Ind. Cream
1/12 Doz. 2712/697 Ind. S. & C. Tray

2712/799—8 in.
Footed Bud Vase

230

2713/2
Goblet
Height 6¼ in.
Capacity 11 oz.

2713/11
Sherbet
Height 4¾ in.
Capacity 7½ oz.

2713/63
Footed Ice Tea
Height 6¼ in.
Capacity 13 oz.

2713/179—8 in.
Berry Bowl

2713/180—8 in.
Bowl Crimped

2713/385
Bread Tray
Length 11 in.

2713/300
Oblong Butter and Cover
Length 8¼ in. Height 3 in.
Width 4 in.

2713/499—4½ in.
Berry Dessert

2713/500—4 in.
Nappy, Crimped

2713/502—4 in.
Nappy, Square

2713/550—8 in.
Plate

2713/686—3 piece
Ind. Sugar and Cream and Tray
Consisting of:
1/12 Doz. 2713/687 Ind. Sugar
1/12 Doz. 2713/688 Ind. Cream
1/12 Doz. 2713/697 Ind. S. & C. Tray

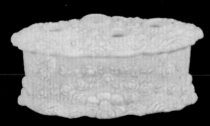

2714/287
Crocus Pot and Cover
Length 8½ in. Width 4 in.
Height 3¾ in.

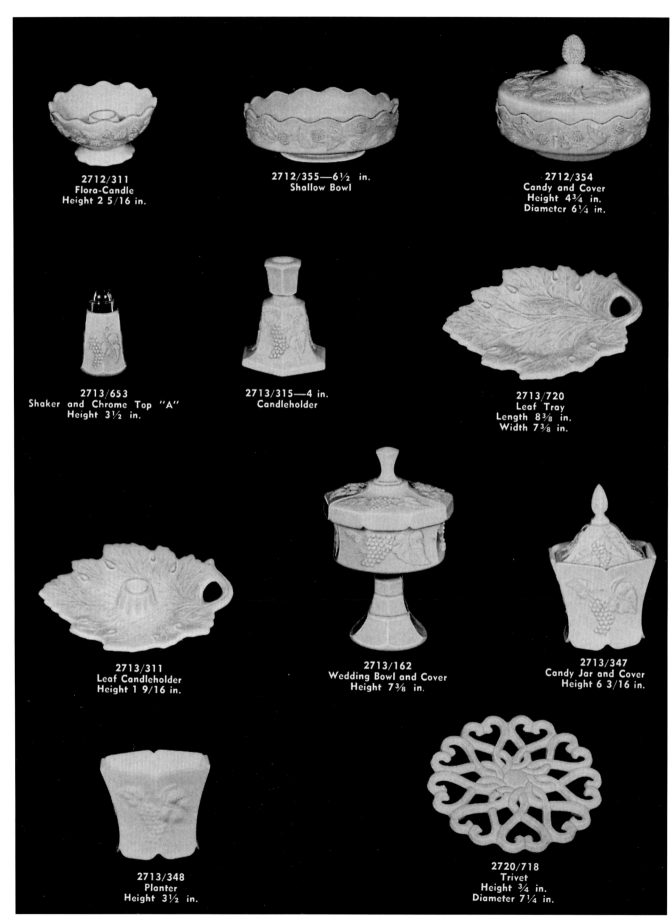

2712/311
Flora-Candle
Height 2 5/16 in.

2712/355—6½ in.
Shallow Bowl

2712/354
Candy and Cover
Height 4¾ in.
Diameter 6¼ in.

2713/653
Shaker and Chrome Top "A"
Height 3½ in.

2713/315—4 in.
Candleholder

2713/720
Leaf Tray
Length 8⅜ in.
Width 7⅜ in.

2713/311
Leaf Candleholder
Height 1 9/16 in.

2713/162
Wedding Bowl and Cover
Height 7⅜ in.

2713/347
Candy Jar and Cover
Height 6 3/16 in.

2713/348
Planter
Height 3½ in.

2720/718
Trivet
Height ¾ in.
Diameter 7¼ in.

EBONY GLASS

September 1953 – 1963

2288 Vase, Handled Tut, 1953-1958; $68.00
2402 Bowl, 9", 1953-1957; $42.00
2402 Candlestick, 2", (pair) 1953-1957; $34.00
2404 Vase, 6", 1953-1957; $55.00
2409 Vase, 7½", 1953-1963; $67.00
2428 Vase, 6", 1952-1960; $55.00
2428 Bowl, 7" Round, 1953-1962; $60.00
2428 Vase, 9", 1953-1963; $68.00
2428 Vase, 13", 1953-1962; $95.00
2430 Bowl, 11", 1953-1957; $45.00
2430 Candlestick, 2", (pair) 1953-1958; $50.00
2430 Candy Jar and Cover, 1953-1958; $65.00
2453 Lustre, 7½", 8 UDP,
    (pair) 1953-1957; $250.00
2467 Vase, 7½", 1953-1961; $68.00
2496 Smoker Set, 5-piece, 1953-1955; $95.00
    Cigarette Box and Crystal Cover
    4 Crystal Oblong Ash Trays
2538 Place Card Holder, 1953-1962; $26.00
2545 Candlestick, 2" Flame,
    (pair) 1953-1958; $35.00
2545 Candle Lamp, 1953-1958; $48.00
    2545 Candlestick, 2" Ebony
    Crystal #26 Candle Lamp Base
    Crystal #26 Candle Lamp Chimney
2567 Vase, 7½" Footed, 1953-1957; $75.00
2592 Cigarette Box and Cover,
    1953-1957; $67.00
    Ebony with Gold, 1953; $75.00
2592 Ash Tray, Oblong, 1953-1957; $22.00
    Ebony with Gold, 1953; $25.00
2618 Cigarette Box and Cover,
    1953-1963; $38.00
2618 Oblong Ash Tray, Crystal,
    1953-1957; $18.00

2626 Chinese Lute Figure, Decoration 522,
    Gold, 1953-1957; $400.00
2626½ Chinese Lotus Figure, Decoration
    522, Gold, 1953-1957; $400.00
2626 Chinese Bookend, 7½", Decoration
    522, Gold, (pair) 1953-1957; $650.00
2629 Chanticleer, 1953-1957; $450.00
    Decoration 522, Gold; $500.00
2636 Bookend, Plume,
    (pair) 1953-1957; $150.00
2638 Candlestick, (pair) 1953-1962; $150.00
2666 Mayonnaise, Plate, Ladle,
    1954-1963; $55.00
    Ebony Mayonnaise, Crystal Plate
    and Ladle
2666 Bowl, 9" Salad, 1954-1962; $30.00
2666 Bowl, 11" Salad, 1954-1962; $40.00
2666 Salad Set, 4-piece, 1954-1962; $85.00
    Ebony Salad Bowl, Crystal Serving
    Plate, Wooden Fork and Spoon
2666 Bowl, Oval, 1954-1957; $38.00
2666 Candle, Flora, (pair) 1954-1962; $38.00
2667 Ash Tray, 5", 1954-1962; $12.00
2667 Ash Tray, 7", 1954-1962; $15.00
2667 Ash Tray, 9", 1954-1961; $18.00
2667 Candlestick, 2½",
    (pair) 1953-1963; $37.00
2667 Cigarette Holder, 1954-1963; $22.00
2668 Candlestick, (pair) 1953-1963; $45.00
2668 Hurricane Lamp, 1953-1963; $70.00
    2668 Ebony Candlestick
    2668 Crystal Hurricane Lamp
    Chimney
4116 Bubble Ball, 4", 1954-1963; $18.00
4125 Snack Bowl, 1961-1962; $22.00

Chinese Bookends, Chinese Lute and Lotus, Plume Bookends

Decorated Ebony Chanticleer, experimental Milk Glass Chanticleer
Cigarette Holder, 2667 Candlestick, 2668 Candlestick

2453
Lustre
8 U. Drop Prisms
Height 7½ in.

2467—7½ in.
Vase

2496
5 Piece Smoker Set
Consisting of:
1/12 Doz. 2496 Cigarette Box & Cover (Cov. Cry.)
1/3 Doz. 2496 Oblong Ash Tray (Crystal)

2538
Place Card Holder
Height 2¾ in.

2545
Candle Lamp, Complete
Consisting of:
1/12 Dz. 26 Candle Lamp Base (Crystal)
1/12 Dz. 26 Candle Lamp Chimney (Crystal)
1/12 Dz. 2545 2 in. Candlestick (Ebony)

2545—2 in.
"Flame" Candlestick

2567—7½ in.
Footed Vase

2592
Cigarette Box and Cover
Length 6 in.   Width 3¼ in.

2592
Oblong Ash Tray
Length 3¾ in.   Width 2¾ in.

2618
Cigarette Box and Cover
Length 5½ in.   Width 4¼ in.

235

2629
Chanticleer
Height 10¾ in.

2636
"Plume" Book End
Height 9¼ in.

2638—4½ in.
Candlestick

2666
Mayonnaise and Plate
and Ladle
Height 3¼ in.

2666—9 in.
Salad Bowl
Height 2¾ in.

2666—11 in.
4 pc. Salad Set
Height 4⅞ in.
Consisting of:
1/12 doz. 2666 11 in. Salad Bowl (Ebony)
1/12 doz. 2666 14 in. Serving Plate (Crystal)
1/12 doz. Salad Fork & Spoon (Wood)

2666
Oval Bowl
Diameter 8¼ in.
Height 3¼ in.

2666
Flora-Candle
Diameter 6 in.

2667—5 in.
Ash Tray

2667—9 in.
Ash Tray

2667—7 in.
Ash Tray

2667
Cigarette Holder
Height 2¾ in.

2667—2½ in.
Candlestick

2668
Hurricane Lamp, Complete
Height 11¾ in.
Consisting of:
1/12 Doz. 2668—Candlestick (Ebony)
1/12 Doz. 2668 Hurricane Lamp
Chimney (Crystal)

2668
Candlestick
Height 2½ in.

GROUPS AND COLLECTIONS

American Milestones

Our American States

Captiva

Centennial II

Crown Collection:

2749 Windsor

2750 Hapsburg

2751 Navarre

2766 Luxemburg

Decorator Collection

Designer Collection:

Images

Impressions

Interpretations

Garden Center Items

Gourmet Collection

1871 Heritage Collection

Group International

Heirloom

Henry Ford Museum

Serendipity Line

AMERICAN MILESTONES/OUR AMERICAN STATES

1971 – 1976
Commemorative Plates

In anticipation of the American Bicentennial in 1976, the Fostoria Glass Company proudly introduced two series of collectible commemorative plates. American Milestones depicted historic events in American history, and Our American States was planned to honor each state in the Union. The designs for both series were executed by Marvin Yutzey and Jon Saffell of the Fostoria design department.

Each plate in the American Milestones was oval in shape, 10½" long, and the entire design was pressed into the plate by the mold as it was made. The rim was left clear while the center portion was etched by sandblasting. An iridescent finish was applied to the total surface, front and back, to achieve a soft rainbow effect. Important to collectors is the fact that each plate was advertised as being made for only one year. On December 31 of each year, the mold for the current plate was destroyed. Detail and workmanship are exquisite. The date of issue and the word "Fostoria" mark each plate.

Our American States were also offered for one year each, but were offered in two groups. The first group, Ohio, California and New York, were offered in the supplementary price list dated July 1, 1971. Each plate came gift boxed in black velvet and white as did the American Milestones plates. Inside each box was a small brochure explaining the commemorative series, stating that the mold would be destroyed in June 1972. A geographical shape of the state, the state bird, tree, flag, and date of entry into the Union are seen on each plate. In January of 1973 five more states were added: Pennsylvania, Texas, Massachusetts, Florida, and Hawaii. The state of Michigan was added in July of 1973. These six plates were available through 1974. A West Virginia plate was made also but was not offered through Fostoria catalogs. It was sold only through the outlet stores. The author has two plates made for bicentennial observances in the Ohio cities of Worthington and Bluffton. The size and basic design, and the Fostoria mark, are the same as for the state plates. Other plates may have been special ordered. A gift-boxed plate should be worth $10.00 more than a plate found without the box.

Old Glory Plate, American Milestones Series; Original Gift Box

239

Old Glory, 1971; $50.00
Star Spangled Banner, 1972; $50.00
Washington Crossing the Delaware, 1973; $50.00
The Spirit of '76, 1974; $50.00
Shrine of Democracy, 1975; $50.00
One Nation Under God, 1976; $50.00

2838/552   2845/552   2846/552   2850/552

2851/552   2852/552   2853/552   2854/552

2871/555

Ohio, 1971; $45.00; California, 1971; $45.00; New York, 1971; $45.00; Pennsylvania, 1973; $45.00; Texas, 1973; $45.00; Massachusetts, 1973; $45.00; Florida, 1973; $45.00; Hawaii, 1973; $45.00; Michigan, 1973; $45.00

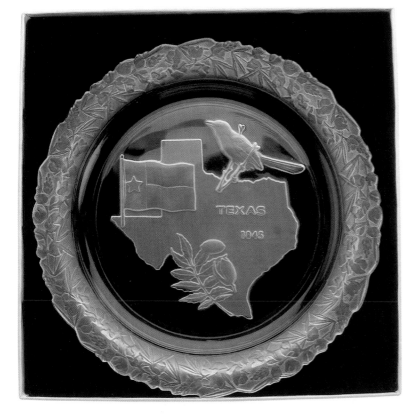

Texas Plate in original gift box

"Our
American
States"
by Fostoria

Texas

Fostoria
LIMITED EDITION

CAPTIVA

July 1983 – 1985
Crystal, Light Blue, Peach

From a letter sent to Fostoria dealers dated July 1983 and signed by Kenneth B. Dalzell, the following statement is taken: "For everyday usage, we are offering a new life-style drinkware and dinnerware collection that is both dishwasher and microwave safe. Captiva is directed to today's life-styles and is available in three colors: Crystal, Light Blue, and Peach."
Stemware is featured in *Fostoria Stemware*, page 187.

705 Mug/Cup, 9 oz.; $18.00
512 Bowl, 6"; $15.00

550 Plate, 8"; $15.00
554 Plate, 10"; $20.00

Color Code
CA18
CA17
CA16

Captiva
Lifestyle Drinkware/Dinnerware
Gift Boxed

554
891
512
892
705
550

Captiva Crystal
CA16/891 13 oz. Goblet/Ice Tea
CA16/892 8 oz. Wine/Juice
CA16/705 9 oz. Mug/Cup
CA16/554 10 in. Plate
CA16/550 8 in. Plate
CA16/512 6 in. Bowl

Captiva Light Blue
CA17/891 13 oz. Goblet/Ice Tea
CA17/892 8 oz. Wine/Juice
CA17/705 9 oz. Mug/Cup
CA17/554 10 in. Plate
CA17/550 8 in. Plate
CA17/512 6 in. Bowl

Captiva Peach
CA18/891 13 oz. Goblet/Ice Tea
CA18/892 8 oz. Wine/Juice
CA18/705 9 oz. Mug/Cup
CA18/554 10 in. Plate
CA18/550 8 in. Plate
CA18/512 6 in. Bowl

Fostoria Glass Company
1200 First Street
Moundsville, West Virginia 26041
800-624-5497

14

©1983 Fostoria Glass Company

CENTENNIAL II

Lead Crystal
Crystal, Cobalt Blue, and Ruby as noted.
Centennial II was listed as a collection in 1970 – 1972.
Some pieces continued to be offered as Lead Crystal Gift Items after 1972.

In anticipation of the American Bicentennial, Fostoria reissued pieces from several patterns made in the early part of the century. All were made in lead crystal, with a few pieces being offered in Ruby and Cobalt Blue. The first Centennial II list appeared in the 1970 Supplement. Other items were added in 1972, 1973, and 1974. By 1976 the pieces still being made were listed as Lead Crystal, and some continued to be made until the factory was closed. There will be some duplication in listings for that reason. Pieces receiving the most attention are the ones made in color. The photograph below shows all those pieces with the exception of the Sherwood Square Vase in Cobalt Blue. Ash Trays, Napkin Rings, Coasters, and Salts were often sold in sets of four. Of note is the 2538 Place Card Holder/Ash Tray which was first listed in 1937 in crystal and colors (see also Ebony Glass, page 233). It was offered for only one year in lead crystal.

2864/123 Ash Tray, 5½", 1974-1977; $5.00
2864/145 Ash Tray "A", 3", 1974; $4.00
2864/147 Ash Tray "B", 2¾",
    1974-1978; $4.00

2864/148 Ash Tray "C", 3⅛",
    1974-1978; $4.00
1913/127 Basket, 11" Flemish,
    1970-1971; $195.00

Ruby Rambler Vase; Cobalt Blue Drape Bowl; Ruby Sovereign Salver, Louise Comport, Rambler Bowl

675/178 Bowl, 8" Round Serving, 1974; $12.00

1704/517 Bowl, 7½" Rosby,
   1970-1981; $18.00

1497/521 Bowl, 8½" Cresap,
   1970-1978; $18.00

1300/217 Bowl, 10½" Drape
   Cobalt Blue, 1970-1973; $250.00

1827/211 Bowl, 10½" Salad, Rambler
   Ruby, 1970-1973; $195.00

2377/355 Bowl, 5⅝" Snack,
   1974-1976; $15.00

2864/327 Candle "B", 2½",
   1979-1981; $10.00

2521/327 Candleholder, Bird,
   1974-1978; $16.00

2883/319 Candleholder, 6",
   (pair) 1974-1978; $24.00

2326/312 Candle Vase, 4¾",
   1974-1976; $10.00

2377/354 Candy Box and Cover,
   1974-1976; $40.00

1229/676 Candy Jar and Cover, Frisco,
   1970-1981; $42.00

2865/377 Coaster A, 3½" (set of 4),
   1973-1981; $12.00

2865/378 Coaster B, 3½" (set of 4),
   1973-1981; $12.00

2865/379 Coaster C, 3½" (set of 4),
   1973-1982; $12.00

2864/380 Coaster, 5½" Wine
   1973-1977; $6.00

1121/219 Compote, 9" Footed, Louise,
   1973-1974; $35.00
   Ruby, 1970-1973; $125.00

1467/509 Hostess Server with Chrome Spoon
   (same as Sweetmeat),
   1973-1982; $12.00

2377/447 Jelly and Cover, 8½" Footed,
   1974-1975; $32.00

2377/448 Jelly, 5⅝" Footed,
   1974-1975; $24.00

2183/475 Marmalade and Ladle, Colonial
   Prism, 1974: $24.00

2867/493 Napkin Ring A, 2" (set of 4),
   1973-1982; $20.00

2867/494 Napkin Ring B, 2" (set of 4),
   1973-1980; $20.00

1704/499 Nappy, 4¾" Regular, Handled,
   1971-1974; $15.00

1704/501 Nappy, 5", 3-cornered, Handled,
   1971-1972' $15.00

1467/516 Nappy, 6½" Shallow, Virginia,
   1972-1976; $12.00

2183/506 Nappy, 5" Colonial Prism,
   1974; $12.00

1467/540 Pickle, 8½" Virginia,

1972-1978; $14.00

2377/454 Pitcher, 7½" Quart, 1974; $27.00

2538/543 Place Card Holder/Ash Tray,
   1974 only; $9.00

1704/554 Plate, 10" Serving, Rosby,
   1970-1981; $15.00

1704/592 Preserve, 3 /12" Footed, Rosby,
   1970-1974; $15.00

1704/451 Preserve, 3½" Square Footed,
   Rosby, 1971-1972; $15.00

2679/591 Preserve and Cover,
   1974-1981; $22.00

1704/360 Relish, 10¼" Tray, Rosby
   1970-1981; $18.00

2867/623 Salt Dip, 2" (set of 4),
   1973-1982; $16.00

1641/630 Salver, 10" Round, Soverign
   Crystal, 1973-1978; $145.00
   Ruby, 1970-1973; $225.00

2183/297 Server and Cover, Colonial Prism
   1974-1976; $47.00

1871/649 Shaker, Chrome Top F,
   (pair) 1973-1981; $28.00

2883/654 Shaker, Chrome Top F,
   (pair) 1974-1975; $20.00

1704/676 Sugar, Rosby,
   1970-1974; $18.00

1704/680 Cream, Rosby,
   1970-1974; $14.00

2377/677 Sugar, 1974-1976; $12.00

2377/680 Cream, 1974-1976; $12.00

2710/687 Sugar, Individual, Daisy and Button,
   1974-1977; $12.00

2710/688 Cream, Individual, Daisy and
   Button, 1974-1977; $12.00

1467/512 Sweetmeat, 5½" Virginia,
   1970-1982; $8.00

2869/583 Tid Bit, Handled 7½",
   1973; $24.00

2000/710 Toothpick, 1974-1976; $22.00

2377/76 Tumbler, 4½", 1974-1975; $12.00

2883/329 Urn and Cover, 7⅝" Footed,
   1974-1979; $24.00

272/754 Vase/Candleholder, 5", 1974; $9.00

272/785 Vase/Candleholder, 8", 1974; $11.00

1300/217 Vase, 4½" Drape,
   1974-1976; $30.00

1605/601 Vase, 7¾" Square, Sherwood
   Cobalt Blue, 1970-1973; $300.00

1827/801 Vase, 9" Footed, Rambler
   Ruby, 1970-1973; $195.00

2377/785 Vase, 8", 1974; $18.00

2883/757 Vase, 6⅜" Bud, 1974-1978; $12.00

2883/761 Vase, 6" Footed, 1974-1978; $22.00

2883/162 Wedding Bowl and Cover, 8",
   1974-1979; $28.00

1913/127

1704/451

1641/630

2869/583

1871/654

2000/710

2183/297

2183/475
2183/482 2183/483

2377/355

2183/506

2326/312

2377/76

2538/543

2377/354

2377/447

2679/591

1300/217

2377/448

2377/677

2377/686

1704/499

2377/785

2377/454

2710/687

2710/688

2883/761

1467/516

1467/540

1704/501

2521/327

1467/512

1704/360

1605/601

2883/162

1704/517

1497/521

1704/554

2864/123

2864/145

2864/147

2883/757

2864/148

2864/327

2864/380

1229/676

2883/654

2865/377

2865/378

2865/379

1704/554

1704/592

2867/493

2867/623

2867/494

1704/676

1704/680

1704/517

1121/219

1827/801

2883/319

2883/329

1827/211

CROWN COLLECTION

2749 Windsor

133 Bottle and Stopper
    Crystal, 1962-1965; $95.00
    Royal Blue, 1962-1965; $125.00
    Gold, 1962-1965; $115.00
314 Candleholder, 3½" (pair)
    Crystal, 1962-1965; $85.00
    Royal Blue, 1962-1965; $115.00
    Gold, 1962-1965; $100.00
386 Chalice and Cover, 8½" Footed
    Crystal, 1961-1965; $85.00
    Royal Blue, 1961-1965; $100.00
    Gold, 1961-1965; $95.00
    Ruby, 1961-1965; $100.00
388 Chalice, 6¾" Footed

Crystal, 1961-1965; $65.00
Royal Blue, 1961-1965; $80.00
Gold, 1961-1965; $75.00
Ruby, 1961-1965; $80.00
676 Candy and Cover, 5½"
    Crystal, 1961-1965; $65.00
    Royal Blue, 1961-1965; $80.00
    Gold, 1961-1965; $75.00
    Ruby, 1961-1965; $80.00
677 Candy, 3¾" Open
    Crystal, 1961-1965; $45.00
    Royal Blue, 1961-1965; $60.00
    Gold, 1961-1965; $55.00
    Ruby, 1961-1965; $60.00

2750 Hapsburg

386 Chalice and Cover, 9¼" Footed
    Crystal, 1961-1965; $95.00
    Royal Blue, 1961-1965; $125.00
    Gold, 1961-1965; 115.00
    Ruby, 1961-1965; $125.00
388 Chalice, 7¼" Footed
    Crystal, 1961-1965; $75.00
    Royal Blue, 1961-1965; $100.00
    Gold, 1961-1965; $95.00
    Ruby, 1961-1965; $100.00

676 Candy and Cover, 5¾"
    Crystal, 1961-1965; $65.00
    Royal Blue, 1961-1965; $85.00
    Gold, 1961-1965; $75.00
    Ruby, 1961-1965; $85.00
677 Candy, 3¾"
    Crystal, 1961-1965; $45.00
    Royal Blue, 1961-1965; $60.00
    Gold, 1961-1965; $55.00
    Ruby, 1961-1965; $60.00

2751 Navarre

195 Bowl, 9"
    Crystal, 1961-1965; $55.00
    Royal Blue, 1961-1965; $75.00
    Gold, 1961-1965; $70.00
    Ruby, 1961-1965; $75.00
198 Bowl and Cover, 8½"
    Crystal, 1962-1965; $75.00
    Royal Blue, 1962-1965; $95.00
    Gold, 1962-1965; $85.00
    Ruby, 1962-1965; $95.00

199 Bowl, 9" Footed
    Crystal, 1961-1965; $95.00
    Royal Blue, 1961-1965; $125.00
    Gold, 1961-1965; $115.00
    Ruby, 1961-1965; $125.00
203 Bowl and Cover, 12⅛" Footed
    Crystal, 1962-1965; $120.00
    Royal Blue, 1962-1965; $150.00
    Gold, 1962-1965; $135.00
    Ruby, 1962-1965; $150.00

2766 Luxemburg

311 Bowl, 7¼" Trindle Candle
    Crystal, 1963-1965; $85.00
    Royal Blue, 1963-1965; $100.00

Gold, 1963-1965; $95.00
Ruby, 1963-1965; $100.00

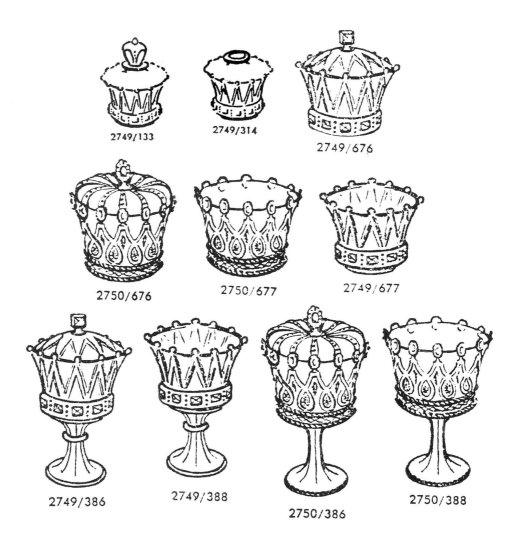

2749/133

2749/314

2749/676

2750/676

2750/677

2749/677

2749/386

2749/388

2750/386

2750/388

"Crowns-in-Crystal"

HANDCRAFTED BY

Fostoria

Fostoria's Crown Collection is fashioned after the famous crown designs of the Old World. Each owes its inspiration to the glittering splendor of an actual royal or imperial headpiece.

Originally, crowns were simple garlands, awarded for achievement in athletics or battle. They had no intrinsic value; the honor, early Romans felt, was reward enough. Rulers wore the diadem, a simple band of linen or silk, of Eastern origin.

Later, rewards became more material. The first soldier to scale a wall received a crown of gold, decorated with turrets. The one given the victor of a sea battle had points, symbolizing the prows of ships.

Crowns, as we know them, are a richly decorated combination of the award for achievement and the diadem which conferred authority.

Now Fostoria offers you these historic shapes in sparkling, hand-molded crystal, to enhance your modern decor with a touch of elegance out of the past. Use "Crowns-in-Crystal" for candy and nut dishes, in centerpiece arrangements, in matching pairs on mantels or end tables.

Hapsburg Gold Chalice and Cover, Navarre Ruby 9" Footed Bowl, Ruby Windsor Chalice and Cover, Hapsburg Royal Blue Candy and Cover, Windsor Royal Blue Candy and Cover, Windsor Gold Bottle and Stopper

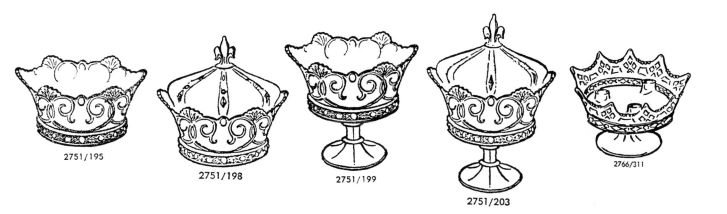

2751/195

2751/198

2751/199

2751/203

2766/311

DECORATOR COLLECTION

1964 – 1970
Teal Green, Lavender, Ruby

The Decorator Collection is an assortment of shapes some of which are drawn from other patterns. The 10" Pitch Vase has the 2666 Contour number but was never listed as Contour. Heights of the Flying Fish and Pitcher Vase will va Prices given are for Lavender and Ruby. Teal Green usually is less.

2424/179 Bowl, 6¾"
   Footed Petal; $30.00
2424/795 Basket, 10" Footed; $45.00
2497/787 Vase, Flying Fish
   (height varies); $40.00
2517/135 Bon Bon, 5" Handled; $25.00

2560/767 Vase, 6" Ruffled; $25.00
2666/807 Vase, 10" Pitcher
   (height varies); $57.00
2692/388 Comport, 6½" Footed; $30.00
2700/152 Bowl, 6" Hanky; $25.00
2718/828 Vase, 12" Footed Bud; $25.00

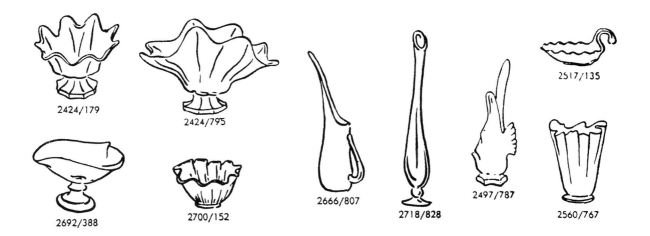

Ruby Pitcher Vase, Lavender Pitcher Vase, Footed Basket, Flying Fish; Teal Flying Fish, Ruby Bon Bon

DESIGNER COLLECTION

Each piece is dated and signed "Fostoria," with no two pieces exactly alike. In 1978 Fostoria sold Images for $25.00 each; Interpretations for $35.00 each; and Impressions for $50.00 each.

Images

IM 02/724-L, 4⅞" Vase, Crystal,
    1977-1978; $65.00
IM 02/725-M, Opal, 1977; $65.00
IM 02/727-N, 4¾" Vase, Purple,
    1977-1978; $95.00
IM 02/728-O, 6" Vase, Opal,
    1977-1978; $85.00

IM 02/731-P, 3¾" Vase, Crystal,
    1977-1978; $57.00
IM 02/739-S, 4⅜" Vase, Brown,
    1978; $50.00
IM 02/740-T, 2¾" Vase,
    Crystal Mist, 1978; $40.00

Impressions

IM 01/711-A, 10¾" Vase, Opal,
    1977-1978; $175.00
IM 01/712-B, 7¾" Vase, Crystal,
    1977-1978; $145.00

IM 01/713-C, Purple, 1977; $185.00
IM 01/714-D, Opal, 1977; $135.00
IM 01/733-V, 5¼" Vase,
    Crystal Mist, 1977; $95.00

Interpretations

IN 03/715-E, Opal, 1977; $95.00
IN 03/716-F, 6¼" Vase, Opal,
    1977-1978; $95.00
IN 03/717-G, 6½" Vase, Opal,
    1977-1978; $95.00
IN 03/718-H, Purple, 1977; $150.00
IN 03/719-I, 6¾" Vase, Crystal,
    1977-1978; $125.00

IN 03/721-J, 8" Vase, Purple,
    1977-1978; $150.00
IN 03/722-K, Crystal, 1977; $145.00
IN 03/735-U, 5" Vase, Crystal,
    1978; $95.00
IN 03/736-R, 6½" Vase, Brown,
    1978; $67.00

Images Purple Vase, Impressions Purple Vase, Images Brown Vase

DESIGNER COLLECTION

A totally new look, the Designer Collection offers uniqueness with each piece individually handcrafted. An original gift for any decor.

IM 01/712 B

IM 01/711 A

IM 01/713 C

IM 01/714 D

IN 03/719 I

IN 03/716 F

IN 03/717 G

IN 03/721 J

IN 03/718 H

IN 03/722 K

IM 02/725 M

IN 03/715 E

IM 02/724 L

IM 02/727 N

IM 02/731 P

IM 02/728 O

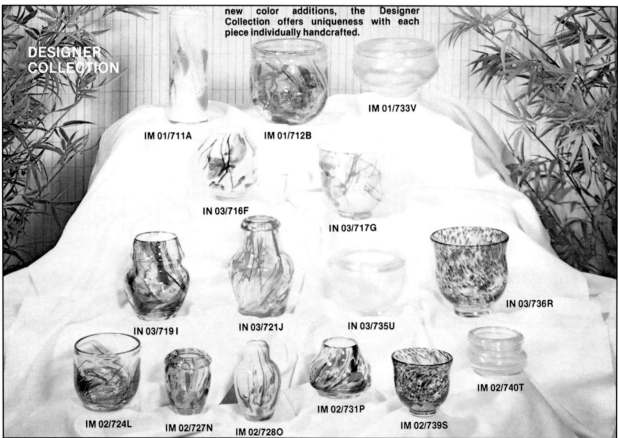

new color additions, the Designer Collection offers uniqueness with each piece individually handcrafted.

DESIGNER COLLECTION

IM 01/711A

IM 01/712B

IM 01/733V

IN 03/716F

IN 03/717G

IN 03/719 I

IN 03/721J

IN 03/735U

IN 03/736R

IM 02/724L

IM 02/727N

IM 02/728O

IM 02/731P

IM 02/739S

IM 02/740T

GARDEN CENTER ITEMS

(also called Garden Club Items)

In the early 1960s the rage in cosmetics was for the matte and frosted look. It was no different in glassware. Every color needed to be viewed as if through a frosted window, "softened," as it were, by the overlay of acid etching.

4166/151 Bowl, 5" Footed
  Silver Mist, 1960-1964; $18.00
2666/189 Bowl, 8¼" Oval
  Crystal, 1960-1961; $15.00
  Silver Mist, 1960-1964; $15.00
4166/199 Bowl, 9" Footed
  Silver Mist Spruce, 1960-1963; $28.00
2368/220 Bowl, 10½" Oblong
  Crystal, 1960-1964; $21.00
2596/215 Bowl, Oblong Shallow
  Silver Mist, 1960; $20.00
2703/189 Bowl, 14¾" Oblong
  Amethyst, 1964; $45.00
  Silver Mist Amethyst,
      1960-1964; $45.00
  Silver Mist Spruce, 1960-1964; $37.00
2692/234 Bowl, Footed Fruit
  Silver Mist, 1960-1964; $22.00
  Silver Mist Amethyst,
      1960-1962; $25.00
4116/291 Bubble Ball, 4"
  Cinnamon, 1964; $12.00
1121/389 Compote, 5¾"
  Silver Mist Milk Glass, 1960-1964; $20.00
  Silver Mist Amber, 1960-1963; $22.00
2364/197 Lily Pond, 9"
  Crystal, 1960-1962; $18.00
  Silver Mist, 1960-1964; $18.00
2364/251 Lily Pond, 12"
  Crystal, 1960-1962; $20.00
  Silver Mist, 1960-1964; $20.00
834/70 Pitcher, Jenny Lind
  Silver Mist Amber, 1960-1963; $54.00
  Silver Mist Milk Glass,
      1960-1964; $45.00

2703/191 Plate, 13" Square Buffet
  Crystal, 1964; $24.00
  Marine, 1964; $30.00
  Amethyst, 1964; $30.00
2725/761 Urn, 5¾" Handled
  Silver Mist, 1960-1963; $10.00
  Silver Mist Spruce, 1960-1963; $12.00
2692/760 Urn, 6" Handled
  Silver Mist, 1960-1962; $20.00
2692/828 Urn, 12" Handled
  Silver Mist, 1960-1962; $47.00
2693/162 Urn, Franklin, and Cover
  Silver Mist Milk Glass,
      1960-1964; $42.00
4152/751 Vase Bowl, 3⅞"
  Silver Mist, 1960-1964; $10.00
  Silver Mist Spruce, 1960-1964; $10.00
4121/754 Vase, 5"
  Crystal, 1964; $12.00
  Spruce, 1964; $12.00
  Chartreuse, 1964; $18.00
4166/757 Vase, 6" Bud
  Crystal, 1960; $18.00
  Silver Mist Amber, 1960; $20.00
  Silver Mist Amethyst, 1960; $20.00
  Silver Mist Milk Glass, 1960; $18.00
2724/779 Vase, 7½" Goblet
  Silver Mist Amber, 1960-1964; $15.00
  Silver Mist Spruce, 1960-1962; $15.00
2577/792 Vase, 8½"
  Crystal, 1960; $20.00
  Silver Mist, 1960; $20.00
  Silver Mist Amber, 1960; $22.00
  Silver Mist Amethyst, 1960; $22.00
  Silver Mist Milk Glass, 1960; $20.00

2703/191

4116/291

4121/754

834/70
Jenny Lind Pitcher
Height 8¼ in.

1121/389—5¾ in.
Comport

2364/197.—9 in.
Lily Pond
Height 2 in.

2364/251—12 in.
Lily Pond
Height 2¼ in.

2577/792—8½ in.
Vase

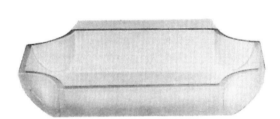

2596/215
Oblong Shallow Bowl
Length 11 in.
Height 2 in.

2638/220
10½" Oblong Bowl
Height 4½"

2666/189
Oval Bowl
Diameter 8¼ in.
Height 3¼ in.

2692/234—6½ in.
Fruit Bowl
Length 9¼ in. Height 5½ in.

2692/760—6 in.
Handled Urn
Height 6 in.

2692/828—12 in.
Handled Urn

2693/162
Franklin Urn & Cover
Height 8½ in.

2703/189
Oblong Bowl
Length 14¾ in.
Width 10¼ in.

2724/779—7½ in.
Goblet Vase

2725/761
Handled Urn
Height 4⅜ in.
Diameter 5¾ in.

4152/751
Vase Bowl
Height 3⅞ in.

4166/151—5 in.
Footed Bowl
Height 5½ in.

4166/199—9 in.
Footed Bowl
Height 6¼ in.

4166/757—6 in.
Bud Vase

GOURMET SERVICE

1977 – 1978
Crystal, Brown, Green

GO05/064 Tumbler, 5⅛", 14 oz.; $5.75
GO05/159 Salad/Soup, 6¼"; $5.75
GO05/396 Cup, Handled; $5.25
GO05/554 Plate, 10½" Dinner; $8.00
GO05/666 Snack Set (Boxed Plate, Soup, and Cup); $18.50

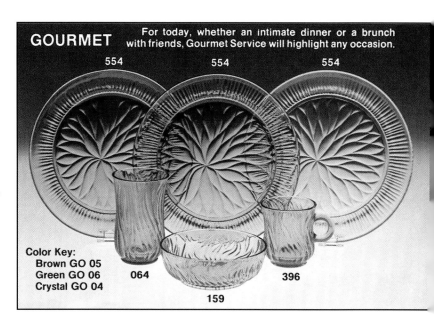

Garden Center Jenny Lind Pitchers in Silver Mist Amethyst and Amber (neither color listed)

1871 HERITAGE COLLECTION

Crystal
1972 – 1973
A few pieces continued to be made as Lead Crystal Giftware through 1982.

521 Bowl, 8 ⅜"; $20.00
506 Bowl, 5" Fruit, 1972-1982; $15.00
354 Candy Box and Cover; $22.00
899 Double Old Fashioned (boxed set of 4); $28.00
871 Highball (boxed set of 4); $32.00
454 Jug, Quart; $45.00
869 Plate, 7" (boxed set of 4); $28.00
550 Plate, 8", 1972-1982; $8.00
682 Sugar/Cover and Cream; $25.00
583 Tidbit Set, 3-piece; $30.00
567 Torte Plate; $30.00

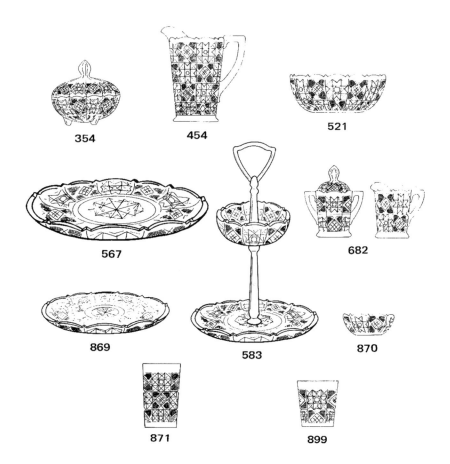

GROUP INTERNATIONAL

Pieces were made in 2795 Shantung and 2796 Coventry (solid colors with crystal middle standard) from 1967 – 1968. The colors listed are from the Morgantown period. One price is given which applies to all colors or combination of color and crystal. Note how different the Candle Lamps in the photograph are from those in the line drawings.

2795/250 Bowl, 12"; $75.00
    Fern Green Bowl
    Tangerine Base
    Mayan Blue Bowl
    Fern Green Base
2795/234 Bowl, 16"; $100.00
    Fern Green Bowl
    Tangerine Base
    Mayan Blue Bowl
    Fern Green Base
2795/325 Candleholder, 8" (pair); $95.00
    Fern Green
    Mayan Blue
    Tangerine
2795/330 Candleholder, 12" (pair); $125.00
    Fern Green
    Mayan Blue
    Tangerine
2795/833 Candle Vase, 18"; $145.00
    Fern Green Bowl
    Mayan Blue Bowl
    Fern Green Base
2795/835 Candle Vase, 22"; $165.00
    Fern Green Bowl
    Tangerine Base
    Mayan Blue Bowl
    Fern Green Base
2796/325 Candleholder, 8" (pair); $95.00
    Fern Green
    Mayan Blue
    Tangerine
2796/384 Compote, 10"; $95.00
    Fern Green
    Mayan Blue
    Tangerine
2796/459 Candle Lamp, 19"; $150.00
    Fern Green
    Mayan Blue
    Tangerine

2796 Coventry Candle Lamps
Tangerine and Mayan Blue

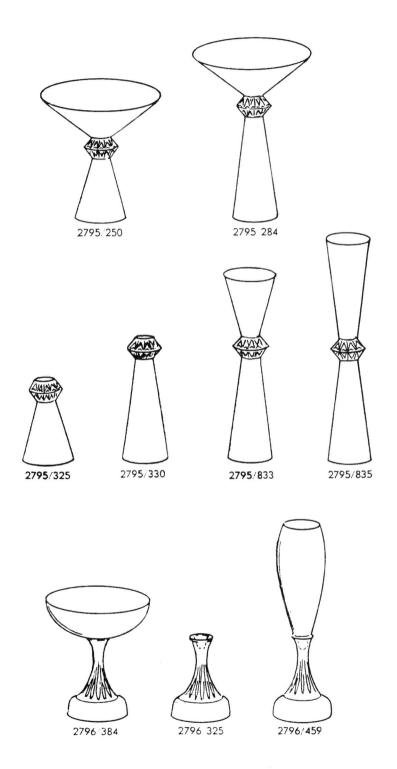

2795/250

2795 284

2795/325

2795/330

2795/833

2795/835

2796 384

2796 325

2796/459

HEIRLOOM

One of the most beautiful of the decorator lines, Heirloom was made from 1959 – 1970 in opalescent colors of Yellow, Blue, Green, Pink, and Opal and in regular colors of Ruby and Bittersweet. Though not listed, pieces have been reported in Crystal.

The 18" and 24" Vases were listed only in 1959. In 1960 a 20" Vase is listed, a possible compromise on sizes, which continued in production through 1962. Two of the few epergnes made by the Fostoria Company were in this pattern. The smaller epergne was formed by turning the 6" Candlestick upside down to fit over a peg in the Oval Bowl. Sizes vary on most pieces as they are all shaped by hand.

The Bittersweet color, a bright orange, was listed in 1960 – 1962. Yellow was not made after 1962, causing it to be one of the more difficult colors to find. Some pieces were made for a very limited time in any color.

A few pieces in Heirloom can brighten any decor. Certainly, Fostoria designed this glassware to be enjoyed for its beautiful color or its unique design. Collectors tend to prefer one color over the others, but a few hardy souls have managed to find nearly every piece in all the colors in which it was made: a stunning collection.

One price is given for each piece and holds for any color unless that color is given a different price.

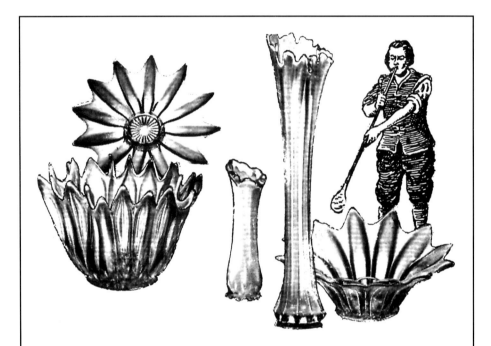

Fine Giftware with Fashion Flair . . .

FOSTORIA'S NEW "HEIRLOOM"

This is an entirely different kind of glassware. The color blendings are unique. All pieces are available in pink, yellow, green, blue and opal. It's made like handmade antique glass. Thus the name, Heirloom, for this group of 'free-form' shapes. We hardly have to suggest the exciting decorative possibilities.

Heirloom's delicate beauty begins in fire. Here you see molten glass being gathered by hand from the furnace.

After molding, the glass, still pliable, is swung by the craftsman to stretch it and form the shapes. Each is unique.

Add a unique continental flair with new handmade Fostoria "Heirloom"

Look closely! You'll see this is an entirely different kind of glassware. One woman who saw it said, "It looks modern, sort of continental, but it's made like handmade antique glass."

Thus the name, *Heirloom,* for this group of "free-form" shapes. We hardly have to suggest the exciting decorative possibilities. Even the few pieces we show here suggest dozens — and there are many more for you to see in person. We'll tell you where — and send you an illustrated leaflet with prices (as low as $1.75). Write today. Fostoria Glass Company, Moundsville, West Virginia.

Working entirely by hand, this artisan uses ancient skills and methods to give an Heirloom vase its final graceful shape.

Fine Crystal with Fashion Flair . . . Fostoria

2720 Basket; $54.00
  Yellow, 1959-1960
  Blue, 1959-1960
  Pink, 1959-1960
  Green, 1959-1960
  Opal, 1959-1960
  Bittersweet, 1960
2729 Bon Bon; $42.00
  Yellow, 1960-1962; $48.00
  Blue, 1960-1970
  Pink, 1960-1970
  Green, 1960-1970
  Opal, 1960-1970
  Bittersweet, 1960-1962
  Ruby, 1961-1970
2720 Bowl, 5⅜" Square Florette; $48.00
  Yellow, 1959-1962
  Blue, 1959-1962
  Pink, 1959-1962
  Green, 1959-1962
  Opal, 1959-1962
  Bittersweet, 1960-1962
2727 Bowl, 6" Hanky; $35.00
  Yellow, 1960-1962; $45.00
  Blue, 1960-1970
  Pink, 1960-1970
  Green, 1960-1970
  Opal, 1960-1970
  Bittersweet, 1960-1962; $40.00
  Ruby, 1961-1970

2727 Bowl, 6" Square; $40.00
  Yellow, 1960-1962
  Blue, 1960-1962
  Pink, 1960-1962
  Green, 1960-1962
  Opal, 1960-1962
  Bittersweet, 1960-1962
2720 Bowl, 6½" Crinkled; $40.00
  Yellow, 1959-1962
  Blue, 1959-1962
  Pink, 1959-1962
  Green, 1959-1962
  Opal, 1959-1962
  Bittersweet, 1960-1962
2183 Bowl, 7"; $35.00
  Yellow, 1959-1962; $42.00
  Blue, 1959-1970
  Pink, 1959-1960
  Green, 1959-1970
  Opal, 1959-1970
  Bittersweet, 1960-1962; $40.00
  Ruby, 1961-1970
2720 Bowl, 8½" Star; $45.00
  Yellow, 1959-1960
  Blue, 1959-1960
  Pink, 1959-1960
  Green, 1959-1960
  Opal, 1959-1960
  Bittersweet, 1960; $55.00
2727 Bowl, 9" Square; $65.00

Yellow Heirloom Winged Vase,
Oblong Bowl, Basket, Bud Vase

Yellow, 1960-1962
Blue, 1960-1962
Pink, 1960-1962
Green, 1960-1962
Opal, 1960-1962
Bittersweet, 1960-1962
1515 Bowl, 10"; $60.00
Yellow, 1959-1962; $65.00
Blue, 1959-1970
Pink, 1959-1970
Green, 1959-1970
Opal, 1959-1962
Bittersweet, 1960-1962
2183 Bowl, 10" Float; $48.00
Yellow, 1959-1962; $54.00
Blue, 1959-1970
Pink, 1959-1970
Green, 1959-1970
Opal, 1959-1970
Bittersweet, 1960-1962; $52.00
2729 Bowl, 10" Oval; $44.00
Yellow, 1960-1962
Blue, 1960-1962
Pink, 1960-1962
Green, 1960-1962
Opal, 1960-1962
Bittersweet, 1960-1962
Ruby, 1961-1962
2727 Bowl, 11" Shallow; $50.00
Yellow, 1960-1962

Blue, 1960-1962
Pink, 1960-1962
Green, 1960-1962
Opal, 1960-1962
Bittersweet, 1960-1962
2727 Bowl, 11" Crimped; $54.00
Yellow, 1960-1962; $60.00
Blue, 1960-1970
Pink, 1960-1970
Green, 1960-1970
Opal, 1960-1970
Bittersweet, 1960-1962; $58.00
Ruby, 1961-1970
1515 Bowl, 15" Oblong; $75.00
Yellow, 1959-1962; $85.00
Blue, 1959-1970
Pink, 1959-1970
Green, 1959-1970
Opal, 1959-1970
Bittersweet, 1960-1962; $85.00
2183 Candle, Flora; $45.00
Yellow, 1959-1962
Blue, 1959-1962
Pink, 1959-1962
Green, 1959-1962
Opal, 1959-1962
Bittersweet, 1960-1962
2726 Candleholder (pair); $67.00
Yellow, 1959-1962; $75.00
Blue, 1959-1970

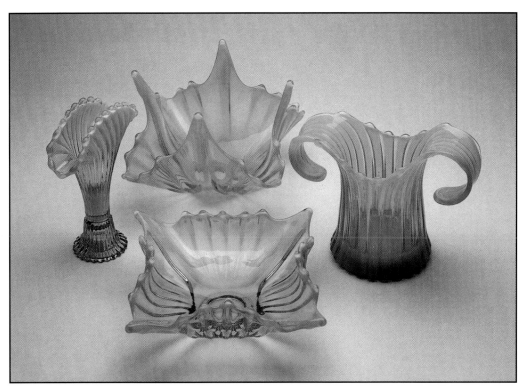

*Yellow Heirloom Candle Vase
(whimsey), Crinkle Bowl,
Handled Vase, Star Bowl*

Pink, 1959-1970
Green, 1959-1970
Opal, 1959-1970
Bittersweet, 1960-1962
Ruby, 1961-1970
2730 Candle, 6" (pair); $95.00
Yellow, 1960-1962
Blue, 1960-1962
Pink, 1960-1962
Green, 1960-1962
Opal, 1960-1962
Bittersweet, 1960-1962
1515 Centerpiece, 16" Oval; $125.00
Yellow, 1960-1961
Blue, 1960-1961
Pink, 1960-1961
Green, 1960-1961
Opal, 1960-1961
Bittersweet, 1960-1961
2730 Epergne, 12" Small; $125.00
2730 12" Epergne Bowl
2730 7" Epergne Vase
Yellow, 1960-1962
Blue, 1960-1962
Pink, 1960-1962
Green, 1960-1962
Opal, 1960-1962
Bittersweet, 1960-1962
1515 Epergne, 16" Large; $195.00
1515 16" Epergne Bowl
1515 9" Epergne Vase

Yellow, 1960-1961
Blue, 1960-1961
Pink, 1960-1961
Green, 1960-1961
Opal, 1960-1961
Bittersweet, 1960-1961
2727 Plate, 8"; $38.00
Yellow, 1960-1962
Blue, 1960-1962
Pink, 1960-1962
Green, 1960-1962
Opal, 1960-1962
Bittersweet, 1960-1962
2727 Plate, 11"; $56.00
Yellow, 1960-1962
Blue, 1960-1962
Pink, 1960-1962
Green, 1960-1962
Opal, 1960-1962
Bittersweet, 1960-1962
2570 Plate, 17"; $75.00
Yellow, 1959-1962
Blue, 1959-1962
Pink, 1959-1962
Green, 1959-1962
Opal, 1959-1962
Bittersweet, 1960-1962
2728 Vase, 4½" Handled; $125.00
Yellow, 1960-1962
Blue, 1960-1961
Pink, 1960-1961

Bittersweet 6" Candles, Oblong Bowl, Hanky Bowl, 7" Bowl

Green, 1960-1961
Opal, 1960-1961
Bittersweet, 1960-1961
1229 Vase, 6" Bud; $30.00
    Yellow, 1959-1962; $35.00
    Blue, 1959-1970
    Pink, 195901970
    Green, 1959-1970
    Opal, 1959-1970
    Bittersweet, 1960; $35.00
    Ruby, 1961-1970
2728 Vase, 9" Pitcher; $115.00
    Yellow, 1960-1962; $135.00
    Blue, 1960-1970
    Pink, 1960-1970
    Green, 1960-1970
    Opal, 1960-1970
    Bittersweet, 1960-1962; $125.00
    Ruby, 1961-1970
1515 Vase, 10" Candle; $85.00
    1959-1961
    Blue, 1959-1961
    Pink, 1959-1961
    Green, 1959-1961
    Opal, 1959-1961
    Bittersweet, 1960-1961
1515 Vase, 11"; $40.00
    Yellow, 1959-1962; $55.00
    Blue, 1959-1970
    Pink, 1959-1970

Green, 1959-1970
Opal, 1959-1970
Bittersweet, 1960-1962; $50.00
Ruby, 1961-1970
2728 Vase, 11" Winged; $150.00
    Yellow, 1960
    Blue, 1960
    Pink, 1960
    Green, 1960
    Opal, 1960
    Bittersweet, 1960
1002 Vase, 18"; $175.00
    Yellow, 1959
    Blue, 1959
    Pink, 1959
    Green, 1959
    Opal, 1959
1002 Vase, 20"; $145.00
    Yellow, 1960-1962
    Blue, 1960-1962
    Pink, 1960-1962
    Green, 1960-1962
    Opal, 1960-1962
    Bittersweet, 1960-1962
1002 Vase, 24"; $195.00
    Yellow, 1959
    Blue, 1959
    Pink, 1959
    Green, 1959
    Opal, 1959

Ruby Pitcher Vase, Oval Centerpiece, Crimped Bowl, 10" Oval Bowl

Blue Winged Vase, 11" and 9" Vases,
Opal Bud Vase, 3½" Candlestick, Bon Bon

Green Candle Vase, 10" Bowl, Flora Candle

Pink Large Epergne,
3½" Candles, 9"
Square Bowl

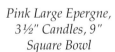

Green 17" Plate,
Flower Float

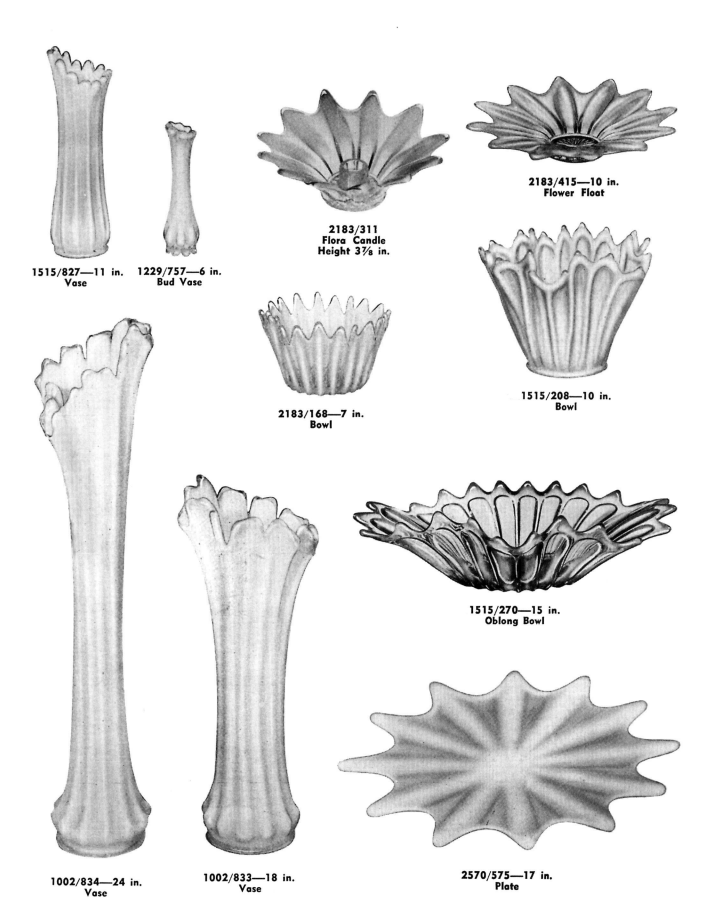

1515/827—11 in.
Vase

1229/757—6 in.
Bud Vase

2183/311
Flora Candle
Height 3⅞ in.

2183/415—10 in.
Flower Float

2183/168—7 in.
Bowl

1515/208—10 in.
Bowl

1515/270—15 in.
Oblong Bowl

1002/834—24 in.
Vase

1002/833—18 in.
Vase

2570/575—17 in.
Plate

1002/834—20 in.
Vase

1515/827—11 in.
Vase

1229/757—6 in.
Bud Vase

1515/208—10 in.
Bowl

1515/270—15 in.
Oblong Bowl

2183/311
Flora Candle
Height 3 7/8 in.

1515/279—16 in.
Oval Centerpiece

1515/311—10 in.
Candle Vase

1515/364
Large Epergne
Height 9 1/2 in.
Consisting of:
1—1515/312 9 in. Epergne Vase
1—1515/413 16 in. Egergne Bowl

2720/168—6 1/2 in.
Crinkle Bowl
Height 4 1/2 in.

2183/415—10 in.
Flower Float

2570/575—17 in.
Plate

2720/126
Basket
Length 12 in. Width 5 in.

2183/168—7 in.
Bowl

2720/170
Square Florette
Width 5⅜ in. Height 3½ in.

2720/191—8½ in.
Star Bowl
Width 8¼ in. Height 2¾ in.

2726/311
Candleholder
Height 3½ in.

2727/202—9 in.
Square Bowl
Height 3⅝ in.

2727/231—11 in.
Shallow Bowl
Height 2 in.

2727/557—11 in.
Plate

2727/239—11 in.
Bowl Crimped
Height 2½ in.

2727/550—8 in.
Plate

2727/152—6 in.
Hanky Bowl
Height 2½ in.

2727/155—6 in.
Square Bowl
Height 2 in.

2728/751—4½ in.
Handled Vase

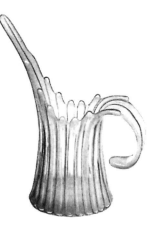

2728/807—9 in.
Pitcher Vase

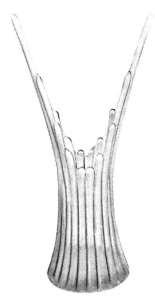

2728/827—11 in
Winged Vase

2729/540—10 in.
Oval Bowl
Width 5½ in. Height 2½ in.

2730/255—12 in.
Oval Centerpiece
Height 3 in. Width 5 in.

2729/135
Bon Bon
Length 7 in. Width 5½ in.

2730/319—6 in.
Candle

2730/364—12 in.
Small Epergne
Height 6½ in. Width 5 in.
Consisting of:
1—2730/254 12 in. Epergne Bowl
1—2730/319 7 in. Epergne Vase

HENRY FORD MUSEUM COLLECTION

Fostoria was quite proud of the Henry Ford Museum Collection and marked pieces with an "HFM." Occasionally, the fire polishing was too intense, and the initials were nearly burned off, but most often they can be seen and felt. Pages from the official brochure published by Fostoria to feature the Henry Ford Museum Collection are included here. The Exeter (6109) pattern and Panelled Diamond Point (2860) were also part of the Henry Ford project. They are featured in *Fostoria Stemware*, pages 133 and 52, respectively.

2770 Argus

The tableware pattern chosen for this collection was Argus, one of the earliest patterns of American pressed flint glass. Stemware is featured in *Fostoria Stemware*, page 50.

Compote and Cover
    Crystal, 1964-1973; $95.00
    Cobalt Blue, 1964-1973; $125.00
    Olive, 1964-1973; $95.00
    Ruby, 1964-1973; $125.00
Dessert
    Crystal, 1963-1982; $24.00
    Cobalt Blue, 1963-1982; $27.00
    Olive, 1963-1982; $24.00
    Smoke, 1972-1982; $24.00
    Ruby, 1964-1982; $28.00

Plate, 8"
    Crystal, 1963-1982; $24.00
    Cobalt Blue, 1963-1982; $27.00
    Olive, 1963-1982; $24.00
    Smoke, 1972-1982; $24.00
    Ruby, 1964-1982; $28.00
Sugar and Cover, Cream
    Crystal, 1964-1973; $115.00
    Cobalt Blue, 1964-1973; $125.00
    Olive, 1964-1973; $115.00
    Ruby, 1964-1973; $135.00

Copper Blue Sandwich Candlesticks, Crystal Four Petal Candy,
Copper Blue Ribbon Comport, Strawberry Diamond Salts and Spoons

Handmade
Flint Glass Reproductions
from the
Henry Ford Museum
Collection
by

The
Henry Ford Museum

It was Henry Ford's wish to "collect the history of our people as written into things their hands made and used." Mr. Ford predicted, "When we are through, we shall have reproduced American life and preserved in actual working form a part of our history and our tradition."

From his idea grew the Henry Ford Museum and Greenfield Village in Dearborn, Michigan . . . the greatest collection ever assembled of objects made by hand . . . by Americans in the early years of our country.

Comprising more than 250 acres, this museum of American life as our forefathers knew it and lived it is seen each year by millions of Americans and visitors from all over the world.

American glass was of particular interest to Henry Ford. And his collection of pressed and pattern glass is one of the largest and most representative in the country.

The Museum has invited distinguished American manufacturers to make and market reproductions of the antique originals shown in the Museum, so that you may enjoy the best of our past in your home today.

Fostoria Glass Company has been appointed the exclusive manufacturer of glassware reproductions—both authentic tableware and prized decorative pieces in fine Flint Glass for today's "collector's look" in decorating.

The
Beauty of Flint Glass

Flint glass was named in England where it was discovered that small pieces of flint stones, ground up and put into the glass as an ingredient, gave crystal a higher quality of refraction. This made a faceted or molded design (such as Argus) gain superior brilliance and sparkle.

Later it was discovered that lead would impart the same quality and it was substituted for flint. The name "flint glass" remains, however, to mean *lead glass of high quality*.

The first flint glass was made in America in 1769. Quantity production became possible with the invention of the hand press in the 1820's, and by 1840, complete table settings were available in pressed glass. At that time, manufacturers began the custom of naming their patterns. Argus, which is reproduced today by Fostoria, was one of the earliest named patterns; original pieces are very rare.

The "HFM" Marking—If you examine a piece from Fostoria's Henry Ford Museum Collection closely, you will notice that the letters "HFM" appear as a signature. Every piece of glassware made for the Museum Collection carries this hallmark.
The letters, of course, stand for the name of the Museum, and distinguish the pieces as authorized reproductions.

Complete Argus service: 10½ oz. Goblet, 4 oz. Wine, 8 oz. Sherbet, 4½ oz. Tumbler/Juice/Cocktail, 10 oz. Tumbler/Old Fashioned, 12 oz. Tumbler/Highball, 13 oz. Luncheon Goblet/Ice Tea, Dessert, Covered Compote, Covered Sugar and Creamer, 8 in. Plate.

Argus

Very few pieces remain today of the original *Argus*, one of the earliest patterns of American pressed flint glass. Some of the reproductions are line for line copies of the original tumblers housed in the Henry Ford Museum. Others have been adapted to provide items which were not used in Early America, but are needed to fit current customs of living.

FOSTORIA has carefully recreated the features distinguishing the originals. The hand-molding produces glassware so durable and sturdy that it is suitable for everyday use. Yet the sparkle and luster imparted by use of "flint glass" invite association with your finest china, silver, and linens . . . giving you a dual purpose type of service. The extensiveness of the line makes possible a coordinated service from cocktails through dessert.

The original *Argus* was made in crystal. The ruby, cobalt blue and olive green were chosen with the approval of the Museum as colors representative of the same historical period and considered most compatible with contemporary decorating trends.

a circa 1830

b circa 1850   c circa 1830   d circa 1850

For detailed
descriptions
of these pieces
see the
next page.

e circa 1850   f circa 1850

g circa 1850

h circa 1835-1845

j circa 1830-1840   k circa 1840   i circa 1835-1845

Decorative Glassware

a   The very early *Four Petal* pattern is known only in a deep bowl, a creamer, and the *Covered Sugar Bowl.* The pattern is especially rare in the electric blue color of the original in the Henry Ford Museum.

b   It is thought that the *Dolphin** was probably copied from imported pieces since the Dolphin was used extensively as a design motif.

c   *The Sandwich Candlestick* reflects the tendency of the early pressed glass manufacturers to rely on elegant imported glass pieces for their design inspiration.

d   The *Pressed Block Footed Bowl* is attributed to Bakewell Pears & Co. in Pittsburgh, but others like it may have been made in Sandwich, Massachusetts.

e & f   A rarity in Ribbon Glass is the original *Compote** with *Rebecca-at-the-Well* pedestal. The figure is also found as a *Candlestick*.*

g   The *Covered Ribbon** Compote was originally frosted by a grinding process. Later acid was used to attain the effect which some collectors mistakenly call camphor glass.

h & i   The *Tulip Vase* was originally designed and catalogued as a celery holder; the *Draped Vase* was designed for flowers. The originals were made at Sandwich, Massachusetts.

j   The general practice in making compotes was to attach unmatched pedestals to bowls or dishes in currently popular designs. One exception is the lacy *Plume Compote* in which the patterns match. The Plume patterned pedestal was also used for compotes with other dish patterns. These patterns were attributed to the Boston and Sandwich Glass Companies.

k   One of the rare lacy salts, the *Strawberry Diamond Salt Dish* was manufactured in Sandwich, and originals today are found rarely in blue, more rarely in green.

Decorative Glassware

2776/327 Candlestick, 9" Sandwich (pair)
 Crystal, 1965-1977; $60.00
 Olive Green, 1965-1971; $70.00
 Copper Blue, 1965-1971; $125.00
2777/327 Candlestick, 9" Rebecca (pair)
 Crystal Mist, 1965-1970; $195.00
 Olive Green Mist, 1965-1970; $225.00
 Copper Blue Mist, 1965-1970; $250.00
2777/388 Compote, 12¾" Rebecca Ribbon
 Crystal Mist, 1965-1970; $150.00
 Olive Green Mist, 1965-1970; $175.00
 Copper Blue Mist, 1965-1970; $225.00
2778/347 Candy and Cover, 8", 4-petal
 Crystal, 1965-1972; $40.00
 Olive Green, 1965-1972; $50.00
 Copper Blue, 1965-1972; $65.00
2779/219 Bowl, 10½" Footed Pressed Block
 Crystal, 1965-1971; $78.00
 Olive Green, 1965-1971; $100.00
 Copper Blue, 1965-1971; $125.00
2780/388 Compote, 8" Dolphin
 Crystal Mist, 1965-1971; $85.00

 Olive Green Mist, 1965-1971; $110.00
 Copper Blue Mist, 1965-1971; $125.00
2786/803 Vase, 9" Sandwich Draped
 Crystal, 1965-1970; $75.00
 Olive Green, 1965-1970; $85.00
 Copper Blue, 1965-1970; $95.00
2787/387 Compote, 6½" Ribbon, and Cover
 Crystal, 1965-1970; $55.00
 Olive Green, 1965-1970; $64.00
 Copper Blue, 1965-1970; $70.00
2788/389 Compote, Plume
 Crystal, 1966-1972; $50.00
 Olive Green, 1966-1971; $54.00
 Copper Blue, 1966-1972; $58.00
2790/818 Vase, 10" Footed Tulip
 Crystal, 1966-1970; $68.00
 Olive Green, 1966-1970; $72.00
 Copper Blue, 1966-1970; $78.00
2793/105 Salt, 3¼" Strawberry Diamond
 Crystal, 1966-1973; $22.00
 Olive Green, 1966-1973; $27.00
 Copper Blue, 1966-1973; $30.00

Copper Blue Rebecca Comport and Candlestick;
Olive Green Rebecca Candlestick; Silver Mist Rebecca Candlestick

SERENDIPITY

A unique assortment, not extremely practical, but certainly interesting. Notice that the drawings of the family paper weights are different from the actual pieces.

2842/112 Ash Tray/Candle, 2",
    1973-1974; $30.00
2842/124 Ash Tray, 9½", 1972-1974; $38.00
2842/311 Candleholder, Individual,
    (pair) 1972-1974; $38.00
2842/327 Candleholder, 9½",
    (pair) 1972-1974; $38.00
2842/539 Paperweight, 1972-1974; $34.00
2856/117 Ash Tray "B", 7", 1974; $38.00
2856/118 Ash Tray "D", 7", 1974; $38.00
2856/139 Bookend "A", 5", (pair) 1974; $65.00
2856/140 Bookend "B", 5", (pair) 1974; $65.00
2856/141 Bookend "E", 5", (pair) 1974; $75.00
2856/539 Paperweight "A", 6",
    1972-1973; $35.00
2856/545 Paperweight "B", 6",
    1972-1973; $35.00
2856/546 Paperweight "C", 6",
    1972-1973; $35.00
2856/547 Paperweight "D", 6",
    1972-1973; $35.00
2857/124 Ash Tray, 10", 1972-1973; $40.00
2857/117 Ash Tray, 7", 1972-1973; $37.00
2858/152 Crimp (Bowl), 5", 1972-1973; $28.00
2858/178 Crimp (Bowl), 8", 1972-1973; $38.00

2858/207 Crimp (Bowl), 10", 1972-1973; $45.00
2825/139 Bookend, 4¾" Small Shell,
    (pair) 1973-1974; $75.00
2825/140 Bookend, 5¾" Large Shell,
    (pair) 1973-1974; $85.00
2866/313 Candle, 2" (pair); $30.00
2866/315 Candle, 4" (pair) 1973-1974; $34.00
2866/319 Candle, 6" (pair) 1973-1974; $38.00
2868/539 Family Paperweight, Child, 4",
    1973; $95.00
2868/545 Family Paperweight, Mother,
    5½", 1973; $115.00
2868/546 Family Paperweight, Father,
    7½", 1973; $125.00

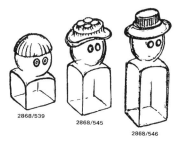

2868/539   2868/545   2868/546

Child and Mother Family Paperweight

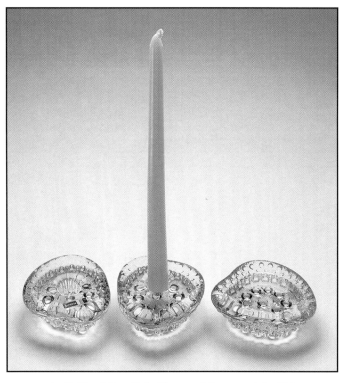

Individual Candleholders and Paperweight 539

Small Shell Bookends, Paperweights A and D

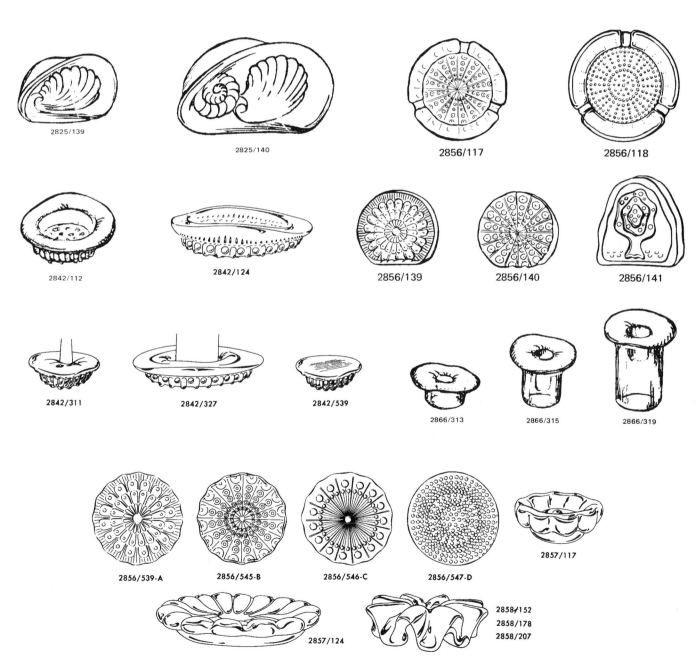

2825/139

2825/140

2856/117

2856/118

2842/112

2842/124

2856/139

2856/140

2856/141

2842/311

2842/327

2842/539

2866/313

2866/315

2866/319

2856/539-A

2856/545-B

2856/546-C

2856/547-D

2857/117

2857/124

2858/152
2858/178
2858/207

GIFTWARE

Bar Boutique
Bell Collection
Blown Stemware and Giftware
Boutique Giftware
Candlestick Collection
Candle Vase Collection
Celestial
Colonial Prism Giftware
Holly and Ruby Giftware
Hostess, Serveware and Heritage Giftware
Lead Crystal Giftware
Light Show Collection
Lotus Giftware
Maypole Giftware
Morning Glory Giftware
Personalized Giftware
Shaker Collection
Starlight
Satin Mist Pattern
Swirl Pattern
Transition
Vase Collection
Virginia Giftware
Woodland Gift Items

BAR BOUTIQUE

A rectangular Tray and insulated Ice Bucket made of heavy plastic were offered in 1984 in the Captiva and Heritage patterns. Also a High Ball and Double Old Fashioned were made in the Captiva pattern. Heritage already had barware and stemware (see *Fostoria Stemware*).

783 Captiva Tray; $22.00
973 Captiva Ice Bucket; $35.00
888 Captiva High Ball; $18.00

339 Captiva Old Fashioned; $18.00
783 Heritage Tray; $22.00
973 Heritage Ice Bucket; $35.00

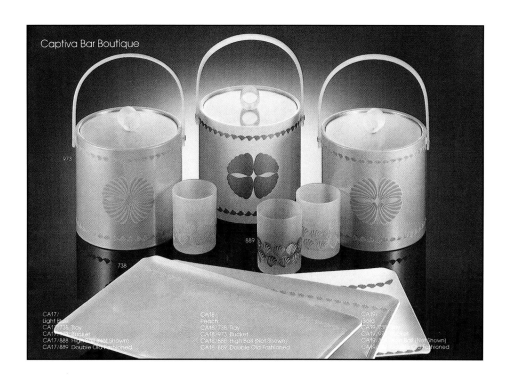

BELL COLLECTION

Offered as a collection 1981 – 1982.

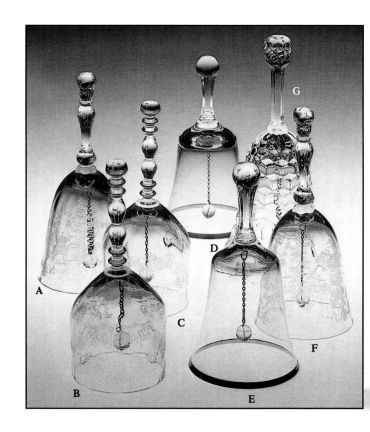

AM01/047 American (G.)(1981-1982); $450.00/market
NA02/047 Navarre
    A. Blue (1976-1982); $150.00
    F. Crystal (1976-1982); $95.00
RI01/047 Richmond (D.)(1977-1982); $40.00
SE04/047 Serenity
    B. Crystal (1977-1982); $85.00
    C. Blue (1977-1982); $125.00
SH03/047 Sheffield (E.) (1977-1982); $35.00

BLOWN STEMWARE AND GIFTWARE

Imported
Stemware 1984 – 1986
Giftware 1985 – 1986

The blanks for the patterns shown here were imported, cut, polished, and marketed by the Fostoria Company. Stemware included a goblet, wine, flute, and ice tea. Prices listed are suggested retail given to Fostoria dealers in 1985 and 1986 and refer to one stem, even though patterns were often sold as sets. Interestingly, the 1985 catalog lists the patterns in the left column as Blown Stemware whereas the patterns in the right column were listed in 1986 as International Hand Cut Lead Crystal. San Francisco and Monarch were the only imported patterns which included giftware.

Athens, $17.50
Aura, $15.00
Bellwether, $17.50
Liana Gold, $17.50
Liana Platinum, $17.50
Northampton, $20.00

Baroness, $20.00
Carmel, $20.00
Countess, $20.00
Monarch, $22.50
San Francisco, $22.50

Blown
Stemware

Athens

Aura

NO06/899

NO06/893

NO06/891

NO06/892

Northampton

Bellwether

Liana Gold
or
Liana Platinum

A. San Francisco Goblet, Flute, Wine, Cordial; B. Monarch; C. Carmel; D. Countess; E. Baroness

San Francisco:
    Salad Bowl; $20.00
    Vase; $20.00
    Pitcher; $25.00
    Wine Carafe; $25.00
    Decanter; $25.00
    Candy Box; $25.00

Monarch:
    Salad Bowl; $20.00
    Vase; $20.00
    Pitcher; $25.00
    Wine Carafe; $25.00
    Decanter; $25.00
    Candy Box; $25.00

BOUTIQUE GIFTWARE

Drawn from previously made patterns.

1372/310 Lamp, Oil Handled Courting (Coin); 1971-1973, Amber; $120.00

1372/310 Lamp, Electric Handled Courting (Coin), 1971-1973, Amber; $110.00

2364/477 Mayonnaise, Plate, Ladle (Sonata), 1971-1974; $32.00

2364/557 Plate, 11" Sandwich (Sonata), 1971-1974; $20.00

2364/579 Plate, Crescent Salad (Sonata), 1971-1975; $18.00

2451/427 Ice Dish, choice of Liners, 1971-1974; $26.00

2584/380 Coaster, Utility, 1971-1982; $5.00

2666/453 Pitcher, Pint (Contour), 1971-1982; $30.00

2666/454 Pitcher, Quart (Contour), 1971-1982; $40.00

2666/455 Pitcher, 3-Pint (Contour), 1971-1982; $50.00

2666/729 Plate, 10" Snack (Contour), 1971-1974; $20.00

2778/347 Candy Jar and Cover, 4-Petal, Crystal, Olive Green, Copper Blue, 1971-1972; $40.00-$65.00

2793/104 Salt, 3¼", Strawberry Diamond, Crystal, Olive Green, Copper Blue, 1971-1973; $22.00-$30.00

2803/380 Coaster, Shell, Crystal, Black Pearl, Lemon Twist, 1971-1973; $5.00-$10.00

2823/421 Dessert, Shell, Crystal Lustre, Black Pearl Lustre, Lemon Twist Lustre, 1971-1973; $8.00-$15.00

2807/378 Cigarette Lighter Set (Glacier), Gold or Silver Top, 1971-1972; $28.00

2364/654 Shaker, Large, Chrome Top B, (pair) 1975-1982; $25.00

2364/655 Shaker, Small Chrome Top C, (pair) 1975-1982; $18.00

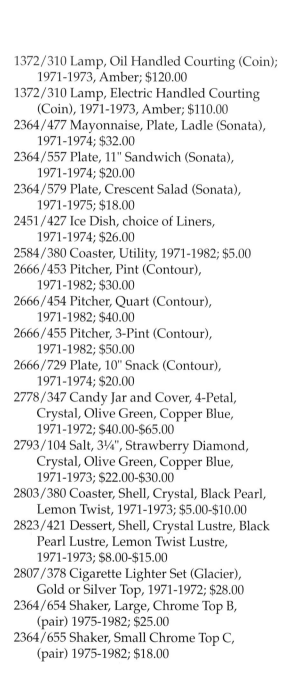

1372/310   1372/311

2364/477
2364/478   2364/479
2364/482

2364/557   2364/579   2451/427

2479/429   2479/431   2584/380

2666/453   2666/454   2666/455

2666/729   2778/347

2793/105   2793/640   2803/380   2823/421

2807/378

CANDLESTICK COLLECTION

Shown as a Collection in 1982.
Drawn from previously made patterns except for CA12/337.

A. CA10/325 Candlestick, 8" (pair); $75.00
B. CA10/314 Candlestick, 3" (Colony) (pair); $40.00
C. CA10/326 Candlestick, 9" (Colony) (pair); $75.00
D. CA10/332 Candlestick, Duo (pair); $85.00
E. CA10/327 Candle Lamp, 9", Blown Shade (pair); $300.00
F. CA11/314 Candlestick, 3" (2324) (pair); $40.00
G. CA11/319 Candlestick, 6" (2324) (pair); $57.00
H. CA12/314 Candlestick, 3" (Kent) (pair); $40.00
I. CA12/323 Candlestick, 7" (pair); $72.00
CA10/461 Shade, 9" Blown, $35.00
CA12/337 Candlestick, 3-Light, 1977-1982; $125.00
CA12/337 Candelabra, 3-Light, 1977-1982; $220.00
CA12/132 Bobache, Wired; $25.00
TR02/981 Prism, 3⅛" Spearhead; $6.00

Crystal Giftware

RO06/605

RO06/615

RO06/606

CA 12/337

LE04/554

Handcrafted
Candlestick
Collection

CANDLE VASE COLLECTION

1977 – 1980
Crystal, Green, and Brown

GL06/313 Candleholder, 2" Stackable (Glacier) (pair); $9.00
GL06/757 Vase, 6" Bud (Glacier); $9.00
HI01/308 Candle, 3" Votive (Highlight); $6.50
HI01/754 Vase, 5" (Highlight); $6.50
FL05/756 Candle/Vase, 6" Flora (Flame); $6.75
FL03/317 Candleholder, 4" (Flame); $6.00
FL03/757 Vase, 6" Bud (Flame); $6.75

CANDLE VASE COLLECTION

The perfect gift, Fostoria's Candle Vase Collection in crystal, green and brown will accent any decor.

The 1704/RO04 Rosby Punch Bowl, Base, and Cup shown on page 285 were offered continually from 1924 to 1982. The plate first appeared with the Centennial II Collection in 1973. See also Milk Glass, pages 204 and 227.

RO04/605 Punch Bowl (Rosby); $125.00
RO04/606 Punch Bowl Base (Rosby); $35.00
RO04/615 Punch Cup (Rosby); $12.00
LE04/554 Serving Plate, 10", 1973-1982; $14.00

CELESTIAL

Crystal 1985
Crystal, Blue, or Sun Gold with Iridescent Finish

318 Candle, 5"; $12.00
179 Bowl, 11"; $12.00
506 Bowl, 5"; $12.00
554 Platter, 11"; $18.00
757 Vase, 8"; $18.00

COLONIAL PRISM GIFTWARE

1980 – 1982
Prices given are 1982 Fostoria prices.

CO13/211 Bowl, 10"; $34.75
CO13/506 Bowl, 5"; $17.50
CO13/512 Bowl, 6"; $17.50
CO13/567 Plate, 14" Torte; $34.50
CO13/649 Shaker, Chrome Top G (pair); $15.00
CO13/297 Covered Server; $43.00
CO13/687 Sugar; $19.00
CO13/688 Cream; $19.00
CO13/300 Oblong Butter and Cover (Colony); $20.50
CO13/620 Two-part Relish; $20.00

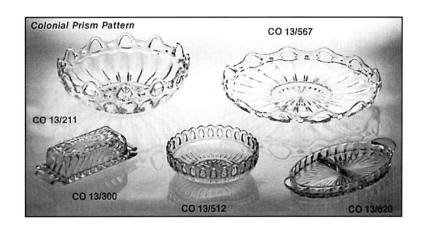

Colonial Prism Pattern

CO 13/567

CO 13/211

CO 13/300

CO 13/512

CO 13/620

Colonial Prism Giftware

HOLLY AND RUBY GIFTWARE

1981 – 1982

HO02/211 Bowl, 10"; $125.00
HO02/315 Candlestick, 4½" (pair); $95.00
HO02/506 Nappy, 5"; $38.00
HO02/567 Plate, 14" Torte; $125.00
HO02/549 Plate, 7"; $35.00
HO02/584 Party Server, two metal spoons; $67.00
CA15/312 Candleholder, Bird; $32.00
CO15/682 Sugar and Cream (Colony); $95.00
CO15/762 Vase, 6" Footed Bud (Colony); $62.00

Holly Party Server, Nappy, Torte Plate, Salad Bowl, Candlesticks

Holly and Ruby Giftware

HOSTESS, SERVEWARE, AND HERITAGE GIFTWARE

After the announcement on May 19, 1982, that all hand-made items had been discontinued, the first letter sent to Fostoria retail dealers contained the notice of additional giftware in the popular Heritage pattern, as well as new hostess items. The letter also states that "beginning September 1, we will have our first full-color gift box. This new gift box will be used for the Heritage stemware, barware, 8" plate, and 5" bowl, plus the new Bennington barware." Thus, many of the pieces sold as Hostess, Serveware, and Giftware were available gift boxed in sets of four.

Hostess, Serveware, and Heritage Giftware were made up of miscellaneous pieces and pieces from the Heritage pattern. There were two pressed Heritage patterns, both lead crystal.

The gold metal trappings were advertised as 24 carat gold plated. Note that the Cake Stand was considered reversable, and when reversed, was called the Chip and Dip. Prices are from the 1985 price list.

Hostess—Gift Boxed

G. HE04/344 Candy Box and
   Cover, Gold Knob; $13.75
H. KI02/047 Bell, Gold Handle;
   $12.50
I. HO04/503 Party Server, 2
   Gold Spoons; $12.50

A. HE03/578 Two-Tiered Server, Chrome; $21.25
B. HE03/583 Tid Bit, Gold Handle; $13.75
C. HE03/380 Coaster, Utility (set of 4); $15.00
D. HE03/382 Coaster, Executive (set of 4); $15.00
E. HE03/894 Bowl, 5"; $7.50
F. HE03/887 Plate, 8"; $8.75
G. HE03/493 Napkin Rings (set of 4); $16.25
I through J (see Shaker Collection)
K. GR05/757 "Grace" Bud Vase; $8.75
L. ME03/757 "Melissa" Bud Vase; $8.75
M. HO04/163 Hostess Footed Compote;
N. HO04/344 Hostess Candy and Cover, Gold Knob; $13.75
O. HO04/509 Hostess Server and Spoon; $11.25

A. HE03/194 Large Bowl, $21.25
B. HE03/639 Cake Stand or Chip and Dip; $31.25
C. HE03/554; 10½" Platter; $21.25
D. (see Shaker Collection)

E. HE03/738 Condiment Set, Gold; $15.00
F. HE03/742; Sauce Set, Gold; $15.00
G. HE04/583 Tid Bit, Gold Handle; $13.75

D. HO04/987 Salad Servers, Spoon
   and Fork, Stainless Steel; $50.00
E. HO04/733 Pastry Server, Stainless Steel
   or Gold; $25.00
F. HO04/732 Cake Knife, Stainless Steel
   or Gold; $25.00

Hostess—Gift Boxed

CA16/293 Jewel Box and Cover (Captiva); $25.00
CA16/293 Place Card Holder, 24K Gold Metal (Captiva); $12.00
SA05/293 Jewel Box and Cover (Satin Ribbons); $25.00
SA05/293 Place Card Holder (Satin Ribbons); $12.00
HO04/304 Flame Snuffer, 24K Gold Metal; $35.00
HO04/292 Mini Box, Hinged Cover; $35.00

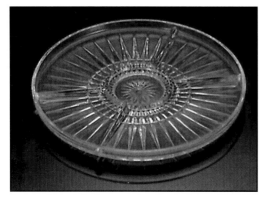

C. HE03/556 Divided Relish; $21.25

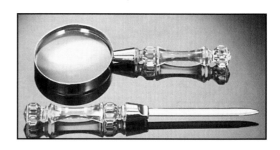

A. EX01/874 Magnifying Glass,
24K Gold; $35.00
B. EX01/875 Letter Opener,
24K Gold; $35.00

LEAD CRYSTAL

The Fostoria Glass Company began listing Lead Crystal in 1970. New items as well as pieces from early patterns were included. Several collections were offered which often included pieces listed in another category. The numbering system had changed in 1957 to include both a line number and a shape number. Then, in July 1976, a prefix of the first two letters of the pattern name were substituted for the first two numbers of the line number. Thus the 1704/676 Rosby Sugar and Cover became LE04/676 when listed as Lead Crystal. The Rosby punch bowl was RO04/605. The numbering system became extremely difficult to follow, making determination of production dates complicated. Not all the catalogs showed every piece and the price lists had no pictures. As much information as could be determined is included. Centennial II was the first large collection of Lead Crystal and many of the pieces from this collection continued to be offered as Lead Crystal; some survived until the end. As many shapes as possible are shown with minimal duplication.

During the period from 1976 to 1982, Fostoria seemed to be majoring in stemware and minoring in giftware. By 1977 there were two sections to the catalogs: Giftware and Stemware.

LEAD CRYSTAL GIFTWARE

Numerical order
Most often the numbers followed as described above. However, notice that
Tid Bit 2878/583 and Tid Bit LE04/583 are not the same.

675/118 Bowl, 8" Round Serving, 1973-1974; $12.00
1871 Shaker, Chrome Top F, (pair) 1974-1975; $20.00
1883/654 Shaker, 4¾",
    F Top, (pair) 1974-1976; $27.00 2183/475 Marmalade
    and Ladle (Colonial Prism), 1973-1974; $24.00
2183/506 Nappy, 5", 1974; $12.00
2222/536 Olive, 7" (Colonial), 1973; $10.00
2326 /312 Vase, 4⅜" Candle, 1972-1976; $10.00
2377/354 Candy Box and Cover, 1975-1981; $40.00
2377/382, Coaster D (set of 4), 1979-1982; $20.00
2377/447 Jelly and Cover, 8½", 1974; $32.00
2377/677 Sugar and Cream, 1974-1981; $24.00
2870/755 Vase, 5½", 1973, $12.00

2878/583 Tid Bit, 7½" Handled, 1973; $24.00
2885/433 Ice Tub, 6" (Stratton); $35.00
CO11/8008/400 Decanter, Quart, Coventry,
    Cut 928, 1975-1981; $95.00
JE 01/293 Jewelry Box and Cover, 1980-1982; $27.00
LE04/123 Ash Tray, 5½", 1974-1977; $5.00
LE04/145 Ash Tray "A", 1974-1978; $4.00
LE04/147 Ash Tray "B", 2¾", 1974-1978; $4.00
LE04/148 Ash Tray "C", 3⅛", 1974-1978; $4.00
LE04/2883/162 Wedding Bowl and Cover, 8",
    1974-1979; $28.00
LE04/2183/297 Covered Server (Colonial
    Prism), 1973-1978; $47.00

LE04/319 Candle, 6", (pair) 1974-1978; $24.00
LE04/2883/329 Urn and Cover,
    7⅝" Footed, 1974-1979; $24.00
LE04/2377/355 Bowl, 5⅝" Snack, 1974-1981; $15.00
LE04/360 Relish, 10¼" Tray, 1970-1978; $18.00
LE04/377 Coaster "A" 3½", 1974-1978; $4.00
LE04/378 Coaster "B", 3½", 1974-1978; $4.00
LE04/379 Coaster "C", 3½", 1974-1978; $4.00
LE04/2864/380 Wine Coaster, 1973-1978; $6.00
LE04/493 Napkin Ring "A", 1974-1978; $4.00
LE04/494 Napkin Ring "B", 1974-1976; $4.00
LE04/509 Hostess Server and Spoon, 1974-1978; $12.00
LE04/512 Sweetmeat, 5½", 1970-1978; $8.00
LE04/521 Bowl, 8½", 1970-1977; $18.00
LE04/540 Pickle, 8½", 1972-1978; $10.00
LE04/554 Plate, 10" Serving, 1970-1978; $15.00
LE04/583 Tid Bit, 7½" Handled, 1974-1978; $18.00
LE04/2679/591 Preserve and Cover, 4½",
    1974-1981; $22.00
LE04/623 Salt Dip, 2", 1974-1978; $4.00
LE04/630 Salver, 10" Round, 1974-1977; $145.00
LE04/654 Shaker, Chrome Top F,

(pair) 1974-1978; $20.00
LE04/677 Sugar, 1974-1978; $12.00
LE04/680 Cream, 1974-1978; $12.00
LE04/2710/687 and 688 Sugar and Cream,
    Individual (Daisy and Button) 1974-1978; $25.00
LE04/2000/710 Toothpick Holder, 1974-1981; $22.00
LE04/1300/751 Vase, 4¼" Drape, 1973-1977; $24.00
LE04/757 Vase, 6⅜" Bud, 1974-1978; $12.00
LE04/761 Vase, 6" Footed, 1974-1978; $22.00
LE05/327 Candle "B", 1974-1978; $4.00
LE05/2377/380 Coaster (Stratton), 1980-1982; $20.00
LE05/517 Bowl, 7½", 1970-1978; $18.00
LE06/377 Bird Candleholder, 1974-1978; $16.00
LE06/676 Candy Jar and Cover, 1970-1978; $42.00
RA03/682 Sugar and Cream (Raleigh) 1982; $24.00
RI02/865 Ring Holder, Silver or
    Gold, 1978-1981; $25.00
ST04/2377/433 Bowl, 6" (Stratton), 1982; $15.00
ST02/8008/400 Decanter, Quart, Stratford,
    Cut 929, 1975-1981; $95.00
ST06/327 Candleholder, Star, 1979-1981; $10.00
VI06/682 Sugar and Cream (Virginia) 1982; $28.00

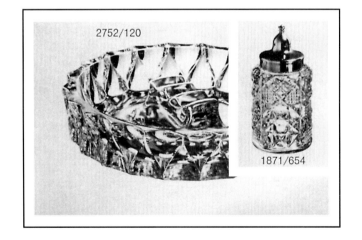

2752/120

1871/654

2828/757

2828/111

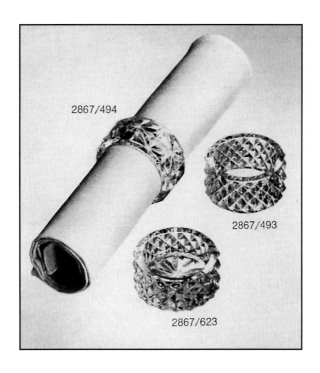

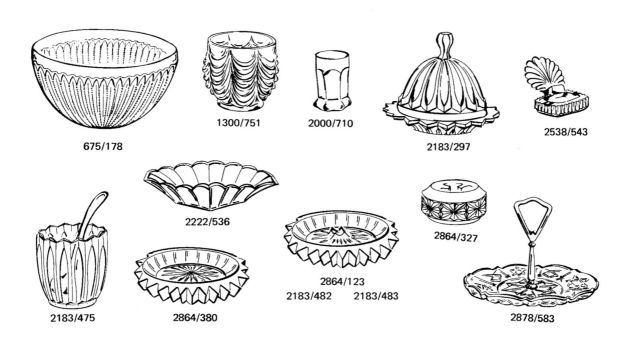

675/178

1300/751

2000/710

2183/297

2538/543

2222/536

2183/475

2864/380

2864/123
2183/482   2183/483

2864/327

2878/583

LE 04/493   LE 04/486   LE 04/509   LE 04/512   LE 05/517   LE 04/521

LE 04/540   LE 04/554   LE 04/583   LE 04/591

LE 04/623   LE 04/630   LE 04/654   LE 06/676   LE 04/680   LE 04/677

LE 04/688   LE 04/687   LE 04/710   LE 04/751   LE 04/757   LE 04/761

LEAD GIFTS

This great American lead crystal meets international standards. The items have deep facets which catch and reflect light. Lead crystal imparts a superior clarity and brilliance.

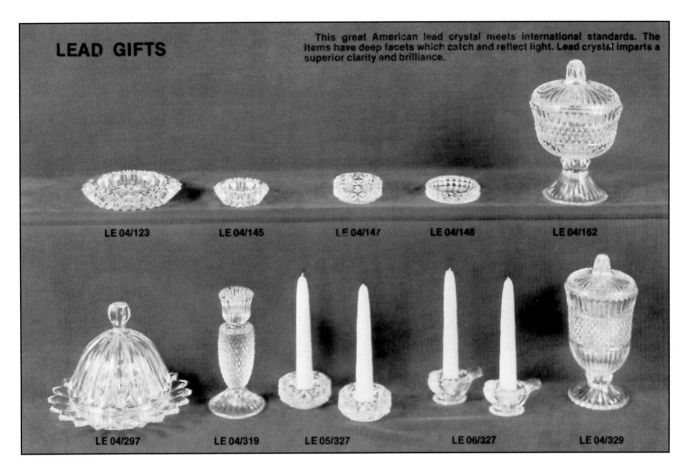

LE 04/123   LE 04/145   LE 04/147   LE 04/148   LE 04/162

LE 04/297   LE 04/319   LE 05/327   LE 06/327   LE 04/329

LE 04/354   LE 04/355   LE 04/360   CO 11/400   ST 02/400

LE 05/380   LE 06/377   LE 04/378   LE 04/379

1121/219

1229/676

1704/680

1704/676

1704/592

1704/499

1467/540

1704/554

1497/521

1641/630

1467/512

1704/517

1704/360

1467/516

LIGHT SHOW GIFTWARE

1985 – 1986

319 Virginia 6" Candlestick (pair); $30.00
469 Virginia Chimney Hurricane; $20.00
466 Virginia Globe Hurricane; $20.00
LI01/467 Glass Light in Crystal, Cobalt, Opal; $35.00
HE03/313 Heritage Candleholder (pair); $12.50
HO04/304 Flame Snuffer; $35.00

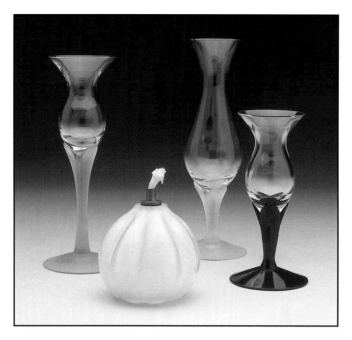

Peach Mist Lotus Candle Vase, Opal Glass Light, Crystal Mist Candle Vase, Ebony Lotus Candle Vase

LOTUS GIFTWARE

1981 – 1982
Crystal Bowl with Crystal Mist, Peach Mist, and Ebony Base
Ebony Base will be the most expensive.
Stemware is featured in *Fostoria Stemware*, page 145.

318 Candlestick, 5½" low; $35.00-$45.00
323 Candlestick, 7½" high; $45.00-$55.00
789 Vase, 8" Bud; $45.00-$55.00

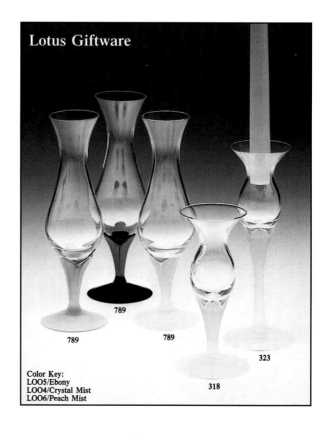

MAYPOLE

1981 – 1982
Light Blue, Yellow, Peach
Stemware is featured in *Fostoria Stemware*, page 146.

195 Bowl, 9"; $95.00
314 Candle, 3" (pair); $95.00
319 Candle, 9" (pair); $150.00
567 Plate, 12" Torte, $110.00
764 Vase, 6" Bud; $58.00

Maypole Giftware

Color Key:
MAO8/Light Blue
MAO9/Yellow
MA1O/Peach

MORNING GLORY GIFTWARE

1982, Crystal and Light Blue (Add 20% for Light Blue)

Morning Glory
Giftware

Color Key:
MOO8/Crystal
MOO9/Light Blu

249 Bowl, 12"; $100.00
314 Candlestick, 3" (pair); $95.00
319 Candlestick, 6" (pair);
$135.00
567 Plate, 14" Torte; $125.00
789 Vase, 8" Bud, Crystal Mist;
$58.00

PERSONALIZED GIFTWARE

"Made from flawlessly clear crystal."
Prices are 1985 Fostoria prices.

Small Crystal Rock:
  PE01/541 Plain Paperweight; $7.25
  PE01/545 Grandpa Paperweight; $9.25
  PE01/546 Pen Stand; $13.75
Heart Shaped Crystal:
  PE02/541 Plain Paperweight; $7.25
  PE02/542 Friends Forever
          Paperweight; $9.75
  PE02/543 Mom Paperweight; $9.75
  PE02/544 Love Paperweight; $9.75
  PE02/546 Love Pen Stand; $16.75
Large Crystal Form:
  PE03/541 Plain Paperweight; $7.75
  PE03/546 Pen Stand; $14.25
  PE03/547 Dad Pen Stand; $16.75

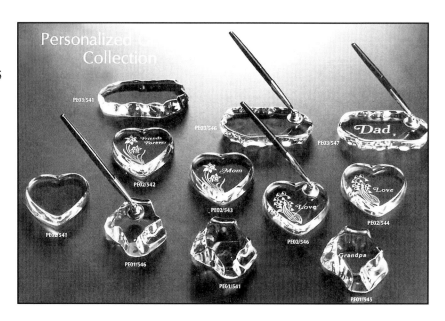

SATIN MIST/SWIRL

1978 – 1979
Gift Boxed
Satin Mist: Crystal, Pink, and Blue; Swirl: Crystal, Apple Green, and Amber

Satin Mist
  238 Bowl, 11" Salad; $22.00
  504 Salad/Dessert, 6"; $12.00

Swirl
  223 Bowl, 10¾" Salad; $22.00
  504 Salad/Dessert, 6"; $12.00

SHAKER COLLECTION

1980 – 1982 except where noted.
Crystal
All priced as pairs.

AM01/649 American, Chrome Top A; $26.00
AM01/650 American, Individual, Chrome
    Top C; $26.00
CE01/649 Century, Chrome Top B; $28.00
CE01/650 Century, Individual, Chrome
    Top C; $28.00
CO01/649 Coin, Chrome Top E; $48.00
CO13/649; Colonial Prism, Chrome
    Top G; $28.00
FA04/649 Facet, Chrome Top A; $35.00
LE07/649 Leonardo, Chrome Top F,
    1980-1985; $27.00
MA07/649 Madison, Chrome Top G; $27.00
RE12/649 Revere, Chrome Top F,
    1980-1985; $15.00
RO06/649 Rosby, Chrome Top G; $32.00
SA04/649 Salem, Chrome Top F
    1980-1985; $27.00
TE02/659 Teardrop, Chrome Top C; $25.00
TR05/649 Transition, Chrome Top G; $26.00
WO01/659 Woodland, Chrome Top A; $27.00
YO01/659 York, Chrome Top C; $25.00

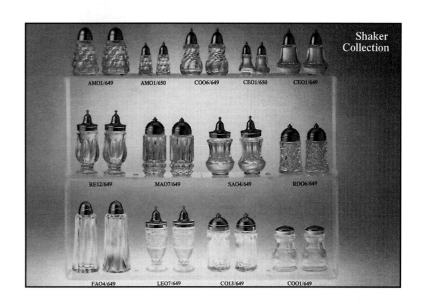

STARLIGHT

1985 Fostoria prices

ST07/179 Bowl, 8"; $25.00
ST07/255 Tray, 12" x 6"; $25.00
ST07/344 Candy Box and Cover;
    $25.00
ST07/560 Tray, 12" Round Serving;
    $25.00
ST07/686 Sugar, Cream and Tray;
    $25.00
ST07/810 Vase, 9"; $25.00

TRANSITION

1985 Fostoria prices
Stemware is featured in *Fostoria Stemware*, page 55.

TR05/123 Ash Tray, 5"; $25.00
TR05/179 Bowl, 8" Serving; $25.00
TR05/319 Candleholder (pair); $25.00
TR05/504 Salad/Dessert, 5"; $25.00
TR05/557 Plate, 11" Buffet; $25.00
TR05/665 Chip and Dip (5" Salad/11" Plate); $35.00
TR05/686 Sugar and Cream; $25.00

Transition

VASE COLLECTION

GR 05/757

ME
03/757

NO 03/758   RE 11/758

GR04/757 Vase, 4¾",
    "Grace"; $10.00
ME03/757 vase, 4¾",
    "Melissa"; $10.00
NO03/758 Vase, 7½",
    "Nostalgia"; $18.00
RE11/758 Vase, 7½",
    "Reflection"; $18.00

VIRGINIA GIFTWARE

Crystal, Dark Blue, Light Blue, Peach, Gray
1985 Fostoria prices

VI05/171 Compote, Footed; $15.00
VI05/319 Candlesticks, 6" (pair); $30.00
VI05/466 Globe Hurricane, Crystal; $20.00
VI05/469 Chimney Hurricane, Crystal; $20.00

VI05/550 Plate, 7", Dark Blue, Light Blue, Peach; $12.00
VI05/554 Plate, 10", Dark Blue, Light Blue, Peach; $20.00
VI05/761 Vase, 7", also made in Ruby; $12.00-$18.00

2921 WOODLAND GIFT ITEMS

1977 – 1978
Crystal, Blue, Brown, and Green
Stemware is featured in *Fostoria Stemware*, page 55.

517 Bowl, 7"; $15.00
317 Candle, 5"; (pair); $20.00
448 Jelly, 4⅝" Footed; $15.00
505 Nappy and Cover, 5"; $15.00

554 Plate, 10" Serving; $15.00
653 Shaker, Chrome Top A (pair); $27.00
506 Nappy, 5"; $11.00

WOODLAND PATTERN
Gift Items

Color Key:
Crystal WO 01
Blue WO 02
Brown WO 03
Green WO 04

505 653 448 506

317 554 448 505

517 506 653

ABOUT THE AUTHORS

Milbra Long has had a life-long passion for beauty. Emily Seate, her daughter, has had a life-long love for words and their presentation on the printed page in order to communicate an idea. For many years, the two women went their separate ways, Milbra into a 23-year career as an elementary school teacher, an antiques store owner with her husband, Frank, and finally, in her own business, Milbra's Crystal. Emily spent time in the military (she likes to say she "retired after four"), married a third-generation Texan, obtained a graduate degree from Texas Christian University, had a 10-year career as an executive secretary, and finally joined Milbra's Crystal in 1991.

The partnership they formed was unique in that it had been forged through an active and ongoing mother/daughter relationship which had long before blossomed into friendship. Emily spent the first few years following Milbra around like a puppy, soaking up information. By 1992 Milbra had shared her dream of creating a reference book for Fostoria collectors, and she and Emily talked for hours about how that could be accomplished. Very soon Milbra's passion for beautiful glass and Emily's love of words created an explosion of excitement.

Fostoria Stemware was a baptism by fire. The nitty-gritty of research, editing, proofing, and questioning demanded all their energies and experience. On July 27, 1994, they each held a copy of their first book and realized they were hooked. They had to tell the whole Fostoria story.

Reality dictated some parameters, and after some thought and discussion, they decided they could cover thoroughly the years from 1924 through the closing of the factory in Moundsville in 1986. But what about the early lamp catalog, the candlestick catalog, and the beautiful early pieces of glass Milbra had in her personal collection? It would be hard to leave those out.

When they concluded that three more books would be required to cover the period from 1924 – 1986, they decided to call the third book after the title Fostoria used on so many of its early catalogs, "Useful and Ornamental." After all, that pretty well summed up the Fostoria Glass Company and its 99 years of glass production. When the series is completed, you will have the legacy of a bygone era, with its impossible conditions, incredibly skilled workers, and extraordinarily beautiful glassware.

Milbra and Emily are delighted to be able to present this next book in the Crystal for America series to you. They welcome your questions and comments, and wish you success in the pursuit of your dreams.

INDEX

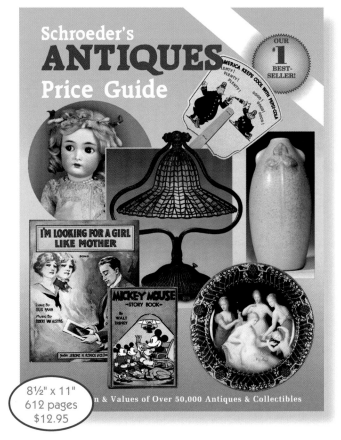